FIGHTING FORCES,

WRITING WOMEN

In this fascinating and persuasive study, Sharon Ouditt examines
the traumatic nature of women's experience during the First
World War. Drawing on propaganda, journals, women's magazines, unpublished memoirs and contemporary fiction, she
reveals the challenge to feminine identity which the war both
demanded and attempted to restrict.

Women, she argues, did not achieve sudden and unproblematic independence through their entry into the public
spheres of work and of politics. Rather they found themselves
having to negotiate complex ideological structures in order to
legitimate their role as 'temporary' citizens – whether as
crusading nurses, land workers or pacifist activists.

Historically meticulous and theoretically informed, this book
will appeal to anyone interested in the ways in which women
managed their involvement in the First World War, in the
relationship between literature and history, and in the war
writing of Virginia Woolf amongst others. At once a work of
feminist history and of literary criticism, this book offers a study
of the ambiguity and flexibility of 'femininity' in the context of
dramatic social change.

Sharon Ouditt is Lecturer in Englis'
The Nottingham Trent University.

FIGHTING FORCES, WRITING WOMEN

Identity and Ideology in the First World War

Sharon Ouditt

London and New York

First published 1994
by Routledge
11 New Fetter Lane, London EC4P 4EE

Simultaneously published in the USA and Canada
by Routledge
29 West 35th Street, New York, NY 10001

Typeset in 10/12pt Baskerville by
Ponting–Green Publishing Services,
Chesham, Buckinghamshire
Printed and bound in Great Britain by
T.J. Press (Padstow) Ltd, Cornwall
Printed on acid free paper

British Library Cataloguing in Publication Data
Ouditt, Sharon
Fighting Forces: Identity and Ideology in the
First World War
I. Title
809.93358

Library of Congress Cataloging in Publication Data
Ouditt, Sharon
Fighting Forces: Identity and Ideology in the First World
War / Sharon Ouditt.
p.   cm.
Includes bibliographical references and index.
1. English literature–Women authors–History and
criticism.   2. World War, 1914–1918–Great Britain–
Literature and the war.   3. Women and literature–Great
Britain–History–20th century.   4. English literature–
20th century–History and criticism.
5. World War, 1914–1918–Women–Great Britain.   I. Title
PR478.W6509   1993
820.9'9287'09041–dc20   93–15511
CIP

ISBN 0–415–04704–8 (hbk)
ISBN 0–415–04705–6 (pbk)

For Martin, with love and thanks

CONTENTS

PLATES

ACKNOWLEDGEMENTS

Many colleagues and friends at the universities of York and Leicester have, often unwittingly, provided support and inspiration for this book and I would like, before I start, to thank those whose names I have *not* mentioned.

Primarily, though, my thanks go to Martin Stannard, whose tact, acuity and assurance propelled me through this project from start to finish. I would also like to thank Nicole Ward Jouve, for encouraging me to begin it in the first place, Jane Aaron, for being an outstanding supervisor and friend throughout and Clare Hanson, for helpful comments on a later draft. Marion Shaw and Joanne Shattock were very constructive examiners. Aleid Fokkema has been an invaluable friend and diligent reader; Rick Rylance and Kelvin Everest have been both supportive and thought-provoking. Sue Roe showed tremendous faith in this project before it was even half-finished and Julia Hall, my editor at Routledge, has been cheerful and assiduous in helping to bring it to a close. My thanks are also due to Dido Arthur and Heather Cowie for providing sleeping space while I was researching the material, to my parents, Sylvia and Reno Ouditt, for maintenance of all kinds at all times and to my smallest, but most vital support-system, Zuli, for making me, amongst other things, laugh.

The staff at Leicester University Library, the Departments of Printed Books and Documents at the Imperial War Museum, the British Museum and Newspaper Library and the Fawcett Library have been consistently helpful. My thanks are due to them and to the following for permission to quote material owned by them: for extracts from the Women at Work Collection, Crown copyright, the Imperial War Museum. For permission to quote from documents and memoirs held by the Imperial War Museum I would like to thank Mrs June Cooper, Mrs V. Corden, Ken Cross, Mr Harrold, Elizabeth C. Leyland and John B. C. McCann. Permission to reproduce May Wedderburn Cannan's *Lamplight* was granted by James Slater; *The Rose of No Man's Land* is quoted thanks to Plymouth Music Co. Inc. for Jerry Vogel Music Co. Inc.

For permission to reproduce plates 1–4 I would like to thank the Trustees of the Imperial War Museum; for plate 5: The Mary Evans Picture Library/Fawcett Library.

Every attempt has been made to obtain permission to reproduce copyright material. If any proper acknowledgement has not been made we invite copyright holders to inform us of the oversight.

INTRODUCTION

It is, of course, understood that introductions are always written last, but I wonder if I might stretch the confessional convention and admit that the concluding chapter of this book was written first. It was a question of the influence of anxiety. 'Why did Virginia Woolf write the way she did?' I was asked, approximately ten years ago, while attempting to gain entry to a certain university. I didn't know. I didn't get the place. But I did become obsessed with the question and permitted it to interrogate me through undergraduate and postgraduate study, through the miners' strike, through the impact of French feminisms, through the Gulf War and through my own negotiations with motherhood, teaching and thesis-writing. My research was increasingly influenced by feminist thinking in Britain, France and America that pointed up the challenges made by Woolf, and by other writers, to cultural paradigms that centred on a pattern of domination that could only ultimately be seen as destructive. The 'Great' War seemed a tragic, if ideal manifestation of this pattern, and I became convinced that Woolf was engaged in a literary and political critique of that war from a stance of radical female alterity. And so I wrote about it. I later became troubled by two things: first, the nature and extent of Woolf's 'radicalism', and second, the feminist context within which she was operating. By her own admission creation is not a single and solitary act. Who, then, were her political and literary sisters challenging (obliquely?), criticising (wryly?), undercutting (amusingly?) a symbolic order that had suffered – in both senses – one world war and was heading for another?

I launched, therefore, a double-headed line of enquiry. One element was concerned with the theoretical problem of defining femininity within a conceptual framework of radicalism and alterity, working with the assumption that women, before they had been granted the vote, were deprived of the status of citizen. The other involved a great deal of archival research, seeking out forgotten novels, reading journals, magazines, pamphlets and unpublished memoirs in order to discover how women, at that historical moment, related their gendered identities to their possible roles in war time. The story refused to emerge as a simple one. The writings spoke to a complex of political and personal issues, to confrontations with authority figures – whether masculine and militaristic or feminine and domestic – to the profound satisfaction of independence found in paid employment, and to the guilt of being required to enact the role of the protected, for whom the protectors lost their lives. My initial theoretical enquiry began to look uneasy in the company of these narratives of disguise, manipulation and compromise. It was necessary to shift the balance.

My problem had been in associating alterity with radicalism in its politically progressive sense. Women's alterity was an accepted trope of the day, but it frequently had more to do with fuelling the home fires and maintaining racial superiority than with enabling a social re-birth. The proximity and inter-changeability of ideas of conservatism and radicalism in relation to discussions of 'femininity' became my subject, and it became imperative to locate the discussion in contemporary discourse. It is likely that women's most commonly articulated (or un-spoken) desire during the First World War was that justice be done to women and that their part in the war, whether as crusading nurse, desolated lover or pacifist activist, be acknowl-edged. How this was managed depended on the individual's relation to the sources of power in her society and on the structure of her political beliefs. The language in which this was articulated, though, involved an intricate dialogue negotiating the allure of a fixed, feminine identity with the necessity of social change. The strategic function of that identity and the extent of that change became the focus of my enquiry.

The task of sorting out material so that it ceased to represent the turmoil of the 'heterogeneous present' and acquired instead some sense of unity or linearity inevitably required the imposi-tion of constraints and classifications. My research, however, had encouraged me to resist the temptation to 'argue' that women's experience of the war was, as Woolf puts it, 'simply one thing'. Rather than arranging the material chronologically, or thematically, then, it seemed more appropriate to arrange it around areas of subject experience. In this way the war years are repeatedly revisited, but from different perspectives. This enforces a kind of blurring, but at the same time emphasises the fact that women's experiences of the war were radically varied in terms of the work performed, the public recognition accorded to it, its political implications and its challenge to feminine identity.

The book is thus divided into five chapters which analyse different areas of experience. It begins with the active inter-vention in the prosecution of the war on the part of Voluntary Aid Detachment (VAD) nurses, Land Army workers and mun-itions factory employees, examines the relative passivity of women who experienced the war on the 'home front' and then looks at feminist pacifist writings before offering a reading of Virginia Woolf as a pacifist war writer. The movement of the whole is from active involvement in the war effort through a conservative form of romantic passivity to active anti-war in-volvement: from the politically central, in other words, towards the marginal. The direction of each chapter follows a similar line, beginning with an examination of cultural formations and ideologies and then proceeding to literary representations which arguably take issue with the dominant constructions of femininity. An example of the political ambiguity that this approach illuminates can be seen in Chapter 1, which deals with the VAD organisation. Vera Brittain's *Testament of Youth* (1933) was a best-seller, and has been serialised on television and re-printed in Virago and Fontana paperbacks. It has clearly been successful in reaching a wide audience and has con-ceivably been instrumental in shaping modern consciousness of women's part in the First World War. When it is compared with some of the institutional directives, however, its glamour as the story of an individualist who endured Armageddon and sur-vived seems somewhat tarnished. *Testament* directly reproduces some of the less palatable ideologies that helped to make the VAD institution successful. Katharine Furse, the director, played the class and educational high standards of the applic-ants as a trump card against possible accusations on the part of the military of 'unladylike' behaviour. The result was that not

3

only were women of lower social status excluded from nursing service, but that they were also encased in an ideological construct that assumed their *moral* inferiority. Brittain maintains the discourse of superior sensitivity, and even uses it to derogate the trained nurses, whom she constructs as envious of the innate capabilities of the volunteers and, in any case, intrinsically dull. The literary effect of Brittain's text has been to promote and validate the woman's story of the war. Its political effect has been, in its silent reproduction of the ideologies exploited by Furse to ensure women's acceptance near the trenches, to advance a feminism predicated on an individualism that was available only to women of a certain class.

It should be clear by now, then, that this book specifically concerns *British* women's experience of the war. Its concern is not to rectify the androcentric bias in literary study of Great War Mythology, which is Claire Tylee's project (Tylee 1990), but to examine the literary and political capital made from the idea of 'femininity' in a historically turbulent situation. My thinking has been influenced by historians such as Joan W. Scott and Patricia Higonnet, and the political philosopher Jean Bethke Elshtain, as well as feminist literary critics – in particular Cora Kaplan – who are interested in the intersections between the way femaleness is represented in public discourse and in private life. I would further situate my work in the context of feminist research that examines the ways in which women negotiate with, and even collaborate with, systems that might be labelled merely or wholly oppressive: Kathryn Sutherland (1991) and Alison Light (1991) have both been instructive in this respect. In order to aid my discussion of the central and the marginal, I make use of Julia Kristeva's distinction between Symbolic and semiotic modalities – not in their original psychoanalytical and linguistic formulation, but, as is more common, metaphorically. The advantage of this is that, in compact form, it opens out the boundaries of debate from a simple male-bellicose/female-pacific opposition into something that takes account of the relative positions of gender, class, race, political or religious orientation in the context of the war – and allows for coalitions and oscillations to occur. The Symbolic Order, briefly, may stand for the 'Law of the Father': government or institutional directives, propaganda, what Robert Graves calls 'newspaper language' – that which follows, in Kristeva's terms, a 'logic of identification' with the values of the nation state (Kristeva [1979] 1986: 194). The semiotic is that which is structurally opposed to and repressed by the dominant ideologies, and may be potentially revolutionary – *or regressive*. The image of maternity as used by feminist pacifists, for example, is on the one hand a powerful locus of radical alterity, or on the other merely a conservative essential already mobilised, for its own purposes, by government propaganda. The same kind of ambivalence is projected onto the single figure of Woolf's Mrs Ramsay, who is at once oceanic and suffocating, alluring and constricting.

It is this kind of ambivalence that lies at the heart of this book. There was – and is – an imaginative persistence in aligning women with cyclically reproduced, permanent values that are placed beyond the boundaries of masculine 'law', and its manifestations worked both for and against women's claim for citizenship. It allowed VAD nurses an identity in the war on the assumption that they would be insulated from its gruesome effects. On the other hand it allowed women to be persuaded to adopt the role of repository of spiritual values. But beyond this, women's alterity was a powerful stance that had the potential to reveal bellicosity as a form of masculine madness.

So this is a study that covers both conservatism and radicalism and tries to identify their common ideological currencies. For, despite the emphasis on difference, there was much scope for alliance. Vera Brittain, VAD Commandant Rachel Crowdy and pacifist Helena Swanwick, for example, all reassembled in 1924 under the auspices of the League of Nations. It seems clear that in the attempt to assert woman's role as citizen, different agendas were set. One involved helping to win the war and implied a radical but temporary release from normal activity; another involved seeking equality with men, which meant resisting essentialist definitions of womanhood or women's sphere; another involved the rejection of war as a means of conflict resolution and saw it as a symptom of a degraded social system that relied on the structural subordination of women, the working classes and small nations. The drama of permanence versus change, implicit in all these positions, is played out in detail in individual texts, whether they be institutional directives, propaganda tracts, magazine or journal articles, memoirs, autobiographies or novels. The power of maternal and sororial metaphors both enabled and obstructed a journey out into history, whose destination lay beyond the boundaries of a purely *literal* maternalism.

The 'fighting forces' of the title refer not only to the women who contributed to the national effort to combat the enemy, but also to the women whose subjectivities were the arena for a battle for power between socially and historically located discourses. They are also women who, as an ideological stance, chose to 'fight' against force as an acceptable means of resolving international disputes. Within these various positions both conservative and radical definitions of feminity intersect. This kind of ambiguity and self-contradiction seems to form the nucleus of what has been, and still is, feminism.

1

NUNS AND LOVERS
Voluntary Aid Detachment nurses in the First World War

'She called to me from her battle-places', wrote May Sinclair, echoing the sentiments of many women who felt they could no longer maintain a passive female role in the face of the summons to active service (Jones and Ward 1991: 15). But what was the nature of this call? By whom was it issued? Those who played their part in the war in the uniform of a Voluntary Aid Detachment (VAD) nurse were attracted by the offer of a coherent and authoritative identity, an entrance on to the world stage, a chance to do as their brothers and lovers were doing – 'Oh, it's you who have the luck, out there in blood and muck' (Macaulay 1915; rpt in Reilly 1981: xxxv).[1] But this form of public recognition was dependent on a feminine piety that implied deference to masculinity, militarism and the patriarchal nation state. And while VADs were offered something resembling equality, that role was deeply sororial, in the tradition of the upper-class family. They found themselves, then, at an ideological junction between a traditional, idealised value system and a radical new order of experience: a complex and ambiguous subject position that was frequently the source of breakdown.

Sandra Gilbert and Susan Gubar in volume 2 of *No Man's Land* (1989) argue that women's release from social and economic constraints proved an unproblematically liberating move which produced a new, 'amazonian' strength and literary self-confidence (cf. Gilbert and Gubar 1989: 259ff). They propose that the war might have threatened a 'female conquest of men' (261) and present women's entry into war work as joyfully liberating, happy and purposeful. Their argument is powerful and, in feminist terms, alluring. But to present the war as the

7

'festival of sexual liberation' of newly-mobilised women who 'swooped over the waste lands of the war with the energetic love of Valkyries' (293) is, first, to elide specific historical details which might offer alternative means of understanding these women's confrontations with profound social change and, second, to present 'woman' as a homogeneous category, totalised and glorified. I shall argue that they present only part of the story and are limited by a feminist desire to seek out and celebrate a 'single battalion of sisters' that might 'persist into post-war patriarchy' (1989: 304).

To attend in detail to the direct accounts of this female experience, as I argue in this chapter, reveals a deeply-structured uncertainty in these women's consciousnesses that Gilbert and Gubar's feminist festival will not allow them to admit. Jane Marcus has already offered a detailed critique of their scholarship, but in the service of an argument concerning an alternative feminist history that confronts the masculine paradigm that Gilbert and Gubar appear to accept. Marcus's argument concerns a neglected 'plot': that of the self-representation of women in suffragette iconology, a record that patriarchal propagandists endeavoured to obliterate (Marcus 1989: 53–6). My focus, however, is different, and is directed towards the experiences of women who were not necessarily feminists but who sought female involvement in the war and were willing to negotiate the terms of their entry. I shall present, then, an account of the ambiguous subject identity of war nurses that examines the lure of old certainties in conflict with new circumstances. This specifically involved the collision of established codes of 'femininity' with the efforts of the VAD organisation to advance women onto the battlefield by canny manipulation of those very codes. The movement out into this particular moment in history was thus fraught with contradictions in aspirant nurses whose texts articulate the strain produced by their being both 'in process' as subjects and 'on trial' as women (cf. Kristeva [1974] 1984: 22; [1977] 1980: 135).

Women, of course, were not invited to join the army and scarcely invited to help it in the field. Many of the more wealthy and leisured women defiantly established their own semi-military organisations,[2] but even the suffragist doctor Elsie Inglis was initially advised by the Royal Army Medical Corps to 'go home and sit still' (Lawrence 1971: 98). The loudest and most persuasive call to women was to come from the Red Cross and Order of St John *via* the VAD organisation. In this, women could make their contribution in an acceptable role: as nurses, offering voluntary aid to the sick and wounded under the auspices of the Geneva Convention and at a safe distance from the front line.[3] This position was seen by many as women's nearest equivalent to that of the fighting male; it both supported his idealised aims and acted as an antidote to their gruesome effects. The Red Cross sign came to symbolise this ambivalent cluster of objectives. For the fighting male, the cross signalled sanctuary. For the nurses it was, like the nun's cross, the badge of their equal sacrifice. In a poem by May Wedderburn Cannan the Red Cross sign is seen to be equivalent to the crossed swords indicating her lover's death in battle:

> And all I asked of fame
> A scarlet cross on my breast, my Dear,
> For the swords by your name.

(Reilly 1981: 16)

Thus the role of military nurse offered a marginalised identity – one in, but not of, the war – which came under considerable pressure as the gendered idealism that it predicated was undermined by the practical experience of the war zone.

For most, however, the shift in identity that they experienced was at once enabled and limited by discourses of militarism and femininity, and by the operation of social class. The VAD was registered with the War Office as part of a scheme for national defence: as such, its identity was military, and in order for women to gain acceptance in war zones (both geographical and hierarchical) it was crucial that they pay careful attention to the etiquette of military procedures. The liberating appeal of this was circumscribed by the VAD authorities' invocation of some apparently more permanent aspects of female social organisation: femininity and class. The 'feminine' in this construction was informed by the operations of middle- and upper-class households where the servant class and the Nanny respectively assured protection from drudgery and instilled in 'young ladies' the principles of obedience and honour. While VADs declared their loyalty to the King, they were simultaneously instructed that their parent organisation was their 'Mother'.[4] The familial metaphor thus domesticated the potentially revolutionary appeal of the VAD, which addressed its members as 'dutiful daughters', putting pressure on them to adopt the reverential role of the Mother in obeisance to the Father – the patriarchal – nation state. This performed the function of guaranteeing the deeply conventional position of the organisation. The competition between these discourses, though, could be radically unsettling to the young recruits forced to negotiate between the power granted to them by their class and patriotic endeavour and the subordination that was a product of their gender and voluntary status.

VOLUNTARY AID DETACHMENTS: THE MAKING OF AN INSTITUTION

There's a Rose that grows in 'No man's land',
And it's wonderful to see,
Tho' it's sprayed with tears,
It will live for years
In my garden of memory.
It's the one red rose the soldier knows,
It's the work of the Master's Hand;
In the War's great curse, stood the Red Cross Nurse,
She's the Rose of 'No man's land'.
(J. Caddigan and J. A. Brennan, 'The Rose of No Man's
Land' (1918); quoted in Macdonald 1980.)

This song conveys the popular received image of nurses during the First World War: a woman in the Red Cross uniform, suggesting a kind of female St George, braves the crashing artillery on the Western Front. Eyes uplifted, inwardly grieving, yet externally serene and efficient, she tends the wounds of the men of her homeland. This stereotype, widely distributed on posters, was as much iconographic as literary. Women had effectively, quickly and cynically been translated into an efficient aspect of wartime propaganda.

All but the most high-minded, however, were rapidly disabused of this glamorous image by the reality of the situation. The original scheme for voluntary aid to the sick and wounded, far from appealing to the pursuit of 'heroism in the abstract' (Brittain 1981: 157), was designed as a practical measure to fill a gap in the Territorial Medical Service between the Clearing

Hospitals and the Military Base. The VAD organisation did not emerge in 1914 as a brave young Sisterhood eager to succour the injured heroes in France; rather it was situated very firmly at home as an auxiliary service in case of invasion. In 1909, in the thick of the Arms Race, the War Office issued the 'Scheme for the Organisation of Voluntary Aid in England and Wales'. A British Red Cross Society (BRCS) document entitled 'The "VADs"', and possibly intended as a press release, is keen to emphasise the military connection:

> The organisation was to be the technical reserve of the Territorial Force Association for mobilisation in case of invasion. The TFA could delegate the raising of detachments to the British Red Cross Society and later to the Order of St John, but they were registered at the War Office and shown in Army Orders.
>
> (Files of the British Red Cross Society, hereafter BRCS, 10 1/6)

In 1910, under the joint administration of these rival voluntary ambulance associations, the organisation eventually came into existence.[5]

From the outset the movement was successful, largely owing to the eagerness of women to be recognised as responsible figures in the matter of national defence (cf. Summers 1988: 253). There were, however, problems. The organisation, although registered with the War Office, received no government funding. All detachments relied on voluntary contributions. This followed the tradition of women's involvement in voluntary work in the earlier Victorian period: if women were to contribute to their country's war effort they could do so, but at their own expense (cf. Summers 1979; Vicinus 1985: 5). In order to become qualified, members were required to sit and pass examinations on home nursing, first aid and hygiene. These naturally required tuition; lectures had to be paid for by the candidates, as did the expenses of sitting the exam. One of the planks of the VAD's ideological platform had always been that each member should receive training to a uniform standard. From the outset, though, because some detachments inevitably had wealthier and more generous members who were prepared to fund their branch's activities, this ideal was qualified by the influence of class privilege. It was also required of members that they obtain some voluntary experience in a hospital. Clearly the chance of doing this, too, varied according to local resources and relied on co-operation from professional nurses, with whom, as we shall see, there was often some friction.

A further source of difficulty was to become more acute as the war progressed: the precise function of the VADs in case of national emergency was never entirely clarified – other than to say that they should 'improvise'. That they were to be merely auxiliary, however, *was* clear. Thekla Bowser, an Honorary Sister of the Order of St John whose laudatory account of British VAD work in the war was published in 1917, proclaims this as a point of honour:

> The highest privilege goes to the man who may fight his country's battles, give his life for his King, risk living a maimed man to the end of his days; next comes the privilege of being of use to these men who are defending us and all we love.
>
> (Bowser 1917: 16)

From this kind of statement it can be seen that the VAD, as a women's organisation, was not in a position to challenge or change the power system, but, in the name of patriotism and the glorification of *man*'s role in battle, saw itself as an aid to the country's war aims at a structurally subordinate and permanently ill-defined level.

In the initial chaos at the outbreak of war, the War Office refused help from the Red Cross and other volunteers with the result that many women joined the French Red Cross in order to gain immediate access to the fighting lines. May Wedderburn Cannan, minor poet and Red Cross enthusiast, writes in disparaging terms of the Liberal government's organisational ineptitude:

> The Medical Services in Whitehall were convinced that they could deal with the situation when actually there was a complete breakdown. . . . There were no motor ambulances in the advanced zone of the British Army and only one attached to the Military Hospital in Versailles. . . . The British Red Cross offered two hundred motor ambulances and they were refused; they offered 1,000 trained nurses and they were refused.
>
> (Cannan 1976: 71)

Katharine Furse, who was to become the Commandant-in-Chief, puts the alternative (pro-Liberal) case that the VADs were organised to act in case of invasion and, as there was no great fear of invasion in August 1914, the machinery was in need of adjustment before adequate use could be made of available resources. It was clear, however, that women were not at all welcome near the fighting lines, and it was only after a personal letter was written to 'someone whose husband was in a high place at the War Office' that any substantial notice of the VAD was taken (Furse 1940: 300–1).

October 1914 saw the first use of British VADs abroad. Katharine Furse, at that time Commandant of the Paddington division, London, left for Boulogne with members from her Division on 19 October, having received orders from the War Office to set up a rest station on the lines of communication on the Western Front (BRCS 10 2/9; BRCS 12 2/2). At first it was not clear whether these upper-class first-aiders would be wanted, but with the first battle of Ypres (October 1914) they were rapidly called upon to help in improvised wards crammed with stretchers – until the trained nurses arrived, at which point the VADs were dispensed with. Following this, they improvised a highly successful rest station, converting railway trucks into storehouses, packing-cases into furniture and condensed milk cans into mugs. Furse records the dismissive attitude with which they were greeted: 'women were such a nuisance in war time and who were these odd women in uniform, anyway?' (Furse 1940: 309). But the success of the rest station, which was to become one of many on the lines of communication, providing drinks and cigarettes for the fighting forces, signalled progress. In January 1915 Furse was recalled to England to found the Central VAD Head Quarters Office at Devonshire House, London. Meanwhile, in France, it was under the supervision of Rachel Crowdy that the network of rest stations, hospitals and hostels – for the relatives of the sick and dying and for ill or over-tired nursing staff – were set up along with canteens for convalescents and clubs for trained nurses. In 1916, the first VAD motor ambulance convoy was established (BRCS 12 2/2).

The organisation, until the war, had been entirely voluntary and dependent on contributions. In 1915, however, the War Office recognised that there were insufficient trained nurses for the military hospitals and suggested supplying VADs as

Plate 1 Katharine Furse, Commandant-in-Chief, Voluntary Aid
Detachments, later Director of the WRNS. (By courtesy of the
Trustees of the Imperial War Museum.)

probationary nurses to be paid and housed by the military authorities (BRCS 10 2/9). The terms of service were that a fully qualified member should do one month's probation in a hospital and if considered suitable should sign a contract for a further six months' service in the same hospital. An allowance was given for food, quarters, washing and travelling and the pay for the first seven months was at the rate of £20 per annum with increments of £2.10s for every subsequent six months agreed to. While this salary marked an important stage in the state recognition of the VADs' contribution to the military enterprise, it is worth noting that they were paid less than some servants (at the time a cook earned approximately £30, a parlourmaid £25 and a housemaid £14 (Terry 1988: 21)) and dramatically less than women munitions workers, whose pay was said to vary between £50 and £250 per annum (see Chapter 2). Their rate of pay, in fact, was approximately the same as that of privates in the army, who also received a separation allowance for their families. This poor remuneration was to become a powerful grievance for some who resented the implication that, where 'ladies' were concerned, patriotism should be its own reward.

Recruitment, however, soared. The age-limit (23–42 for foreign service, 21–48 for home service) inevitably led to attempts at deception from enthusiastic prospective candidates, as was indeed the case with males wanting to join the army. The 20-year-old Vera Brittain was not the only one to be delighted at being taken for 23 by a severe-looking Matron (cf. Brittain [1933] 1979: 180). Soon after war broke out as many as 600 members per week were appointed to military hospitals at home and abroad (BRCS 10 1/6). The organisation expanded in 1916 by opening up a General Service Scheme which, like the Women's Army Auxiliary Corps, employed women as dispensers, clerks, cooks, telephone operators, store keepers, X-ray attendants and laboratory attendants.

By 1916, then, the VAD organisation had 80,000 members and a clearer identity in the war. Its uniform was established, its functions on the lines of communication were highly valued and it had even gained limited government funding. But the ambitions of the organisation's leader went beyond this. Furse wanted equal recognition for women's war work, an efficient, centralised method of recruitment and training for women as 'leaders'. [7] In 1916 she had assumed that women's conscription into the army was imminent, but she was wrong about this, and the reasons for the military establishment's refusal to conscript women, even as auxiliaries, were intimately connected with the function of gender in wartime propaganda. To have conscripted women would have been to accord them equivalent status in the emergency and to have broken the stereotypical presentation of women as war's 'other' on which so much of the 'home fires' mythology depended. Furse believed that this barrier could be eroded, but this reveals a confidence in individualism over the more permanent structuring forces of her culture's ideology. She had openly colluded in the appeal to class and femininity as a certain kind of power base *because* of its unthreatening nature. That equality should be out of the question ought not, therefore, to be surprising. Indeed, the foundation of the VAD, on close examination, is seen to be precariously constructed upon aspirations towards militarism and equality that are consistently undermined by the conservative pressures of class and gendered identity. This comes vividly to life in the personal testaments of the recruits, but has a prior existence in the structure of the organisation.

IDEOLOGICAL STRUCTURING/ DISCOURSES OF GLORY?

The militarisation and professionalisation of nursing is a story that exists as a sub-text to this one and is told in full elsewhere (Vicinus 1985; Summers 1988). What I want to illuminate here is the network of ideological assumptions that lay behind the VAD's directives and propaganda and their uneven reception. The institution was poised between appeals to militaristic discipline and to civilian femininity. Precedents, of course, were scarce. With the exception of professional nursing forces such as the Queen Alexandra Imperial Nursing Service, women's work had not previously entered the sphere of martial activity on a large scale: it was not until July 1917 that the Women's Army Auxiliary Corps was founded, with the Women's Royal Naval Service and the Women's Royal Air Force following soon after.[8] What, then, were the consequences of Furse's negotiating a stake in militarism while maintaining that her organisation did not intend to depart from the feminine ideal?

16

It is perhaps worth remembering that the most generalised concepts of middle-class femininity in the early twentieth century did not cast women as creatures of discipline. Few had attended boarding school; intellectual training at university, although possible, was rare; military training was all but unheard of. Women, as Virginia Woolf argued explicitly in *Three Guineas* and implicitly in *Jacob's Room*, were excluded from most forms of institutionalised discipline. Furse, in urging on her recruits the importance of good behaviour, emphasised the point that 'the desire of all concerned is to make the employment of women a success' (BRCS 10 1/3). But this was no straightforward matter, for what was the nature of the 'success' to which Furse aspired? And on whose terms was it to be negotiated? Admittance to the battle zones was in the gift of the military authorities. For reasons of tradition, security and discipline, the latter were reluctant to admit women onto their territory. Those in Furse's position, then, inevitably had to bid for the small freedoms at first allowed them by moving between the opposed poles of militarism and femininity – and the reception of the VAD uniform points this up nicely.

Uniform is crucial to military organisation. It also might be said to act as an interface between the individual and the institution she represents; indeed it is often the means of transformation from the former to the latter. The VAD in civilian clothing might have been identified by its wide variety of coded signals, suggesting her parents' social status and her role as their daughter. In uniform, however, having invested herself with the prescribed lengths, breadths, colours and fabrics of the institution that had accepted her, she was required entirely to subjugate her appearance and behaviour to the demands of that institution: to become its representative. This apparent loss of freedom, therefore, can be seen as a means of gaining access to new and more glamorous freedoms: to be a nurse in wartime was a fitting occupation for a woman. And furthermore, it offered the enticing illusion of a coherent identity. Furse notes the excitement of being in uniform in the first months of the war, when free travel on public transport was amongst the perks. If the men were hurrying to transform themselves into parcels of patriotism it was clear that their female counterparts were equally anxious to seek a similar identity.

If uniform appealed to discourses of militarism it had a concomitant function and a crucial one in this context: it helped to subdue expressions of individuality and, in this case, of 'femininity' that might border on the sexual. This concern provides a constant sub-text to Furse's documents. The regulations were oppressively specific: collars were to be stiff, white, 2⅜ inches deep; cuffs stiff, white, 3⅜ inches deep; belts stiff, white, 3 inches deep – and so on (BRCS 8/3). No hints of individual taste were allowed; no additions or alterations, no veils or bow ties or collars worn over the coat – and strictly no paint, powder, scent or jewellery as, in Furse's words, 'the using of such things invites criticism, and may bring discredit on the Organisation' (BRCS 10 2/12).

The effect of uniform on subject position, though, belies the rigid codes that Furse administered. Radclyffe Hall's Stephen Gordon welcomes it as a reward for good service, and as an escape from the gendered constrictions of civilian dress. 'The good workman is worthy of his Sam Browne belt' (Hall [1928] 1982: 275), she declares, grateful for a brief release into masculine identification. On the other hand, Dorothy Nicol, in her unpublished memoir, enthuses: 'No bride could have been more excited over her trousseau than I was over my kit', using the image of marriage to connote devotion to her country.[9] Uniform had a certain mystique – it was a prize, a symbol of one's coming of age, of having entered the Symbolic Order. Lesley N. Smith, however, in her *Four Years Out of Life* (1931), shows a greater consciousness of the loss of autonomy that uniform suggests: 'On 8th November, 1915, I was called up by the War Office and, in company with fifty other hats (navy felt, price 15s 6d) and fifty other coats (navy serge, price 27s 6d) I reported in London' (1931: 24). A certain (upper-class) individualism makes her fearful of submerging her identity in a metonymical stream of hats and coats. Later on in the book, once the nurse's uniform has come to represent death and human degradation, she describes how one nurse, Gracie, defies the tendency to merge with a decaying system by holding on to vestiges of traditional femininity:

Gracie still wore a wide silk petticoat beneath her cotton uniform and swung her skirts, with a feminine rustle of silk, down the dilapidated duckboards. Her sheer lawn caps were hand-stitched in a convent and seemed to retain something of the delicate refinement of the embroiderers, and she miraculously never became draggle-tailed but flicked her crisp linen aprons in a challenge to the wind and filth.

(1931: 176)

At once coquette and Carmelite, she stands out, like the 'Rose of No Man's Land', needing something over and above militaristic ritual to shield her from the real conditions of the Front. If uniform is an interface, she needs the additional protective armour of silk and chastely-stitched caps to protect her identity from absorption by the general degradation. Many feminists might regard the above passage with distaste, seeing Gracie as a mere victim of male stereotyping, her uniform nothing more than her badge of slavery. It is possible, however, to read the passage otherwise. Femininity, in its most conservative form, can be seen to be a powerful agent in the preservation of a subject identity quite separate from, and opposed to, the military ethic which promises only death and disintegration.

In placing these strict regulations on the wearing of uniform the authorities presumably hoped to standardise feminine identity. Inevitably, however, the signals transmitted by clothes and their wearers could not be closed off and neatly contained within a single ideology. This is suggested by the use of a stack of metaphors in a short story by Mary Borden, in which a nurse is described as she makes an unexpected appearance in a town square in Belgium:

She was a beautiful animal dressed as a nun and branded with a red cross. Her shadowy eyes said to the regiment: 'I came to the war to nurse you and comfort you'. To them she is an enigma, to the officers she is a tease, to the town she is like a white peacock.

(Borden 1929: 34)

Rather than symbolising a fixed order, this nurse sends out messages which are received variously as repressed animal passion, sanctified self-sacrifice, mystery, flirtation and vain self-possession. The layers, the crispness and fastidiousness of the uniform were expected to signify discipline, restraint and subjugation to a fixed and solid order. The multiple ways in

19

which it was received by both male 'outsiders' and female 'insiders' indicates that the subject positions available to women in that period could not be contained by a simple, rigid structure. The texts suggest first that the possibility of an unfractured identity is illusory, and second, and more interesting from the point of view of a gendered analysis of warfare, that 'femininity' in all its undisciplined plurality was more durable as a cultural formation than anything uniform could do to it.

If femininity was durable in a way that outstripped authoritative control, the characteristics of social class were invoked to set the seal on the organisation's reliability. The VAD recruitment campaign worked on the assumption that upper- and middle-class women would be seen best to represent England; working-class women would not. The appeal was to that class whose static, Victorian value system could overcome, by sheer 'character' and 'breeding', any of the possible dangers that might affront the woman on active service.

One of the better-known Red Cross posters for the recruitment of nurses, by Alonzo Earl Foringer, depicts a seated female figure, robed and veiled with the Red Cross sign on her cap, gazing heavenwards while she cradles a tiny wounded soldier on a stretcher. The icon is a bizarre intersection of the madonna and child and the Pietà. It emphasises the 'holiness' of the war at the same time as it encourages women to adopt a Marian role. The caption reads: 'The Greatest Mother in the World.' Gilbert and Gubar see in this confirmation of the nurse's power over immobilised men (1989: 288); Marcus reads it as an iconoclastic reversal of a suffragette forcible-feeding poster (1989: 64). While the former seems misguided in comparison with the latter, which may carry some historical weight, neither considers the ideological conjunction between class and Christian submissiveness that recruiting depended on. 'You are being sent to work for the Red Cross', Furse informed VAD volunteers in a 'sealed letter'. 'You have to perform a task which will need your courage, your energy, your patience, your humility, your determination to overcome all difficulties.'[10] This appeal was based on the one issued by Kitchener to the men in the first Expeditionary Force. The latter centres on the need for discipline, responsible behaviour, avoidance of wine and women. Furse's, while often following the syntax of the Kitchener paper, emphasises humility, unselfishness, the importance of giving 'generously and whole-heartedly, grudging nothing'. The values are more spiritual than practical and they appeal to the self-denial promulgated by Christianity, to patriotism and to a general subservience to patriarchy: 'If you see others in better circumstances than yourself, be patient and think of the men who are fighting amid discomfort and who are often in great pain' (ibid.).

The perpetuation of this value system was ensured by a recruitment procedure that was detailed and rigidly selective. Each candidate had to send in her Qualification Form (showing she had passed the first aid and home nursing examinations), signed by her Commandant and counter-signed by the County Director, before her references could be taken up. References were to include a Matron's report on her hospital experience, a reference regarding the nationality of her parents, one from 'a Lady' testifying to her character and one from her school or college as to her qualifications and character. A medical certificate was required, to be posted to the Headquarters by the doctor, and each candidate was interviewed by a Matron. Brittain describes the belittling effect of this experience in an image which suggests the closed world of her class and a nascent resentment at being on the wrong side of the authoritative fence: 'I stood [. . .] all through the interview, and know now just how a servant feels when she is being engaged' ([1933] 1979: 179). This demand for women of 'good background', though, had its drawbacks. Many of the women had been educated to rely upon the enormous servant class for the drudgery of daily housekeeping. Brittain, as she records to her shame, did not know how to boil an egg; Ruth Whitaker had never washed a cup; the fictional Nell Smith (in 'Not So Quiet . . .', see later) had never cleaned a room. These practical handicaps, however, diminished in significance because the training proper to their class had also provided them with a model of behaviour based on the nursery and on their Nanny's strict, cautionary reminders that obedience was all, as Dorothy McCann recalls in her unpublished memoir:

> One evening Matron told me that I was to be head cook from the next morning and my friend was to be my assistant. When I told her I couldn't cook she said 'Nurse, there is no such word as can't'.[11]

In such texts the school-room adage typically comes into play and transforms a class-based disability into a possibility. These women would not demand their rights, would not complain, but they would perform, as Thekla Bowser puts it, 'the lowliest task from the highest motive' (Bowser 1917: 23).

Class-bound assumptions about the superiority of 'psychological fitness' over 'practical ability', then, lent these women the self-confidence to break the mould of their assumptions regarding 'fit work for ladies' (cf. Brittain 1981: 220). At the same time, however, their education gave them a certain complacency about their ability to act independently within rigid structures of discipline. This was frequently proved to be misplaced. As the glamour of their role in the war diminished, many found themselves psychologically unfit to deal with the prolonged rigours of their job, and this was rarely ameliorated by clashes with the organisation's hierarchy.

At the root of these women's crises of identity lay, perhaps, the hypocrisy of propagandist recruiting procedures, which journalist and novelist Evadne Price exposed. Price, under the pseudonym Helen Zenna Smith, wrote the novel 'Not So Quiet . . .' Stepdaughters of War (1930) as an equivalent to, and complement of, Erich Maria Remarque's All Quiet on the Western Front (1929). 'Not So Quiet . . .' is indeed written with what has been called 'the determination to call a spade a bloody shovel' (Cadogan and Craig 1978: 48), but it sets out a plausible counter-version of the ideological drive behind the conservative propaganda:

> It astounds me why the powers-that-be at the London headquarters stipulate that refined women of decent education are essential for this ambulance work. Why should they want this class to do the work of strong navvies on the cars, in addition to the work of scullery maids under conditions that no professional scullery maid would tolerate for a day? Possibly because this is the only class that suffers in silence, that scorns to carry tales. We are such cowards. We dare not face being called 'cowards' and 'slackers', which we certainly shall be if we complain. [. . .] Poor fools, we deserve all we get.
>
> (Price 1930: 50)

There was, however, a further possible motive for selecting

members from that class, and one aided by the 'holy mother' image: their sense of decorum and simple ignorance might have caused them to seem less likely to become romantically entangled with the men. To have done so would have been to impair the honour of the organisation and to have confirmed the worst assumptions of those who believed women incapable of making their employment a success. In her autobiography Furse dwells on the need to 'establish a reputation for almost exaggerated seriousness' (1940: 321) and sent home her most efficient, skilful and restless driver, who made the mistake of becoming engaged while on active service. Ironically, this woman was to become Mrs Graham Jones, the leader of the first VAD motor ambulance unit in France and, it has been suggested, the prototype for *'Not So Quiet . . .'*'s ruthless and inflexible Commandant, the hated 'Mrs Bitch'.[12] A riposte to this obsession with 'exaggerated seriousness' comes in *'Not So Quiet . . .'* from the aristocratic but down-to-earth Tosh:

> Personally, if I were choosing women to drive heavy ambulances their moral characters wouldn't worry me. It would be 'Are you a first-class driver?' not 'Are you a first-class virgin?' The biggest harlot or the biggest saint . . . what the hell does it matter as long as they put up a decent performance behind the steering wheel and can keep their engines clean? You can't get up to much immorality with dying men, can you?
>
> (Price 1930: 126)

Price thus reverses the opposition between 'psychological fitness' and 'practical ability', but it is interesting that even in this text, which scores most of its points by attempting to violate the sensibilities of the educated classes, the debunking has to be done through the acceptable voice of the aristocracy. Working-class women were the victims of these recruiting procedures not only because they were excluded from this area of war work, but, more importantly, because the ideological framework within which Furse, her supporters and those she was trying to convert operated, persisted with a symbolic representation of working-class women as degraded and lascivious – little more than potential prostitutes (cf. Kaplan 1988: 55–75). Given the military establishment's fear of sexually transmitted diseases – brought to public attention in the nineteenth century by the

Contagious Diseases Act (1866; cf. Walkowitz 1980; also Enloe 1983: 18–45) – extreme and socially prejudiced measures were taken to assure the military that their forces were not being exposed to a massive, avoidable risk.

EARLY VOLUNTARY AID DETACHMENT RESPONSES: WOMEN IN POWER

The image of the Holy Mother may have been a powerful recruiting icon, but it bore little resemblance to the complexities involved in maintaining power positions within the organisation. VAD members were frequently caught between the older, traditional rituals of the nursing profession and the new discipline of militarism, a conflict which was further exacerbated by a general clash between middle-class individualism and the systematised order essential for the smooth running of a complex institution. Nursing Sisters, for example, were often sent VAD probationers who were unwilling to obey the received doctrines; commandants had to devise new role models as a means of maintaining order. The problem was that these women had no clear role models for power (unlike, for example, Wilfred Owen, who assumes the public school model in spite of his own social origins), and the recruits under their command, often accustomed to social seniority, frequently resented authority structures in which they were (doubly) subordinate.

Violetta Thurstan's *Field Hospital and Flying Column* (1915) exemplifies the old school of professional nursing. In this text, remarkable for the way in which a maternal discourse can insulate a narrative that consistently deals with the effects of martial brutality,[13] Thurstan herds her 'large family' of nurses into accommodation, brimming with patriotic pride in the 'gallant little Belgian army' (1915: 9), pouting with distress at losing her portmanteau full of clean aprons, and concluding with a resigned cheeriness: 'But such is war!' (1915: 21). Like the Nanny of a household whose masculine activities do not concern her, Thurstan governs her own cosy world with all the efficiency that circumstances permit. The complexities of power relations amongst women are to her immaterial. She faces gunfire with the air of a bemused child and indeed relates the incident as if it were a bed-time story: 'it was not a very pleasant walk as bullets were flying freely and the mitrailleuse never stopped going pom-pom-pom' (1915: 59). We can see here a governing discourse which sanitises and domesticates the most violent of experiences. The patriarchal establishment need have nothing to fear, Thurstan's text seems to say: this nurse runs no risk of losing her femininity.

Katharine Furse, on the other hand, clearly thought that the best way to achieve recognition in the fighting zones was to imitate the rituals of the military. She thus delights in describing much respectful standing to attention and the liberal use of the word 'Sir' when addressing those in authority (Furse 1940: 307–9), and is not alone in celebrating women's success in this role. The eponymous heroine of Radclyffe Hall's short story 'Miss Ogilvy Finds Herself' is presented as the perfect military leader, who had always (like Stephen Gordon in the novel which developed from this) adopted a masculine identity. The war, at last, provides a space in which she can act authentically. At the age of 56 she crops her hair, sets off for London and is soon leading an ambulance unit in France. A 'cold, hard-faced woman who commanding, domineering, even hectoring at times, had yet been possessed of so dauntless a courage and of so insistent a vitality that it vitalised the whole unit' (1934: 4), she rapidly gains the admiration of the young women under her command who, like her, had pounced on the opportunity for adventure and comradeship. The story suggests the possibility of hundreds of Miss Ogilvys seeking to revolutionise their identity in a dream of authority that is unimaginable in the codes of conventional femininity.

The lesbian 'hero' thus finds liberation in a masculine subject position. Not surprisingly, however, this role is infrequently adopted in the fiction of the period. Indeed it is more common to find attacks on women who adopt a 'masculinised' construction of leadership – and the reasons for this might involve a resistance to the 'false' claims on power positions that it appeared to some that women made. Evadne Price's 'Mrs Bitch' is an extreme example. Unlike her masculine counterpart, Himmelstoss, in Remarque's *All Quiet*, this brutish leader retains her command without retribution. Universally loathed for her sadistic exercise of power and for her relentless pursuit of superhuman standards of perfection, she inspires the (seemingly inevitable) question: 'Why is it that women in authority

almost invariably fall victims to megalomania?' (Price 1930: 61).
Rather than presenting masculine identification as liberating,
this text acts as a warning against female misuse of power in a
rigidly hierarchical system.

VAD recruits, then, who had not been involved in the organisation before the war and who were not trained nurses, had to
find some way of engaging with an often contradictory battery
of authority figures. Professional nurses were frequently an-
tagonistic to the 'untrained women' who, with a handful of
certificates and a few months' experience, threatened to diminish their authority and devalue their expertise.[14] The VADs,
answering their country's call in good faith, were often shocked
to find themselves treated as servants by those they were helping
to fight the same cause.

Furse admitted to flawed administration here. The hierarchy
of the organisation was such that VADs were always subject to
orders from the Matron and so could be asked to perform any
task from scrubbing floors to assisting with amputations at any
stage in their service. Their 'willingness' was to be an index of
the idealism with which the movement began. This lack of
internal structure, though, rendered VADs vulnerable. They
could not break their six-month contract without running the
risk of being refused another position, and breaking a contract
while on foreign service meant relinquishing the right to work
overseas. As the organisation developed in size and scope,
however, and became more aware of the needs and grievances
of its members, many of whom were becoming increasingly well
qualified and experienced, efforts were made to offer a system
of promotion. In 1917 Furse decided to introduce a grading
system for nursing members in military hospitals to ensure
them senior and responsible work once they had served long
enough and proved themselves capable to the satisfaction of
their Matron. Red stripes were worn on the uniform as a means
of signalling this new status. The success of any VAD's career,
nevertheless, still largely depended on the personal relationship she had with her superiors. Official complaints from VAD
members centred on the want of encouragement from trained
nurses and the uncertainty of the service: they could be moved
from a responsible to a menial occupation with no explanation.
On the other hand, the Matrons' complaints about VADs
constantly returned to lack of discipline, reluctance to accept

criticism, and 'independence'. Clearly there were clashes of ideals here. The Matrons and Sisters wanted to do their job unhindered by well-meaning 'ladies' who had no long-term commitment to the standards and principles of the profession. The VADs, on the other hand, resented being subject to an impenetrable authority structure, exercised by women who were often their social inferiors.

Most accounts of VAD work from middle-class women of 'good background' articulate a strong sense of difference between themselves and the trained Sisters, a difference frequently founded on the institutional habit of making 'mysteries of trifles' (Brittain 1981: 312), and epitomised, perhaps, by the bathetic dramatisation by Thekla Bowser of the keeping of the linen at VAD headquarters:

> The linen is kept strictly on military principles, and the first sight of the books which are sent down by the Military Authorities is quite enough to frighten the ordinary woman; but the linen store-keeper bravely tackles them and surmounts all difficulties. She gradually falls into the routine which is much easier that it looks . . . .
>
> (Bowser 1917: 187)

While in Violetta Thurstan's text there is a dislocation between the severity of the experience and the domesticity of the language, here the opposite is the case. A combative discourse is employed in order to elevate the performance of this simple, administrative task to the status of a military exercise: 'bravely tackles', 'surmounts all difficulties', 'falls in' is evocative more of an outpost skirmish than an hour in a central London storehouse. The passage juxtaposes order and ordinariness, encouraging the typical, timorous woman to muster courage, master the task and discover the joys of discipline. Far from attaining an elevated sense of identity in the ranks of Kitchener's nurses, though, most recruits were more likely to bewail being treated as 'Very Able Dusters'.[15] Discontinuity between propaganda and individual experience is predictable and arguably commonplace in war writing. Bowser's assertion, however, that 'a common chord of love and tenderness' (1917: 16) would break down class barriers between women ran counter to the very cultural formation upon which the VAD selection procedure relied. The collision between the two hierarchical systems – class and rank – destabilised the disciplinary ideal of both the VAD and the nursing profession and the social ideal of those who mistakenly thought that a common purpose could smooth over the deep and traditionally divisive structures that were part of their national consciousness.

Olive Dent, in *A VAD in France* (1917), voices her contempt for the professional nurses in jaunty, self-congratulatory tones. She and her companions were not 'overwhelmed with or impressed by our manifold shortcomings. Also we were so lacking in awe as to prefer having more faith in the knowledge of the Government than the opinion (or possibly prejudice) of an individual nurse' (1917: 29). Her confidence in her own judgment of the profession into which she has sought part-time entry is, as far as she is concerned, backed up by the patriarchal authority system. VAD Ruth Whitaker describes how social jealousy intersected with professional jealousy when she was posted to Malta, where 'the Sisters were rag-tag and bob-tail, scraped together after the best had gone to France' (Whitaker, IWM: 96). Snobbery from the lower ranks must have been hard to support – especially when these upper-class young ladies were on visiting terms with the local gentry and were aided in their social climbing by the Matrons ('mainly from Queen Alexandra's Nursing Service, highly trained and gentlewomen'), thus rendering the Sisters socially irrelevant:

> Many of the VADs knew the Methuens and were welcome at the palace, and both Matrons and the Methuens did their best to ease the way for us. When a Governor visited a hospital he always chatted with the VADs and this was resented.
>
> (Whitaker, IWM: 96)

In turn, many VADs resented their professionally subordinate position: Nurse Gratton in Lesley Smith's *Four Years Out of Life* (1931) expresses the seething discontent of a VAD at being under the authority of a Matron, 'whose normal environment was a genteel suburb'. Enid Bagnold's response, however, is more ambivalent. Born into a military family (her father was a colonel), she finds the structures of power tempting, but to be resisted in order to maintain an 'individuality' which, for her, is a self-consciously artistic distance. The 'untrained' stand a good chance of escaping repressive uniformity, but they have to fight against 'the ardent longing to be alike' (Bagnold 1918: 34). For Bagnold, however, this is not essentially a problem. The first words of *A Diary Without Dates* are 'I like discipline. I like to be part of an institution' (1918: 3). She goes on, several pages later:

> Let them pile on the rules, invent and insist; yet behind them, beneath them, I have that strong, secret liberty of an institution that runs like a wind in me and lifts my mind like a leaf.
>
> (1918: 19)

She gains a curious sense of freedom, then, as a result of the restrictions placed on her. So secure and exhilarating is her sense of 'strong, secret liberty' that she can happily use the structure of the institution as a mask, beneath which she can operate freely, without risk of contamination. Her sense of security, however, was misplaced: this manifestation of 'independence' culminated in her dismissal from the Royal Herbert Hospital on publication of *A Diary Without Dates*, for breach of military discipline (Sebba 1986: 61).

In *Testament of Youth* Brittain is similarly damning of the professionals. Having witnessed their 'starved and dry' responses, she expresses 'a deep fear of merging [her] own individuality in the impersonal routine of the organisation' ([1933] 1979: 211). Matrons and Sisters, as she explains, feared the undermining of their authority should VAD nurses be eligible for registration after the war, but:

> Actually this fear was groundless; all but a very few VADs were only too thankful when the war was over to quit a singularly backward profession for their own occupations and interests, but many 'trained women' having no such interests themselves, could not believe that others were attracted by them. The presence of Red Cross nurses drove some of them almost frantic with jealousy and suspicion, which grew in intensity as the VADs increased in competence.
>
> ([1933] 1979: 309)

Brittain betrays her elitism in this contemptuous portrait of a 'backward profession' which had failed to recognise the, in her view, superior qualities of 'educated women'.

We can see, then, that the cultural 'controls' of class and

femininity are used by those keen for women to succeed in order to mollify the military establishment's distrust of women in combat zones. Their power and persistence, however, proved to be fundamentally divisive. Class is used by those such as Brittain as a platform from which to disparage women who were attempting to establish public recognition of their professional status as nurses. Set against each other, each fiercely protective of her individual or professional space, the independent lady and the trained nurse both lose out to patriarchy through an inability to band together and establish a power base. It seems to be the case, then, that the ideological structures that ensured these women their ticket out to the war, equally ensured that they made a round trip. Their overwhelming effect was to prevent any serious challenge to existing power structures and so to return most women at the end of their four years to their point of departure: the home.

THE VOLUNTARY AID DETACHMENTS' STORY: PRIVATE LIVES

While Furse was bidding for new freedoms for women, playing the 'permanent' elements of their value system (class, femininity) against their 'progress' into the active life of the nation, the recruits frequently found themselves overwhelmed by the violent experience of warfare, the victims of private grief and, like the soldiers, unable to marry their war experience with the discourses that hitherto had governed their private lives. The Symbolic Order was revealed to be riddled with cracks and inconsistencies. The stasis of Edwardian younglady hood was profoundly disrupted, but the effect, rather than being revolutionary, was often merely fragmentary.

'Seeing life'

Of course the recruits initially co-operated with, and indeed celebrated, the opportunities offered to them by the institution. Their primary impulse was simple: to break away from the constraints of the family house. Of her experience in the 1st London General Hospital, Vera Brittain was to write: 'After twenty years of sheltered gentility [. . .] I was at last seeing life' ([1933] 1979: 213). She, like other VADs, found herself suddenly released from the passive, chaperoned Edwardian existence characteristic of provincial female life. Many of the recruits had been educated at home. Dorothy Nicol had her fair share of governesses as had Ruth Whitaker, who notes with some asperity that money spent on her brothers' education was denied her: 'It was always "the dear boys" and "the poor girls"' (Whitaker, IWM: 38). Lesley Smith describes the insulated seclusion of the pre-war days in terms that form a consistent theme in war literature, illustrating the mythological Arcadian calm that prefaced the storm: [16]

> To a girl of twenty-three the tennis parties, the garden parties, the weddings and dances seemed as inevitable and unchangeable as the calm prosperity of every day life.
>
> (Smith 1931: 1)

Small wonder then that the war generated profound excitement. VAD Dorothy McCann recalls her amusement when, the night before her unit was due to leave for France, a Sister came round at midnight to check that they were all still present: 'As though we would try to run away from what we thought was the greatest adventure in our lives!' (McCann, IWM: 1). If the first priority was to escape the parental home, the romance of the job centred on escaping the country. 'Foreign service was the thing, and I hardly dared admit even to myself how incredibly lucky I was to have the chance to go' (Nicol, IWM: 10).

For Brittain, France was the only place to be: it represented 'the heart of the fiercest living' where nothing was permanent and there was 'titanic, illimitable death' ([1933] 1979: 372). E.M. Spearing in *From Cambridge to Camiers* (1917) speaks of a 'curious community of suffering' particularly notable after the Somme battles of July 1916, 'in which one is glad to have been allowed to take one's part' (Spearing 1917: 59), and Sarah Macnaughtan writes 'there is a splendid freedom about being in the midst of death – a certain glory in it, which one can't explain' (Macnaughtan 1919: 10). Paradoxically, to be at the site of death was seen to be equivalent to being at the heart of life. It was, effectively, an entry into history. As Radclyffe Hall writes in *The Well of Loneliness*, 'War and death had given them a right to life, and life tasted sweet, very sweet to their palates' ([1928] 1982: 275).

Comradeship was a crucial element in women's new order of

experience. 'There was always a jolly atmosphere in the mess for we were all in the same boat. We loved our work' writes McCann (IWM: 2). A number developed close female friends and a concomitant sense of bonding and belonging. Bagnold, drawing attention to the patients' lack of distinction between trained and untrained nurses, writes: 'How wonderful to be called Sister! Every time the uncommon name is used towards me I feel the glow of an implied relationship, something which links me to the speaker' (Bagnold 1918: 5). In a similar vein, although with something more of the grim desperation that was to characterise 'front line' narratives, the narrator of Mary Borden's short story 'Blind' says:

> We are locked together, the old ones and I, and the wounded men; we are bound together. We all feel it. We all know it. The same thing is throbbing in us, the single thing, the one life.

(Borden 1929: 154)

Being trusted simply to act – to take on duties for which experience is lacking, whether it be becoming head cook or taking charge of a ward for the first time – gave many of these women a sense of their responsibility and of their own capability: 'I had only been capable because they believed in and trusted me', says Dorothy Nicol (IWM: 46). As Ruth Alleyndene says in Vera Brittain's novel *Honourable Estate*, 'At least this century, if it did smash the world for thousands of women, has given them the compensation of work' (1936: 546). Remembering this, it is easy to see the root of their antagonism to those among the 'trained' who obstructed the VADs' route to responsible employment.

The next best thing . . .

There is, then, considerable evidence to support Gilbert and Gubar's case that war offered the 'delight of (female) mobilisation' (1989: 293) and I have no quarrel with this as an articulation of the aspirations of many women. I disagree, however, with their suggestion that the war 'overturned [. . .] the rule of patrilineal succession, the founding law of patriarchy itself' (1989: 280). While it is true that some women took on the tasks of their dead or absent male relations and that many returning soldiers felt alienated from the activities on the

Home Front, this claim is surely unhelpful as a description of the war's *general* effect on women. Exuberance takes over from analysis in their failure to acknowledge the concrete mani-festations of western capitalist culture's systematic devaluation of women. While enjoying the liberties of employment, women were simultaneously wrestling with the fact that they were constructed, unmistakably, as secondary and temporary work-ers. While their *experience* contradicted gendered stereotypes, it was contained within an immediate framework that made strategic use of conservative definitions of femininity, and within a cultural system that showed few signs of revolutionising its patriarchal principles.

Hence the cry 'My God! If only I were a man!' (Hall 1934: 10), which resonates throughout women's texts of this period.[17] Radclyffe Hall is making a special case here (cf. Newton 1984: 557–75), but nevertheless, for most women being a nurse was the 'next best thing' to being a man and going to the Front (Brittain [1933] 1979: 213–14). Much of the official discourse, as we have seen, emphasises the importance of women's secondary contribution to the war in terms that accept mas-culine priority. 'The daughters are wanted by the Country as well as the sons' says Katharine Furse in 'The Ideals of the VADs' (BRCS 10/1). But the sons, of course, take first place in her ideological construction of nationalism. The early part of Brittain's *Testament* and most of her diary might seem to offer a radical critique of women's subordination. Both documents are written in terms which register the determination of this middle-class young woman to achieve equal rights with her male contemporaries – particularly her brother and his friends – at the expense of her female friendships.[18] Her ambition to overcome the constraints placed upon her sex leads her to strive for equality with her lover, Roland Leighton. The context of the struggle changes, however, when he leaves for the Front. On beginning probation work in the local Buxton Hospital she says:

> I shall hate it, but I will be all the more ready to do it on that account. *He* has to face far worse things than any sight or act I could come across; he can bear it – and so can I.
>
> (1981: 186)

Thus while she courts suffering on a level that approaches

Roland's patriotic sacrifice, she implicitly recognises the poverty of the response she is invited to make.

Brittain sees herself as 'everynurse' and Roland as the archetypal British soldier. Nursing is seen to be the perfect complement to his role and if he must suffer physically, she 'should at any rate equal the agony mentally' (1981: 222). There is, however, a fundamental flaw in this aspiration and one which she sees as giving men a permanent advantage: she is not called upon to die. In that sense, as much as she may relish doing something 'irrevocable' (1981: 289) – signing on for six months service – which smacks of being taken over by the military machine just as Roland has been, her status will always be secondary, subservient. She longs to be heroic; the system permits her only to be auxiliary. The inevitable sense of devaluation, then, can never be relieved.

Devotional glamour

The system itself nevertheless offered one means of compensation. The discourse of 'devotional glamour' exalted the female predisposition towards nurturance and self-immolation, admitting them to a 'natural' order. Ruth Whitaker, like so many others, talks of women 'desirous to find sublimation and fulfilment in service' (Whitaker, IWM: 106), and takes pride in her diligence, particularly when the soldiers admit their dependency on her generous and omniscient care: '"You know what I want before I do myself, Sister"', she quotes. '"What should I do without you?"' (IWM: 127).[19] It was not a simple matter for many of these women, in the face of their experience, to appreciate the more radical objectives of feminism. Dorothy Nicol, for instance, cannot help but admire the soldiers: 'The pity of it, the utter senselessness of it, and through everything, the amazing bravery of the men, their uncomplaining and never failing sense of humour' (IWM: 23).

May Sinclair, however, *was* an active feminist, but one who was rapidly seduced by the alternative glories of warfare. She joined Hector Munro's voluntary ambulance corps in 1914, and articulates her excitement in hedonistic terms: [20] 'It is only a little thrill so far (for you don't really believe that there is any danger), but you can imagine the thing growing, growing steadily, till it becomes ecstacy' (1915: 14). Sinclair, in spite of her principles, is in love with the power that war represents. That this new focus should entirely obliterate the structure of her former ideals, she registers as 'odd', but inexorable:

> Odd how the War changes us. I who abhor and resist authority, who hardly know how I am to bring myself to obey my friend the Commandant, am enamoured of this Power and utterly submissive.
>
> (1915: 27)

Vera Brittain also takes on the discourse of glamorous submission, but in her case the emphasis is different. In place of a vibrant, almost Lawrencian self-indulgence, there is a puritan reserve that seems to belong more to the generation of a Dorothea Brooke. Brittain (also, of course, a feminist) looked forward to nursing as 'stern labour for love's sake' (1981: 215), tackled her tasks with a 'devotional enthusiasm' and comments in *Testament*:

> Every task, from the dressing of a dangerous wound to the scrubbing of a bed mackintosh, had for us in those early days a sacred glamour which redeemed it equally from tedium and disgust.
>
> ([1933] 1979: 210)

The *Diary* is characterised much more by the discourse of Puritanism and the growth of the soul[21] than is the more self-assured *Testament of Youth*, although she does veer back in *Testament* to the language of exaltation – particularly when the event in question relates, no matter how obliquely, to sex. On one occasion she describes her reactions to washing a soldier: 'towards the men I came to feel an almost adoring gratitude for their simple and natural acceptance of my ministrations' ([1933] 1979: 165). Although she appears to be in control in the retrospective account, and to some degree mocks her earlier, naive self, she remains in the grip of a Puritan discourse which transforms a rather mundane activity into something resembling a religious rite. The event is perceived neither as ordinary nor, as one might expect from one of Brittain's limited exposure to naked male flesh, as shocking. The impact is held in bounds by an etherealised terminology.

Glamour and exaltation, then, on the one hand compensated for not being invited to make the supreme sacrifice, but on the other drew an ideological veil over many of the challenges and changes that the new experience offered to these women. The power of this discourse, however, was neither universal nor ineluctable. The trauma of the daily experience of nursing – especially on the Western Front – destabilised for some women what had come to be their way of identifying themselves. The complexity and ambiguity of these women's experiences was largely owing to the violent clash between the conservative ideologies that enabled them to get out to the war and the failure of those ideologies to mediate or account for the trauma that later beset them. The fissures in the dominant discourse in some cases created new ways of seeing: in others it did nothing but confirm an increasing sense of alienation.

CHALLENGE TO FEMININE IDENTITY

Many of the novels, autobiographies and sketches published during the war set themselves the task of managing and guiding public response to the traumatic events. [22] Thurstan, Sinclair (both 1915), Dent, Spearing and Bowser (all 1917) are largely concerned to demonstrate women's ability to act within a framework of acceptable female role models – as prescribed by the VAD command. (Bagnold (1918) is something of an exception to this, as indeed her dismissal suggests.) The texts published in the late 1920s and 1930s, in the boom of war writing and often in response to male war stories, present more ambiguous images of war nurses. Indeed, they were often written with the express purpose of revealing the horrific nature of nursing men wounded by a new, mechanised and chemical armoury. Such stories do not attempt to match those of the men for gruesome detail. However, the details of how women encountered and comprehended their experiences reveal a genuine clash between their troubled gendered identifications and the public passport of devoted service that sent them out 'into history' in the first place.

The shock of the real

The VADs, by and large, led rough lives but, as we have seen, complaining, in general, was not advisable: the last thing they wanted was to be sent home as 'unsuitables' and thus to prove to the world that women were incapable of acting sensibly in time of emergency. This would have been equivalent to cowardice – and women, of course, not suffering physically as much as the men did, were constantly encouraged to remember this.[23] The reality of nursing conditions, nevertheless, even through the lens of devotional zeal, was guaranteed to challenge basic assumptions concerning personal comfort and hygiene. Most of the 'hospitals' in France were composed of a precariously arranged series of tents. The nurses would share a bell tent or an Alwyn Hut (a shanty made from wood and canvas), which would frequently collapse during bad or windy weather. Hot water was rarely available to the nurses. They had to endure muddy treks in order to wash at all and found that during the winter their clothes, if taken off, would freeze solid in the night. They had to cope with the usual infestations of mice, rats and fleas; Dorothy McCann describes how their overalls were slotted with tape which could be drawn tight in order to keep the lice out. Nurses, of course, also died – from accidents, illnesses and air raids.

Physical discomfort was augmented by the gradual erosion of customs and practices associated with a well-bred form of femininity. The heroine of Evadne Price's 'Not So Quiet . . .' (1930), Tosh, symbolically cuts off her hair, simultaneously liberating herself of a feminine encumbrance and a seething crop of fleas. While Tosh's female identity is amply com-pensated for (by her self-advertised 'breasts of a nursing mother' (1930: 15)), Nell's (the narrator) is uncertain. She observes the scenario envious of Tosh's emancipatory gesture, but oscillating between admiration for this image of 'masculine' freedom and the shelter of feminine conservatism, policed by her fear of her mother's disapproval.

Lesley Smith narrates an episode similarly concerned with the subversion of decent middle-class behaviour. She describes her humiliation at nearly fainting while helping the Medical Officer replace tubes in a pus-ridden shoulder: 'A year ago I'd have felt rather pleased with myself for being so sensitive; but sensitiveness had lost its value. It didn't help' (1931: 65). Exit 'femininity' with its tenderly nurtured 'sensitivity'. But what is its replacement? These texts, having begun with an enthusiastic response to the call of their country, typically become domin-ated by images of alienation, dislocation and even madness –

motifs of literary modernism. In one of Mary Borden's sketches, 'Moonlight', femininity is replaced by absence of feeling. For her, there is a simple, if devastating equation:

> There are no men here, so why should I be a woman? There are heads and knees and mangled testicles. There are chests with holes as big as your fist, and pulpy thighs, shapeless; and stumps where legs once were fastened. There are eyes – eyes of sick dogs, sick cats, blind eyes, eyes of delirium; and mouths that cannot articulate, and parts of faces – the nose gone, or the jaw. There are these things but no men; so how could I be a woman here and not die of it?
>
> (Borden 1929: 60)

It is an image of Hell, of neurosis. Not only were these nurses experiencing an erosion of their own subject identities, the 'men' they were treating bore increasingly little resemblance to the 'flower of English manhood' whose departure they had so enviously applauded. Far from bolstering their own sense of strength (as Gilbert and Gubar would like us to believe (1989: 263, 286)), this observation led to an impression of physical and mental fragmentation. The patients and wards were named after parts of the body: knees, arms, shoulders – 'heads' was one of the most distressing. These 'untrained women' would frequently be left in sole charge of two wards full of dangerously wounded men. After her experience in the 'heads' ward Lesley Smith's narrator describes the infiltration of her own consciousness by grotesque images from the Front – both audible and visible – 'I was trapped in their horror. I saw and admitted the triumph of ugliness and evil, and knew that wherever I went afterwards, I would take my own Bedlam with me' (1931: 93). Consistent with the war's mythological structuring, the observable realities of ugliness and evil displace the abstractions of glory and honour to occupy a permanent place in these women's minds. Nell Smith is haunted by processions of mutilated men and Brittain, after the war, suffered the recurring fear that her own face was disfigured: that she was growing a beard. As one who had always been conscious of her own 'chocolate-box prettiness' ([1933] 1979: 211), the effects of the horrors of war ate into the most obvious elements of her gendered identification.

Brittain describes her daily activity as not merely changing dressings, 'but of stopping haemorrhages, replacing intestines and draining and reinserting innumerable rubber tubes' ([1933] 1979: 374). She frequently drank tea and ate cake in a theatre with a 'foetid stench, with the thermometer about 90 degrees in the shade, and the saturated dressings and yet more gruesome remnants on the floor' ([1933] 1979: 374). Lesley Smith's Nurse Kay, assisting at an amputation, falls back with the leg, on which she has been pulling, still in her hands; Mary Borden describes working in conditions so crowded that a human knee is mistaken for a ragout of mutton, and narrates in a deadpan voice:

> There was a man stretched on the table. His brain came off in my hands when I lifted the bandage from his head. When the dresser came back I said: 'His brain came off on the bandage.'
> 'Where have you put it?'
> 'I put it in the pail under the table.'
> 'It's only one half of his brain,' he said, looking into the man's skull. 'The rest is here.'
> I left him to finish the dressing and went about my own business. I had much to do.
>
> (Borden 1929: 142–3)

Like so much VAD writing, this shocks through juxtaposition of a flat narrative tone with its hideous subject matter. Borden prefaces her collection of sketches and stories with the fore-warning that they are 'fragments of a great confusion'. She goes on to say that she has 'blurred the bare horror of facts and softened the reality in spite of myself, not because I wished to do so, but because I was incapable of a nearer approach to the truth' (1929: preface, np). The deadpan tone, then, registers her instinct to close down certain sensory perceptions in order to retain a functional level of sanity. It also points towards the incapacity of ordinary discourse to relate the events of the 'forbidden zone' in terms over which the author feels she has a secure level of authoritative control. The events break the frame of what is humanly endurable or capable of being articulated in the language of the well-educated woman.

Home and away

The revelation to these cushioned female patriots of the appalling effects of martial combat inevitably led to a sense of dislocation between the home and the Front. An event common to the narrative trajectories of these texts is the realisation that these daughters can no longer communicate with their mothers. Female experience of the war, so long silenced in our literary history, thus directly parallels that of the male, but the fracture that occurs is rather between mother and daughter than between father and son. Lesley Smith's Nurse Gratton says: 'you know what it's like at home now. You saw it yourself on your last leave. It was no use talking, they didn't understand us and what's worse they didn't even like us' (1931: 281). The challenge to the family structure is an index of a shift in value systems which results in a loss of appropriate language or discourse with which to negotiate the barriers between home and Front. Variations on Nurse Gratton's statement have a pivotal function in these texts, announcing the threat of an eternal estrangement from the apparently 'cyclical' mother–daughter bond that ensured, through a conspiracy of complacent subordination, the perpetuation of patriarchal ideology.

Evadne Price is more graphic than her contemporaries in her concern to expose the hypocrisies of the older generation.[24] Her heroine, Nell Smith, comes to despise the hollowness of women who sit on endless, futile committees and, dealing in the currency of cliché and platitude, pack their sons and daughters off to become heroes. She imagines she is taking her mother and future mother-in-law, Mrs Evans-Mawnington, on a guided tour of the war-victims she sees every day:

> Out of the way quickly, Mother and Mrs Evans-Mawnington
> – lift your silken skirts aside . . . a man is spewing blood
> [. . .]. It isn't pretty to see a hero spewing up his life's
> blood in public, is it? Much more romantic to see him in
> the picture papers being awarded the V. C., even if he is
> minus a limb or two. [. . .] Spare a glance for my last
> stretcher, . . . that gibbering, unbelievable, unbandaged
> thing, a wagging lump of raw flesh on a neck, that was a
> face a short time ago [. . .]. For all you know, Mrs Evans-
> Mawnington, he is your Roy.
>
> (1930: 91, 95)

The juxtaposing of silk and blood, public ceremony and human agony, although somewhat crude literary devices, make the political point in what might be read as a parody of the guided tours undertaken by propagandists such as Mrs Humphry Ward (cf., for example, Buitenhuis [1987: 58–9] 1989). Price emphasises the complete severance of one generation of women from the next. As the novel's relationship to Remarque's *All Quiet* suggests, these women felt better able to communicate with their male contemporaries and to shed some of their sexual inhibitions than to continue a relationship with those who had encouraged them to enter the war in the first place. Allegiance shifts from one of gender to one of generation.

This transition of allegiance, however, could not be unproblematic. While women were learning to deal with war's psychic and physical mutilations, their parents still hailed them as dutiful daughters. Vera Brittain's account discusses the clash between home and Front, the daughter and the worker, and its implications for women's identity as active citizens. As the Allies began to suffer defeats in early 1918, the older generation left on the Home Front became increasingly depressed and anxious. War conditions there may not have been volatile, but they were certainly wearing. Traditional dependency on daughters for housekeeping and nursing invalid parents did not die in this emergency and VADs, unlike soldiers, did not receive a dependency allowance. Dorothy Nicol was summoned home to care for her mother much against her will, as was Vera Brittain, who, in retrospect, expresses the dilemma that many women faced:

> What exhausts women in war time is not the strenuous and unfamiliar tasks that fall upon them, nor even the hourly dread of death for husbands or lovers or brothers or sons, it is the incessant conflict between personal and national claims which wears out their energy and breaks their spirit.
>
> ([1933] 1979: 422–3)

While both soldiers and nurses experienced the culture shock of a return to civilian life, for those like Nicol and Brittain the identity crisis was intensified through being psychically – and practically – torn between the ancient ties of family and the new, compelling need to work. Had Brittain, for example, been part of the military system proper, it would have been necessary to settle the family crisis without her, and although her family accepted this, she was supremely irritated by the trivialities of civilian existence, by London's being 'more interested in obtaining sugar than discussing the agony of the last few weeks in France' ([1933] 1979: 430). On hearing that the very hospital in which she had been serving had been bombed, resulting in the deaths and injuries of several Sisters and VADs, she expresses her disappointment in military terms: 'I felt myself a deserter, a coward, a traitor to my patients and to the other nurses' ([1933] 1979: 433). She had missed her chance to be heroic. The world of the Front goes everywhere with her, becomes the 'real' world. But the demands on daughters remain unaltered.

The challenge to feminine identity – sexuality

An aspect of 'daughterly' behaviour was faultless sexual conduct, which, as we have seen, was understood to be an unquestionable appurtenance of middle-class 'femininity'.[25] But what was the result of fracturing this rigid, symbolic code? A 'festival of female sexual liberation?' I have already questioned the general validity of Gilbert and Gubar's equation between male immobilisation and female libidinal release on the level of its imaginative construction of power relations. On a practical level it seems equally questionable because of the structural tenacity of the discourses that shaped 'feminine' consciousness. Throughout this chapter I have suggested that a challenge to secure subject identity does not unproblematically entail freedom from the conscious and unconscious constraints of that position (if this were so the feminist project now would be much further advanced than it is). Instead such challenges were frequently capable of destabilising the structures of that identity without offering any viable alternatives.

Price's Nell Smith describes her uncertainty as to her qualifications for 'womanliness'. The nature of her job, her initiation into sexual knowledge, her exposure to and use of coarse language all affect that status of which she was once so sure. Her own sexual experience is associated with mental collapse, and the discovery of lesbianism in the midst of the unit is a significant factor in this. The book, indeed, is deeply homophobic, the lesbians being named 'Skinny' and 'Frost'. Skinny is 'yellow and corpseish' in comparison with Tosh's 'pink and white prettiness'; the former uses 'vile language' as against Tosh's 'good-natured swear-words'; the adjectives 'hideous', 'grotesque', 'foul' and 'shameful' are unapologetically applied to Skinny (1930: 109, 111, 113). Nell witnesses the increasing madness and subsequent death of one of her co-workers and, finally, the heroic Tosh dies in her arms, the victim of an air raid. On the way home, suffering from a nervous breakdown, Nell sleeps with the young, healthy, virile Robin, just on his way out to the Front for the first time. She hopes that this experience will halt the procession of maimed and mutilated men that occupies her mind. It is a last resort and it is unsuccessful, merely confirming the distance between her and the old value system in which she has to try to find a place. Far from releasing her, in the context of a world that has not directly witnessed what went on in France, this experience of 'sexual liberation' only confirms her failure and breakdown.

Radclyffe Hall's Miss Ogilvy, on the other hand, *is* sexually unfettered by her war experiences. Her successful adoption of a masculine role in the war gives her the confidence to reject her uncomfortable social identity as one of three spinsters and to release herself into post-war solitude on a barely inhabited island. There she rekindles the spark of adventure and sets about unshackling herself from her inauthentic identity. At this point the narrative disarmingly shifts key from social realism to psychological fantasy. The description of the central figure shifts from 'she' to 'he'; the landscape is transformed from paths and thistles into rolling hills and lush forests. Miss Ogilvy appears to have a deeply sub-conscious inherited memory of the island but this is only fully revealed to her when she takes on the character of a strong, powerful, primitive man who has no memory of Miss Ogilvy and who is in love with a young girl, a 'ripe red berry sweet to the taste' (1934: 24). Their gender roles are highly stereotyped: he is the epitome of robust virility; she tiny, earnest and helplessly sweet. Their language, too, is primitive, and in an act that brings to mind the implications of the Kristevan 'semiotic', they consummate their love to the murmers of 'the word that had so many meanings' and which only they could understand. The Symbolic Order of rational language, linear time and monolithic sexual identity is thus fractured; the potentially revolutionary traces of a mode of being that pre-existed, and might disrupt it, seep through culture's cracks. The twentieth-century Miss Ogilvy dies having thus 'found herself'. The war experience releases in her the potential to recognise the direction which her sexuality should take, but the circumstances of her post-war world are not such that she could practise lesbianism openly. It can only be realised through a fantasy of the 'pre-historic' self.

Brittain also experienced release from sexual inhibitions as a result of her nursing, although less dramatically. She looked upon her exposure to naked male bodies as an element of her education and admits to feeling 'grateful for the knowledge of masculine functioning' ([1933] 1979: 166). Nevertheless, three years of nursing experience, which included watching syphilitics die and becoming acquainted with methods of birth control,[26] taught Brittain to discuss sexual matters in a more open and mature fashion. This seemed refreshing and natural in the company of similarly liberated women such as Winifred Holtby. Suspicion, however, prevailed in the conservative Oxford women's colleges to which they both returned:

> who knew in what cesspools of iniquity I had not wallowed? Who could calculate the awful extent to which I might corrupt the morals of my innocent juniors?
>
> ([1933] 1979: 476)

While the Nell Smiths and Miss Ogilvys go mad or die, the more conventional others faced the problem of rehabilitation into a world that chose to ignore their sufferings and experiences. Oxford saluted the activities of its male students, but suppressed those of its female students. The social and political world was anxious to return to the *status quo ante-bellum*: while it was forced, finally, in 1918 to offer women over the age of 30 the vote (many VADs were under 30), it was reluctant to register the extent of the experiences that had apparently driven women to demand this right. Women had done their bit, filled the gaps. They should now go home and try to forget.

It is, of course, important to remember that some women gained from the war. Katharine Furse, Rachel Crowdy and Violetta Thurstan all went on to do public work;[27] VADs Ruth Manning, Dorothy Nicol and Ruth Whitaker respectively trained in the Almoners Institute, became a physiotherapist and supervised the National Kitchens and Restaurants in South West London. It would be wrong to suggest that all women were merely victims of the ideological stances they had been bred to support. Many of them, however, like the male war writers, although for different reasons, characterise their experience specifically in terms of loss, and particularly loss of youth. The titles *Four Years Out of Life* and *Testament of Youth* illustrate this as does Dorothy Nicol's statement: 'I had left something of myself behind in Camiers that I never found again' (IWM: 57). Evadne Price characterises Nell Smith's generation as 'the race apart, from whom youth has been snatched before it has learned to play at youth' (1930: 203). Brittain's post-war lament, 'I'm nothing but a piece of war-time wreckage, living on ingloriously in a world that doesn't want me' ([1933] 1979: 490), suggests failure, disconnection, breakdown, and the term 'ingloriously' points up the lack of heroic status she feels to be partly responsible for her alienation. Such narratives suggest, then, a kind of 'death of the heart'.

'*Not So Quiet . . .*' ends in a way that imitates *All Quiet on the Western Front*. In the latter text, an epigraph written in the third person informs us that Paul Muller has died on a quiet day in October 1918. Nell Smith, however, goes on living. From a corps of forty, she is the only one to escape an air raid without physical injury. Again there is a third-person epigraph telling us, not that she died, but that 'Her soul died under a radiant silver moon in the spring of 1918 on the side of a blood-spattered trench' (1930: 239). Paul Muller's face shows 'he could not have suffered long' and that he was probably 'glad the end had come ' (Remarque [1929] 1963: 192). Nell Smith's eyes are 'emotionless' and the expression resigned, 'as though she had ceased to hope that the end might come' (1930: 239). Nell Smith's vision can be seen as metaphorical of women's post-war lot. Women are not asked to fight, although they are expected to mop up the ghastly effects of the fighting. They are not asked to die, although their friends, lovers and brothers continue to be killed all around them. The result is a profound sense of alienation and uselessness; a kind of spiritual death. 'At first I thought we were really doing something', says Lesley Smith (1931: 209). But, in the words of Mary Borden, 'Everything is arranged. It is arranged that men should be broken and that they should be mended' (Borden 1929: 117). Significantly, the role of women in the operation is omitted from this evocation of the mechanised absurdity of the war-time production line.

Subdued, guilty, but nevertheless responsible for their part in the war, women after 1918 were still 'hailed' by discourses of class and femininity that were seen to be more deeply-rooted than the emergency measures brought in to help manage the crisis. The void that 'everywoman' Nell Smith faces is one created by the violence perpetrated on the structures that supported and maintained her sense of identity, in collaboration with the assumption that she can simply reactivate her former roles – that, indeed, she has barely strayed from them. The texts of the VADs play out this post-war crisis in various ways. What seems clear, however, is that if there were a 'single battalion of sisters' ready to do battle with post-war patriarchy, its members were fighting the forces of their own ideological construction as much as that of their ostensible enemies.

2

COUNTRY AND TOWN, AGRICULTURE AND MUNITIONS

The proper lady and the woman worker

Not all women's war work could offer the glamour, pity and exhilaration that were generally thought to be the reward of the successful war nurse. The power of the Western Front could hardly be matched by the glower of English skies, English rain – and English industrial practices. Agriculture and munitions workers remained close to home, bounded by the shores of England, which were protected by that symbol of Imperialist power, the Royal Navy. In a macrocosm of the conventional domestic arrangement, they were protecting the homeland while being protected by the fighting forces. But it was surely not as dreary and conventional as all that? For while the VADs carried the burden of their angel/nun images of English womanhood right into the 'heart of the fiercest living', workers on the *home* front, in the *mother* country, relinquished their stays for breeches and abandoned their hearths for lathes and the lure of high wages. In fact they found themselves shattering the image of womanhood that the propaganda sought to protect.

An examination of two contrasting spheres of women's war work, agriculture and munitions, forms the focus of this chapter. These recruited, respectively, the smallest and the largest number of home front women and present two dominant images of the First World War's transgressive female forces: the former because of their radical attire, the latter because of the danger of the work and the large amounts of money the workers were reputed to earn.[1] The contrast also illuminates the powerful way in which the idea of England was dichotomised, by those concerned with the future of the race and the politics of the nation, into country and city. The former represented home, peace and regeneration on the one hand; backwardness, ignorance and stasis on the other. The city, meanwhile, was seen to figure moral degeneration, filth and decay on the one hand, while on the other indicating progress, intellectual achievement and social and political challenge (cf. Williams 1973: 1; Howkins 1986). This manner of constructing national identity and women's role in its future had powerful implications for the policing of women's involvement in war work and for the ways in which the participants sifted through the contradictions surrounding gender and class that confronted them.

The work of feminist writers, literary critics, political activists and psychoanalytical theorists this century has frequently indicated an imaginative persistence in western capitalist culture in aligning women with apparently permanent values that are cyclically reproduced and placed beyond the boundaries of masculine 'law'.[2] This aspect of our cultural consciousness was manipulated by suffragist pacifists in order to suggest radical alternatives to war (see Chapter 4) and has indeed been mobilised by modern feminists to challenge patriarchal linearity. In the early part of the century, though, it was used by propagandists to depict women as 'naturally' conservative. It has been suggested that images of femininity can be strategically invoked in war situations to reinforce a patriotic faith in civilisation (Higonnet et al. 1987: 1). If men had to go out and fight, this had to be constructed as a necessary evil – just as entering the Victorian industrial marketplace had been – to ensure protection and progress. In order to justify the brutality and horror of their duty, however, the fighters needed a concrete image of what they were fighting for. The propaganda industry provided paintings, posters and postcards, many of which pictured images of England and of loyal, waiting women; and propaganda writers spoke of justice, honour, the race – and women doing their bit (cf. Darracott 1974; Holt and Holt 1977; Sanders and Taylor 1982). Englishness and womanhood were frequently conflated into an image of blossoming pastoral simplicity, which easily slipped into the ideology of the rural organic myth. The position of industrialised women working in under-ventilated factories to produce armaments, however, was more deeply troubling to the pastoral image of England and, as I shall argue, required greater imaginative efforts on the part of propaganda writers to align a nurturant female identity with a dangerous, mechanised occupation directly connected with the means of destruction.

The challenge to women's identity in these new roles arose from their position as farm labourer or industrial worker. What *seemed* to be on offer was access to areas of employment and a scale of female employment previously unknown. The advantages would be financial independence, industrial liberation and a role not only in the war, but in the agricultural and industrial life of the nation. These aspirations, though, were held in check by the class template, which assumed that middle-class women would take the top jobs and then leave at the end of the war – thus keeping the working-class women in their subordinate place until the men came back, at which point they would be ejected from the engineering trades and sent back to traditional female employment. So the potential revolutionariness of these new roles was caught in conflict with the authorities' desire to preserve and protect.

This chapter, then, is divided into two halves. The first deals with the Land Army and investigates documents, memoirs and works of fiction to see whether the alternativism of country life could be added to the armoury in women's battle for social change. The second deals with munitions workers, and builds on the image of women as 'other' to war to see what part it played in industrial propaganda.

'OUR FRONT IS WHERE THE WHEAT GROWS FAIR': WORKING ON THE LAND

Paul Fussell devotes an entire chapter of *The Great War and Modern Memory* to the literary tradition of England as Arcadia. Englishness meant, to those who defended it, a rural pastoral idyll; a church clock standing at ten to three, roses growing around a cottage gate – peace. Brooke, Sassoon, Thomas all enlisted to protect 'English soil' and the 'woodland brown', where Housman heard 'the beechnut rustle down' (Dakers 1987: 12; *A Shropshire Lad* [1896], XLI). The soldiers went off with copies of *A Shropshire Lad* and the *Oxford Book of English Verse* in their packs, became saturated with a national vision inspired by Cowper, Clare and Wordsworth and grew nasturtiums in the trenches (Fussell [1975] 1977: 231–69). The 'pastoral oasis' became war's ironic 'other': both haven from

49

horrific destruction and yardstick by which to measure that destruction. It is only a small step, then, to see the implications for gender in this national vision. The garden of England is liberally sprinkled with shepherdesses, lasses, simple maids: moreover the earth, England, as Edward Thomas put it, once threatened with invasion, 'becomes "she"' (cf. Dakers 1987: 15). 'The earth, because my heart was sore,/ Sorrowed for the son *she* bore' says Housman; 'A dust whom England bore, shaped, made aware,/ Gave, once, *her* flowers to love, *her* ways to roam' writes Brooke in his poem of archetypal upper-class sentiment, 'The Soldier'. England, then, is Mother; her earth a metaphorical womb, which nurtures the 'sturdy seedlings' (Frost, 'Putting in the Seed') which protect their mother country. In a national consciousness reared on pastoral verse and driven to defend its territory from Prussian invasion, what was to become the ironic 'other' in war literature, the pastoral, is fused with war's alternative, mythologised 'other' – woman. In this case, then, woman's political relation to military practices is seen as one of radical separation, which suited the military authorities admirably.

Before proceeding to the narratives, it will be useful to set up the context in which these women were working. Britain's agriculture was in a neglected state immediately before the war: wheat, butter, ham, bacon, cheese and lard were all imported on a large scale on the assumption that the Royal Navy could keep open the import channels and that agriculture need not really be affected by the war (Armstrong 1988: 156). The British government, committed to free trade, was reluctant to interfere in matters of trade and industry, and it was not until 1916 and the Lloyd George coalition that measures were taken to control imports and distribution and to encourage arable production by placing a guaranteed minimum level on the rapidly inflating prices of wheat and oats (Armstrong 1988: 157).

Problems of farming methods and economic intervention by the government were compounded by the question of labour. There had been a shortage of agricultural labour since the late nineteenth century, which was accompanied by a powerful 'back to the land' movement. This played the degeneration of urban developments against the moral and racial regeneration afforded by the values permanently typified by the English countryside. Lord Walsingham, a Norfolk landowner, wrote in 1899:

Take the people away from their natural breeding grounds, thereby sapping their health and strength in cities such as nature never intended to be the permanent home of men, and the decay of this country becomes only a matter of time.

(Quoted in Howkins 1986: 66)

The war took even more workers away from the land, leaving the countryside and womanhood as the symbolic zone charged with the task of preserving and nurturing England's national characteristics. There was, however, a potential national emergency on the horizon. Should the war outlast the harvest of 1916, 'England's bread' would be in seriously short supply.

The national organisation of women's land work, however, was initially slow, chaotic and deeply unglamorous in comparison with that of the VADs. This can partly be explained by the *laissez-faire* attitude of the government towards food production, partly by the lack of an early propaganda campaign and, once the munitions industry had been developed, by the competition from better paid and more appealing jobs in industry. There was widespread prejudice against women on the part of farmers, an insufficiency of housing and, perhaps most important, no Katharine Furse to act as pioneer. Before the Land Army was established in July 1917, the Board of Agriculture and Fisheries, headed by Lord Selbourne, was made responsible for finding solutions to the labour problem by recruiting women. The rather complicated route went via county-organised War Agricultural Committees in conjunction with local Labour Exchanges, but it still took until November 1915 – over a year after the declaration of war – for Lord Selbourne to consider the institutionalisation of Women's Committees to promote women's employment on the land (Files of Women's Land Work, hereafter Land, 1/8). No attempt was made to make the work attractive – unlike VAD work. 'Patriotism' was the only lure, and, unaccompanied by devotional or exhilarating propaganda, it was ineffective. Furthermore, farmers were doggedly resistant to employing women, let alone paying them a decent wage, training them and adapting farm machinery to suit female needs. The counter-balance to this, though, was the threat of a blockade. The British Isles had to make themselves self-sufficient.

51

These tentative and parochial beginnings were not helped by the lack of clear guidance on matters of pay and instruction. 'It is not incapacity or unwillingness to do the work that will prevent women becoming farm labourers', wrote 'Cockney Harvester' Amy Drucker, 'but the inability to live on the wages at present proffered' (Drucker 1916: 21). Lord Selbourne emphasised the need to offer women workers competitive payment, but left adjudication largely in the hands of the farmers themselves, with the inevitable result that daily pay was erratic: anything between sixpence and three shillings (Land 1/8). Furthermore, farmers often actively discriminated against women, preferring to employ boys at even cheaper rates or refusing to train them in appropriate methods. Again, unlike the VAD, there was no national training scheme. Edith Airey, who was brought up in a Sussex village, left her childhood home for a munitions factory following her and her sister's experiences on a nearby farm where they were the only two women working under a foreman, 'who didn't take kindly to having women around and would sort out most unpleasant jobs for us'.[3] His antagonism eventually got the better of them and they 'downed tools', having survived the harvest and the winter, when they were abandoned in a field with a pile of muck to spread. 'It was so heavy', says Edith Airey, 'that we could scarcely lift the fork'. Lacking instruction, they were bound to fail.

Olive Hockin, however, in *Two Girls on the Land* (1918) describes how her false belief in the supremacy of physical strength was eroded by the experience of trial and error in handling a plough:

> [F]or a week I was black and blue with stiffness and bruises, only to find in the end that no pulling and lifting had ever been necessary. To feel the balance – something as of a bicycle – and to bring round the horses just to the right point, does not really need much strength, but it does need judgment and some experience, and is therefore, given the opportunity, as much within the reach of a woman's powers as of a man's.
>
> (Hockin 1918: 14–15)

Given the chance, then, women discovered that in many cases expertise was as serviceable as developed muscles and that the division of tasks into masculine and feminine was merely conventional. It was in the interest of the male labourers and the farmers that women should be paid at a lower rate for doing 'inferior', 'light' tasks and that financial interest had become a powerful social construct.

Something had to be done, though, to combat the farmers' conservatism. In February 1916 Lord Selbourne issued a rather dreary appeal to women to 'Contribute to Victory', but it seemed to hint at a way forward:

> My appeal is not addressed alone to the wives and daughters of agricultural labourers, but to the women of every class; and the less a woman needs to earn money for the support of herself and family, the more insistent would be my appeal to her patriotism.

(Land 1/2)

Once again, if patriotism could be construed as a substitute for wages, then the land could be worked and the farmers need not lose much by it. Role models in the higher social classes were thus sought out. 'More satisfaction has been expressed with the work of the educated women, than with that of the industrial women', we hear from the Middlesex Division (Land 1/35), and a circular to the Women's County Farm Labour Committees specifically asks for more appeals to be made to educated women (Land 1/38). Land work's bad reputation for the 'unavoidable mixing of classes' (Letter to headmistresses from WNLSC, Land 5 4/14) was seen as one of the most influential drawbacks in recruiting large numbers of 'ladies', so the patriotic appeal of the work had somehow to be elevated in order to remedy the situation. The report of a women's mission to French farms in 1916 helped. The members of this deputation had their eyes opened to the scope of work that women could do – ploughing being a notable example – and used this to 'arouse the patriotism and imagination' of the women in England (Land 1/17). A propaganda poster issued jointly by the Boards of Trade and Agriculture advanced a patriotic challenge to Englishwomen, using the tactic of shame: 'French women are doing all the work of the Farms', it read, 'even where shells are bursting close to them'. Could not Englishwomen then 'help their country with as good a heart' as these? (Land 1/44).

In an attempt to present work in terms of equality with the

soldiers, Lord Selbourne devised a 'certificate', 'emblazoned with the royal arms in colours', to be issued to women land workers. It was not, of course, a record of individual women's personal achievements, but merely a general statement of objectives. It read as follows:

> Every woman who helps in agriculture
> during the war is as truly serving her
> country as the man who is fighting in
> the trenches, on the sea, or in the air.

(Land 1/21)

A comparison of this with the parallel developments in the VAD organisation, which spoke to its members' courage, humility and daughterly duty, can only reveal the low level of devotional and glamorous appeal that the Board of Agriculture was capable of generating. The early uniform was equally dreary – regulation coats, skirts, gaiters and boots were recommended, with the discreet addition of armlets for those who had done thirty days land work (Land 1/30) – and the lack of structure and identity was not repaired by the fact that, prior to the formation of the Land Army, various other competing and overlapping organisations were in existence.[4]

As potential employment, then, land work for women was uninviting. Chaotic and unglamorous in comparison with its rivals, and beset by an inflexible conservatism, the work needed an organisational centre and some powerful propaganda if it were to succeed in recruiting enough women to maintain a useful level of food production.

Out of the towns and on to the downs

The Women's Land Army ultimately came into being in July 1917 and succeeded in placing 23,000 women on the land before October 1919 (cf. Horn 1984: 134). The enrolment procedure was far less arduous than that of the VAD organisation;[5] Mrs M. Harrold, whose land work included pulling flax to make aeroplane wings, emphasises the comparative informality of the operation in her unpublished memoir:

> Our uniform was sent by parcel post which we had to
> collect from post office, we did not all have the sizes

meant, for, as it was all together there was quite a tussel
[sic] by some & the smaller sizes were snatched & we
weaker ones had to accept what was left.[6]

The discourses of the organisation were much less concerned
with the ideology of patriotic self-sacrifice than the VAD, but
more interested in sensible, workmanlike, healthy toil in the
fresh air. This is articulated in the Land Army Handbook
(issued June 1918), and particularly in the Land Army Song:

Come out of the towns
And on to the downs
Where a girl gets brown and strong
With swinging pace
And morning face
She does her work to song
The children shall not starve
The soldiers must have bread
We'll dig and sow and reap and mow
And England shall be fed

(Land 6 1/4)

The rules governing dress and behaviour in public were less
stringent than those imposed on the VADs, and the distance
from the military influence of the fighting lines might have
encouraged this. There was, nevertheless, a certain anxiety
about maintaining a dignified feminine presence in spite of the
masculine garb (breeches were now a part of the uniform) and
strenuous activity:

The government has given you your sensible uniform and
expects you to make sure that it is always treated with
respect. It looks much better without jewelry or lace frills,
for when you are at work the smartest thing is to look
workmanlike. Keep jewelry and lace for the days when you
wear ordinary clothes. You are doing a man's work and so
you are dressed rather like a man; but remember that just
because you wear a smock and breeches you should take
care to behave like a British girl who expects chivalry and
respect from everyone she meets. Noisy or ugly behaviour
brings discredit not only upon yourself, but upon the
uniform and the whole Women's Land Army.

(Land 6 1/4)

The emphasis is on counteracting any tendency to behave in the revolutionary, unfeminine fashion which the liberation from conventional clothes, influences and occupations might encourage. Thus Land Army girls were advised against smoking in public, entering bars and walking about with their hands in their breeches pockets (Land 6 1/4). Further, with the air of instructing school children, the Land Army Handbook required each recruit to 'promise':

I   to behave quietly
II   respect the uniform and make it respected
III to secure eight hours rest each night
IV   to avoid communication of any sort with German prisoners

Some aspects of the organisation imitated those of the conventional army. For six months' service the worker could earn a stripe, four of which qualified her for a diamond. There were efficiency tests in aspects of farm work, high marks in which might signal eligibility for promotion. They had a 'Roll of Honour' to record deaths in service, due to accidents with farm machinery or animals, and a record of Distinguished Service in the Land Army, which echoes the rhetoric of the newspapers, but with inevitably bathetic results:

> Miss J Barr, Hertford. For exceptional courage and devotion to duty in saving valuable pigs from drowning.
> Miss Kitty Botting, Nottingham. For exceptional courage in rescuing a fellow landworker from a boar which was attacking her.
> Miss A Bohills and Miss K Harrison. These two women were employed at a very lonely farm in Northumberland and have shown great devotion in sticking to their job under very difficult circumstances.
>
> (Land 6/21)

One might argue that men could hardly fail to smirk at this record given the obvious comparison with the real acts of bravery reported daily in the papers. As such it can be seen as a way of devaluing women's work, while pretending to applaud it.

Plate 2 Woman carter by Horace Nichols. (By courtesy of the Trustees of the Imperial War Museum.)

A peaceful avocation

Many land workers left memoirs of their experiences, which are striking in the consistency of their representation of agricultural work. Warm summer weather is described far more often than the harsh winters which tend to characterise munitions work, thus reproducing the mythology of the 'back to the land' movement. The attraction of the work lay in its access to a kind of 'natural' order where the psychic and social wounds of the city could be healed and a robust physical health developed. This appears in vivid contrast to the horrors of war itself, the trauma, human degradation and physical wreckage with which the VAD nurses were involved. But is there more to this than the simple contrast suggests? 'Agriculture is the antithesis of warfare', said R. H. Rew of the Agricultural Section of the British Association in September 1915:

> farming is pre-eminently a peaceful avocation, and farmers are essentially men of peace. The husbandman is not easily disturbed by war's alarms, and his intimate association with the placid and inevitable processes of Nature engenders a calmness of spirit which is unshaken by catastrophe.
>
> (Land 1/6)

This, initially, seems to hint at an alternative ideology that might *disrupt* the bellicosity of contemporary culture. If farming is 'peaceful' and farmers are 'men of peace', why should they support the war aims that are ruining their livelihood? The statement also has implications for women's involvement in land work. Could it possibly strengthen their mythological alterity and provide a power base for political dissidence? These are questions that arise in the narrative accounts of the work, but are usually stifled. Rew's statement is merely a way of articulating the permanent value system that is necessary to provide the solid, reliable bass line that supports the coloratura of battlefield cries, with an expression of permanence, continuity and the irreducible universality of Nature. It hints at being pacifist, but is simply passive: the concern lies with the future of the race rather than the future of the world.

On a simple, practical level women were thought to have no relation to military practice, which made their work on the land all the more fitting. The first-hand accounts, though, are not even concerned to reconstruct a rural environment that will be the preserve of moral values. Those written by working-class women recreate an atmosphere of plenty, of luscious fruits and pleasant groves in a setting far from war, from the complexities of social hierarchies and from the politics of race. Their concern is largely with the abundance of fresh produce and with unfamiliar sensory perceptions (it is worth remembering that land work was frequently recommended as a 'cure' for munitions work). Rosa Freedman, who joined the Land Army having been in domestic service since the age of 13, describes a particularly idyllic scene:

> We picked raspberries, gooseberries, blackcurrents, plums and apples, climbing tall trees with baskets tied around our waists. I remember that place especially as there was a boy about ten with a beautiful voice who sang in the church choir. It was very cheering to hear that boy singing.[7]

She was similarly struck by the sense of community she had with her landlady, who would 'come out to the fields with our tea, in a pot wrapped in a towel, with some lovely thick slices of bread and butter, and she would sit down with us. Her husband was in France' (ibid.). Plentiful resources and absence of men combine to create absence of stress. Mrs M. Bale, whose husband had been posted to Malta with no hope of leave before the end of the war, joined the Land Army with her sister and describes running a market garden full of strawberries and 'other orchards too with apples galore as well as plums, pears, walnuts and bush fruit'.[8] The unpublished 1917 diary of C. M. Prunell[9] abounds with descriptions of blossoms and wildlife and is occasionally illustrated with drawings in pencil and watercolour. From a description of Primrose Day (19 April), through to the first sound of the cuckoo and to the gathering of the swallows, the diary is a testament of country living which recreates the image of England to be found in Georgian pastoral poetry – 'The hedge-sparrows in the furze bush have hatched safely and today are flown' (27 May); 'The elder blossom is at its very best now and very heavy scented; the scent is so strong that you cannot be near it very long these days' (21 June). Pastoral oases indeed.

Olive Hockin's *Two Girls on the Land* displays a similarly detailed – and enraptured – account of the flora of Devonshire, but her absorption in the 'back to the land' mythology that declares nature's moral laws to be far superior to those of 'civilisation' brings her narrative to an unexpected juncture:

> In Nature, herself so beautiful, whose means and ends seem so wonderfully inter-adapted, it would often seem as though man alone were the jarring note. Wherever he comes, comes also death, cruelty, destruction, and ugliness. He kills, not only for his own essential need, as do the hawk and the wolf, but for pleasure in the name of Sport or Science. In the name of 'Liberty, Justice, and Honour' he kills off the best even of the human race. . .
>
> (1918: 68)

The logical conclusion of this might be thought to be a condemnation of the war, elicited by a heightened awareness of nature's organicism in comparison with man's brutality. It indicates a turning point, a kind of ideological junction at which the narrator could go either left or right. As it turns out, Hockin's sentimental merging with the countryside makes no inroads into her uncomplicated patriotism and her anger is directed against the male labourers who kill small, defenceless animals for food, instead of the male governers, who were largely responsible for the holy crusade language to which she refers. This is, to a large extent, in line with the propagandist assumption that women, while remaining 'other' to war, are nevertheless deferentially loyal to the ruling-class ideology that defends war. The corollary of her argument, then, is not a sudden conversion to pacifism, but a reinforcement of old imperialist values in the context of her own well-bred compassion in opposition to the 'brutality' of the village men.

Hockin's observations are based more on ignorance and sentimentality than concern for social engineering. Not so the ambitions of Viscountess Wolsely. She, in her book *Women and the Land* (1916), outlined a project for the re-establishment of women on the land in order to secure the 'moral and physical health of future generations' (1916: 19). She imagined a new world order in which a peasant class would live a thrifty, wholesome life in a rural community. Her appeal to the 'real countrywoman' (1916: 180) was not merely for the duration of the war, but for a national future that would involve married life, a homestead and a wounded soldier (1916: 178–80).[10] This is the logical extension of the conservative appeal to rural values, and it is one in which Olive Hockin, to her credit, has little faith.

Unbounded confidence

Hockin's text, then, plays out the conflict between a farmer and two of his female labourers in the context of an impoverished rural setting.[11] The conflict is a complex one: the farmer is genuinely resistant to female labour and has no qualms about exploiting the women. They, however, are of a higher social standing and expect him to accept their help with deference. It bears some relation, then, to the conflict between trained Sisters and VADs – but with the added complications of gender and genuinely hard, poorly paid physical labour.

Initially the narrator is equipped with the 'unbounded confidence in [her] own ability to do any mortal thing [she] wished to do' (1918: 8) that we have seen to characterise many of the VAD workers of her class. At first she considers the work 'wholesome, interesting, and beautiful [. . .] – work that should appeal to all that is best in men or women' (1918: 11). Almost immediately, however, she is faced with a power struggle that centres on gender, class and skill. Having stressed her qualifications to her (socially inferior) potential employer who, in spite of the labour shortage, is still reluctant to employ a woman, she comments on the incongruity between the farmer's attitude and:

> the condescending frame of mind in which we ladies prepare to stoop to 'menial labour' by way of tiding over his time of enforced shortage of labour! The idea that it could be anything but a favour to allow anyone, be it man, woman, or child, to work for ten or twelve or fourteen hours a day for the munificent daily dole of two shillings and sixpence had never yet occurred to the Devonshire agricultural potentate.
>
> (1918: 11)

She makes the mistake of expecting the farmer, who has lost all his skilled labourers to the war, to be grateful, not so much for her offer of help, but for her *condescension*. He, on the other hand, considers himself generous to employ a person so unlikely to be able to handle farm machinery, at any wage at all. The power battle commences.

The narrator and her friend agree to work twelve hours a day, but have to fight for their allotted free time. Employed on an individual basis rather than as part of an organisation, their rights are harder to obtain – the farmer will prevail upon them to do one more thing, until, eventually, he must be refused:

> 'Can't help it, Maester', I answered, feeling that some time or other we should have to make a stand. 'We've been working the livelong day the whole week through, and if I don't get a breather on a Sunday I shall bust!'
>
> (1918: 31)

This confrontation is represented as a perfectly reasonable and civil request not to be exploited more than is absolutely necessary. Further confrontations, though, reveal a more overt attitude of class superiority. In this text, as in others principally concerned with land work, the war is mentioned infrequently; but here its introduction reflects badly on the farming community:

> 'An' what d'ye think o' this yurr warr, Maester?' asked Withecombe, his mouth quite filled with bread-and-jam.
> 'O-o-oh – ay. . . . Well. . . . They'm *fightin'!*' is Maester's profound comment.
> 'They du tell as they Germans be a-sinkin' all our ships,' contributed Peter Whidd'n.
> ''Tis toime it stopped, that it be,' chimed in 'Arry 'Ickey.
> 'Let them as made the war go out and fight, that's what I says. It bain't no workin' man's warr.'
> 'You'm be right there,' answered Peter Whidd'n. 'Let them as wants it goo an' fight.'
> 'Is it true, Maester,' says Withecombe, 'that you beant allowed to sell your wool? Well, well, 'tis time it wur stopped, so it be, interferin' on a man's own farm –'
> Such are the war echoes that reach our Dartmoor uplands. Verily, until the famous prohibition of wool-selling in 1916, I believe the farmers hardly knew their own country was involved.
>
> (1918: 77)

There is a clash here between the simplistic patriotism of the well-to-do labourer and the equally entrenched lack of faith in that cultural phenomenon of the farmers. The narrator's tone, however, is deeply patronising. She assumes that her position is unquestionably correct, that daily conversation should be characterised by well-informed discussion of the latest developments on all Fronts – that a patriotic commitment to the war is not only the norm, but a mark of intelligence. She dismisses, as a rather quaint form of stupidity, the notion that the war may not seem a righteous cause to the working people who suffer its effects, rather than taking seriously the political objections to it. The style of the recorded conversation reduces the farmers to comic, bucolic stereotypes, ignorant of the appropriate social priorities.

As the account progresses, however, the narrator develops a greater consciousness of the assumptions and prejudices of her own class. Her experience of direct substitution of her way of life for that of a farm labourer – albeit on a limited time-scale – forces her to recognise the value and importance of the labouring classes where previously they had seemed to her merely a functional, and largely invisible element in the social structure:

> Whether I was unusually snobbish or exceptional in taking my own class for granted, I do not know. Perhaps not, for even now I find it very difficult to get people to see my point. People of the comparatively leisured middle classes do still seem to think of themselves as 'the nation', while the lower classes they tolerate as being put there by Providence, to make things and move things and clean things and generally to minister to their needs.
>
> (1918: 124)

A basic narrative trajectory emerges: the middle-class woman is alerted to the deficiencies of her previously secure world vision. The oafish labourer, uninformed and ungrateful, before too long assumes the status of a mythical deity: 'Like Atlas [he] bears the world upon his shoulders' (1918: 124). He is overworked, highly skilled and uncomplaining in spite of atrocious conditions and the ever-present threat of starvation. He does 'the work that matters' but receives abysmally little for it. It is difficult, though, to relate this heroic portrait to the real, flesh-and-blood labourers, who are depicted so contemptuously. In order to make sense of her change of mind, the narrator has to present 'Arry 'Ickey and his mates in terms of classical mythology. These people are literally unrecognisable to her as ordinary human beings.

The account, nevertheless, ends with the humbling of middle-class 'unbounded confidence'. The two workers acknowledge their failure to come up to the excruciating physical standards demanded of them, and anticipate a healthier post-war political climate in which the cycle of poverty and ill-health that oppresses both men and women in agricultural communities will be recognised and addressed by the government. 'Let us hope those days are gone for ever – that now the country will spend on wages and homes for the living the millions it has been forced to spend on workhouses and homes for the dying' (1918: 157). The rural organic myth, here, is turned inside out. Lacking organisational support, or the protective packaging of 'femininity' that the VADs had, this particular middle-class foray into working-class life reveals some of the desperate privations of the 'peasant class' that Viscountess Wolsely was so eager to resurrect and which the structure of the capitalist economy continued to reproduce.

The benightedness and oppression of agricultural life is dealt with in the context of feminist politics in Winifred Holtby's *The Crowded Street*. Before turning to this, though, it will be interesting to look at fictional renderings of land work that are more attuned to the ideological mainstream of the war years to see in what terms its appeal to women was registered.

Harvesting romance

Berta Ruck's *The Land Girl's Love Story* (1919) is interesting as an exercise in how to tailor the conditions of land work to the conventions of the romance. As an ideological vehicle it is strikingly cohesive: the trajectory of the love story is supported by the details of government propaganda to produce some lively escapism in which true love and war work are securely housed within the walls of patriarchy, patriotism and conventional femininity.

The plot follows the fortunes of Joan, an ex-London typist who removes herself from the stifling city to the regenerating countryside where she meets the hero: aloof, handsome and teasingly aggressive. The details in many cases are well-researched. Joan, for example, is attracted to the Land Army by a recruiting rally held in Trafalgar Square. Such a rally was held on 19 March 1918 when there was a particular need for new recruits (Land 6/72);[12] Ruck's recruiting officer points up the drawbacks of the work but weighs them against the conditions of the soldiers in France, advancing a moral and patriotic case for accepting low wages:

> I have put before you the disadvantages of this life. Long hours. Hard work. Poor pay. After you get your board and lodging a shilling a day, perhaps. Very poor pay. But, girls – our boys at the Front are offering their lives for just that. Won't you offer your services for that – and for them?
>
> (1919: 24)

Even the uniform is portrayed in terms that coincide with the romantic novel's need not to stray from conventional images of feminine attractiveness: the recruiting officer is described (rather improbably) as wearing 'the Land Girl's uniform that sets off a woman's shape as no other costume has done yet' (1919: 24). The more luxurious appurtenances of femininity, however, such as lace or silk underwear, are condemned as fussy and impractical: 'Working as a man, you simply can't wear the clothes you wore when you were just sitting still as a girl!' (1919: 82). The lure of masculine attire, though, is ultimately restrained in its appeal by the return to 'normality' once the war is over.

Furthermore the Land Army is depicted as a melting pot where all social classes come together and customary divisions break down. Joan's fellow workers include Sybil Wentworth, who has only known London in the 'season', and Lil, who was a maid and amongst whose 'mates' were 'a girl from Somerville, a pickle-factory hand, a student of music, and Vic the cockney' (1919: 86). Vic (rather like Evadne Price's Tosh) comes over as the natural leader:

> The forewoman took Vic's advice; Sybil deferred to her. Yet she belonged to the class that we have seen blackening Hampstead Heath on Bank Holidays, grimy and anaemic, made ugly by the life and toil of town. The country, the air, the healthy work have beautified them back into the mould that Nature meant; have given them back shapeliness and colour.
>
> (1919: 87)

With the exception of Vic's authoritative position, a positive gesture towards social equality, the above could almost have been written by Viscountess Wolsely. It signals a 'return to Eden'. The combination of the 'back to the land' mythology and the 'communal life set to laughter' (1919: 87) is seen, at least temporarily, not only to eliminate social barriers but also to restore to their natural beauty those made unattractive by the city and who, in their turn, disfigured England's capital by their very presence. The image of the working classes 'blackening' London's green spaces suggests more than degradation as a result of class or race (cf. Showalter [1990] 1992: 5–6). 'Blackening' also suggests a form of cultural inferiority that corresponds to anonymity. The Land Army offers a chance to recapture one's individuality.

The novel rapidly condenses the national propaganda for joining the Land Army – from an invitation to return to nature to a challenge to emulate the French women – into a couple of pages of snappy dialogue. Space is also allotted to anti-German propaganda. German POWs were frequently sentenced to labour on farms (Virginia Woolf often saw them on her walks across the Downs) and it has already been noted that Land Army girls were forbidden to talk to them. In one scene from the novel, Muriel Elvey, who is *not* a land girl but who is a rival of Joan's for the affections of her aloof Captain, in the tradition of an Austen character such as Maria Bertram, reveals her flirtatious foolishness by conversing with a prisoner in German while Joan (who had been to finishing school in Berlin) looks on with admirable restraint. Joan patriotically declares that she 'didn't want any German to get a word from the lips of an English girl' (Ruck 1919: 307), and coyly recalls 'the fate of other pretty girls, in countries less fortunate than ours, laid waste by these men' (1919: 310). Within the structure of the standard romance scenario, the 'Hun' takes on the role of the villainous, reckless rake and, in an act of evil destruction which might be construed as a rape-substitute, sets fire to a barn full of recently harvested corn – 'England's bread' (1919: 319).

This, however, is all largely background to the central romance between Joan and Captain Holiday, the convalescent officer who establishes his manly power over the not-too-passive heroine by demonstrating the correct manner in which to shovel muck.[13] She reciprocates with maternal grace by sheltering him from thunder, which he, in his (very mildly) shell-shocked state, perceives as gun-fire. Again, the structure of their relationship is not dissimilar to that between Elizabeth Bennett and Mr Darcy, or Emma and Mr Knightly. The war setting temporarily unsettles gendered stereotypes, with Joan developing her musculature and the Captain suffering a degree of emasculation, but the two eventually resolve their differences and difficulties – his arrogance, her prickliness – and their irresistible attraction to each other wins through. The whole thing closes in a neat matrix with the right girls finding the right partners and celebrating this and the declaration of peace with the self-satisfied comment: 'It is true, isn't it? We did do our little bit to help!' (1919: 344). In this novel, then, the ideological boundaries of war are unquestioned and this effectively closes down any significant changes in the way the female characters might identify themselves. The period of the war fits in perfectly with the period of courtship in a romantic novel, with its implications of fantasy, self-discovery and self-determination. The conservative consequences of the potentially revolutionary effects of land work are, however, passively accepted and merely merge into the eternal cycles of love and marriage.

In May Sinclair's *The Romantic* (1920), work on the land, rather than simply providing a vehicle for romance, operates as a kind of psychological litmus test. A reverse love story, the novel is largely concerned with the experiences of Charlotte Redhead and John Conway in Belgium as part of a motor ambulance convoy – a setting similar to that of *A Journal of Impressions*, mentioned in the previous chapter – but their success in this, and as a romantic couple, is foreshadowed by their discordant reactions to the English countryside.

Before they set off for the fighting lines they spend some time working on a farm. Charlotte has a romantic and deeply sensual attachment to the land, which is what inspires her to take up farm work in the first place:

Suddenly she stood still. On the top of the ridge the whole sky opened, throbbing with light, immense as the sky above a plain. Hills – thousands of hills. Thousands of smooth curves joining and parting, overlapping, rolling together.

What did you want? What did you want? How could you want anything but this for ever?

(1920: 15)

This ecstatic appreciation of the landscape acts in the novel as an index of Charlotte's physical warmth and of her love of her own country. It also indicates a deep, moral sanity. Little attention is paid to the details of farming, but the idyllic atmosphere provides a striking contrast with the dangers and horrors Charlotte and John are to confront as part of an ambulance team in Belgium. In terms of the book's organisation, the work is indeed 'the antithesis of warfare', but also a preparation for it. A dialogue concerning the nature of the land suggests something of what is to come. Charlotte asks John:

> 'Aren't you glad you came? Did you ever feel anything like the peace of it?'
> 'It's not the peace of it I want, Charlotte [. . .]. It's the fight. Fighting with things that would kill you if you didn't. Wounding the earth to sow in it and make it feed you. Ploughing, Charlotte [. . .]. Feeling the thrust and the drive through, and the thing listing over on the slope. Seeing the steel blade shine, and the long wounds coming in rows; hundreds of wounds, wet and shining.'
> 'What made you think of wounds?'
> 'I don't know. I see it like that. Cutting through.'
> 'I don't see it like that one bit. The earth's so kind, so beautiful. And the hills – look at them, the lean, quiet backs smoothed with light. You could stroke them. And the fields, those lovely coloured fans opening and shutting.'

(1920: 32–3)

The masculine voice brings the two halves of the antithesis together. Charlotte's attitude remains gentle, 'natural', organicist, sensual. John's 'unnatural' link of nature and warfare and his use of violent *sexual* imagery are a signal, in this text, of his pathological state. His desire to control and wound the land rather than nurturing and respecting it points up an emergent psychotic pattern in him: he is to be revealed as impotent, a coward and a compulsive liar, who cannot balance his conflicting desires for punitive self-control and violence. The female character, at one with the land, can negotiate her own fears about war's dangers and sublimate them to the task to be performed. The destructive male cannot master his terror. He runs away from the wounded while under fire – and is shot. This is a more complex version of Hockin's division of feminine compassion from masculine aggression, with the emphasis falling not on a sentimental concern for small animals but on psychological make-up and the celebration of female courage and patriotism.

If Ruck's novel represents the countryside at its most idyllic, and Sinclair uses that image as an index of psychological health, Winifred Holtby's *The Crowded Street* (1924) provides the counter-version of the organic myth. In this the country, instead of representing regeneration, peace and healthy toil, represents backwardness, ignorance and a bleak, terminal hopelessness.[14] If *The Romantic* reverses the conventions of the love story, *The Crowded Street* does away with them altogether. The symbolic trajectory of the novel is directly antithetical to *The Land Girl's Love Story*: the central character, Muriel Hammond, moves away from tranquil provincial security and follows her feminist mentor Delia Vaughan to the metropolis, the only place where civilised, political ideals can be sincerely pursued. Land work is marginal in this text. It is Muriel's sister, Connie, who works on a farm, which occupies a symbolic space effectively beyond the boundaries of civilisation, a place of uncontrolled sexuality, religious mania and dense, impenetrable customs, inaccessible to human reason. Once Connie Hammond has become embroiled in this complex, her only honourable exit is through death.

The novel tries to unravel the problems concerning decorum and female middle-class identity and the decorous, but vulnerable, centre of the novel is Mrs Hammond, Muriel and Connie's mother. From the outset Mrs Hammond is opposed to Connie's proposal that she should work on a farm. At a time when magazines were depicting 'ladies' helping in hospitals and 'it had become the fashion for beauty to go meekly dressed, with clasped hands, and the light directed becomingly upon a grave profile' ([1924] 1981: 129), the rebellious Connie seeks liberation amongst the mud and turnips of a sheep-fold. Her mother's reaction is predictably dismissive: 'And in any case, her father won't hear of it. The breeches, Muriel' ([1924] 1981:

128). Her concern, not atypical, as we have seen, is that this 'doubtful profession' lacks not only a suitably dignified uniform, but role models amongst the female aristocracy.

Thus far Connie is to be envied. She wins her domestic battle and escapes the limited role model offered by her mother. Her new work offers community and a release for her high spirits. The rural organic myth, however, is allowed no foothold in this text. The farming family that employs Connie is seen as ignorant, stubborn and vengeful.[15] She becomes pregnant and her father persuades her to marry the son of the family, a 'terrible young man' named Ben Todd, for whom Connie has little affection. Thraile, in the North Riding, is a 'bleak country where everything was just a little sinister'. Farm machinery causes near-fatal injuries interpreted as the vengeance of the Lord for past sins; a crippled and embittered old man rules the household. When Muriel travels up to Thraile to help her sister, she sees herself entering a battle between civilisation and brutality – of the benighted, religious kind. The Todd family is unwilling to do what is in its power to help Connie and her timid husband make the most of their situation; its members are also incapable of caring for Connie when she is seriously ill. Causation, as far as the Todds are concerned, is in the hands of the Lord. The atmosphere of threat that they generate and their uncanny, mystical, non-rational belief system are beyond Muriel's limited combative powers and even beyond her mother's controlling force. Connie dies of pneumonia, having discovered that she has been betrayed by a fellow worker into believing that the man she really loved – an army officer – had married someone else.

Even the vision of comradeship amongst workers, then, is ultimately undermined. In this novel, women's relation to the land in the context of war is seen to be entirely negative and ultimately regressive in an historical context where women are fighting for the vote and for equal citizenship. Any manifestations of alterity are locked into an impenetrable, conservative stronghold. The city is the seat of rational discourse and women can only make progress and forge an identity for themselves if they take some part in influencing public opinion there. It is towards the towns, then, that this influential feminist writer urges women; the country is no place to develop an identity based on independence and equality.

WORKING IN THE MUNITIONS FACTORIES

The second half of this chapter will focus on an area of women's war work that did not naturally lend itself to the discourse of nurturing or sheltered alterity. Munitions work, in common with land work, was an area of occupation traditionally male and working class but entered by large numbers of women of all classes during the national crisis. It was seen as antithetical to land work in two major ways. First, in terms of England's division into the 'imagined communities' of the country and the city, industrialism was associated by its critics with unnaturalness, unhealthiness and lack of moral balance. Second, rather than being the antithesis of warfare, the work was responsible for producing the means of warfare: shells, guns, aeroplanes. Conventional feminine identity was seen to be secure in rural seclusion: its association with factories and bombs was more problematic for the writers of propaganda. They nevertheless had a demanding task to perform. With a shortage of shells and a shortage of labour, it became necessary to make the employment of women in engineering trades appear attractive, desirable and, at least in the short term, natural.

The main and most illuminating source for this section is propaganda written to publicise the work and boost recruitment. Literary propaganda during the First World War was initially organised secretly by C.F.G. Masterman, who called a meeting of some of the more influential academic and literary figures in the country and persuaded them to advertise the righteousness of the British cause. A.C. Bradley, J.M. Barrie, Mrs Humphry Ward and Thomas Hardy were among them. Unofficial organisations boosted the output. The work was distributed under the imprint of commercial publishing houses and was sometimes prefaced by a disclaimer of government help, although writers were frequently offered tours of the Front and factories in order to aid their projects. The appearance of individual sincerity and absolute spontaneity was crucial to enlist the support of America, to conciliate opinion at home and to persuade thousands of women to throw their industrial weight behind the munitions factories.[16]

Munitionettes

The most arresting aspect of munitions work was its direct contact with the war's armoury, and the workers were frequently made aware of their responsibility for the soldiers' protection. Any badly finished piece of work could mean the death of one of their own side; slack production could result in an insufficiency of weapons that might mean overall defeat. The military importance of their work was, then, in a sense, greater than that of the VADs'. The formal channels through which women sought their identity as munitions workers, however, had more to do with the conservative structure of industrial practices than martial conventions. They were frequently brought up against the conflict between their temporary but widely publicised national value and their more permanent image of mother of the race, which was seen as an emblem of constancy and continuity.

Working women, of course, had had a long history of employment in factories. The cotton, linen, tailoring and hat-making industries, though, were run down at the beginning of the war, rendering many women unemployed.[17] The move from these traditional industries to engineering was hardly straightforward. The capitalist businessmen did not trust the physical and mental capacities of women and saw them as a bad investment; labouring men feared that their jobs would be undercut or severely devalued by 'dilution' with female labour (Braybon 1981: 45, 72). The severe shortage of shells on the fighting fronts in 1915, however, meant that some dramatic industrial reorganisation had to take place. The Ministry of Munitions was created and Lloyd George successfully orchestrated its development. On 17 July 1915 the Pankhursts organised a march proclaiming Women's Right to Serve, which culminated with a deputation to Lloyd George and met with a favourable reception from both Minister and press (cf. *The Times* 17 July 1915: 3). By December 1915 400 women were employed at Woolwich Arsenal. When the armistice was signed there were 27,000 women to be demobilised from this one site (cf. Emp 29/15 and 29/25, Imperial War Museum).

Soldier women

Propagandist writing of the time was keen to develop the image of an army of plucky young women who were as much a military asset as the weapons they were making. Indeed, the propagandists were more successful in this strategy than the Board of Agriculture, and, as the women were not actually invading military territory, their temporary champions were less chary than the military authorities proper of using martial metaphors. Boyd Cable, a popular author and journalist, whose *Doing Their Bit: War Work at Home* (1916) had a preface by Lloyd George and a note explaining that it was written between December and January 1915–16, a crucial time for the shell shortage, introduces his material as an ideological hand-grenade:

> I hope the Front may read these chapters, and I hope the Front will tie a stone to this book and sling it over to any near-enough portion of the Hun lines, because what I have to write is so very cheerful telling for the Front to hear that it would surely be highly unpleasant for the Germans to digest.
>
> (1916: 13–14)

Sir Hall Caine was one of the original fifty-four British authors to sign Masterman's 'Author's Manifesto', pledging support for the war (Buitenhuis [1987] 1989: 19). His *Our Girls: Their Work for the War* (1916) promises to reveal the secrets of 'the mighty army of women in our munitions factories' (Caine 1916: 9). Mrs Alec-Tweedie's *Women and Soldiers* (1918) was equally avid to demonstrate the fiery patriotism and majestic competence of (the right sort of) women. Her munitions workers are like footsoldiers, and have answered 'the call of the drum' – she describes them as a demure battalion: 'Neat khaki caps and neat khaki overalls made them both trim and smart and a veritable little soldier-women's army' (1918: 30).[18]

The metaphor, however, was far from being inappropriate. Unlike the VADs and even the land workers, munitions employees had no organisational independence. Government intervention, as well as introducing male conscription and the infamous DORA, limited industrial freedom by enforcing the abandonment of union practices in munitions and introducing a leaving certificate, without which workers could not move from one factory to another (Braybon 1981: 55). An article in *The Common Cause* publicises the 'deplorably low' pay for cartridge work (13s per week) and argues that for the poorly paid classes of women the Munitions Act 'has meant that they have been prevented from bargaining for a reasonable wage' (*The Common Cause* 17 March 1916: 650). Protective legislation was put aside, thus exposing women to dangerous conditions which damaged their health (Rowbotham 1973: 110; Braybon 1981: 114). Working with TNT, for example, could cause severe irritative and toxic symptoms as well as the change in skin colour that earned its handlers the name 'canaries'.[19]

In keeping with the army spirit, however, the numerous calls to patriotism and hard work, usually from ruling-class sources, smoothed over the difficulties, practical and ideological, and made a virtue out of bad conditions and low wages. Mrs Alec-Tweedie, for example, tells the story of a parlourmaid whose fiancé is about to leave for 'somewhere in France':

> 'Tom,' she said, 'you are off to do your bit, God bless you, and you will be constantly in my thoughts and my prayers; but I do not suppose we shall meet again for many months – perhaps longer – and I am going to spring a mine upon you, not a German mine, old chap, but a truly British one. While you are at the front firing shells, I am going into a munition factory to make shells. The job will not be as well paid as domestic service, it will not be as comfortable as domestic service; it will be much harder work, but it will be my bit, and every time you fire your gun you can remember I am helping to make the shells.'
> 'Well done, my girl, it is splendid of you, but can you stand it?'
> 'I *will* stand it,' she replied with that determination which one knows to be the British characteristic, even when it means getting up at five o'clock every winter morning and not returning for fourteen hours at a spell.
>
> (1918: 29)

The proximity between shell-makers and shell-firers is used often as a link between soldiers and factory workers. Sometimes the connection combines romance with a demonstration of true British pluck, as above; sometimes it is retaliatory, as in Caine's description of a woman making shot 'for them as killed my Joe' (Caine 1916: 38), or Pamela Butler in Irene Rathbone's *We That Were Young* ([1932] 1988) who hopes that her shells will kill the man responsible for the death of her fiance.

Munitions factories were of course prime targets for enemy zeppelin raids, events that engendered a trench spirit in the workers as they waited for an attack in darkness and surrounded by high explosives. Mrs G. Kaye, a Principal Overlooker at Woolwich, describes her reaction to the 400 women and girls under her charge: 'I used to feel very proud of their wonderful pluck when all our lights were put out when the zeppelins used to come over.'[20] 'The heroism of the battlefields has frequently been equalled by the ordinary civilian in the factory', writes L. K. Yates in *The Woman's Part. A Record of Munitions Work* (1918: 12). Mrs Alec-Tweedie makes more explicit the connection between patriotic commitment in trench and factory as the workers wait for the all clear:

> The hours wear on. It grows colder.[. . .] The cold seems to penetrate their very soul; but the women say nothing. They know their men face the guns day and night. Big guns, little guns, every kind of hell fire. They know a shell or a rifle-bullet may end a man's life any minute. They know these men at the front never shirk, why should they? The only people who shirk are the slackers at home, the 'down tools,' the wasters, the scum. No soldier shirks his duty, no woman worker turns chicken-hearted.
>
> (1918: 33)

This articulates the Establishment conspiracy to defeat working-class activism generally. Furthermore, the slippage between industrial reality and trench imagery is clearly calculated to smother in women the inclination to pursue their rights, by offering to increase the burden of guilt that is in any case the lot of the non-combatant. Further analogies aid this strategy. The roar of the machines is like the roar of guns – although one can leave at the end of a shift (Alec-Tweedie 1918: 32); the stamina needed to complete a forty-eight hour shift is similar to that needed on the 'dark glutinous desolate Front', but without the feature of permanent discomfort (Rathbone [1932] 1988: 274). Industrial injuries were quite common: as well as losing hair and teeth as a result of handling TNT, workers might also become trapped in the machinery. Rathbone describes in graphic detail a worker's hair being ripped out by the wheel of a drilling machine ([1932] 1988: 266), and another worker having her finger torn off, 'the white muscles hanging from it like strings' ([1932] 1988: 269). In Bessie Marchant's novel *A Girl Munition Worker* (1916), a character loses a foot as a result of an explosion. These token war wounds, however, are not described to demonstrate the hazards and insufficient safety procedures of many munitions factories but to elevate their victims to the status of 'soldier-women'. That this status is second class is underlined by the comparisons with the 'real' danger zones. This strategy, then, by constantly reaffirming women's *relative* safety by way of honouring the fighting males, not only hindered the long-term improvement of industrial conditions but also effectively ensured that, no matter what their sacrifice, women would continue to be socially constructed as permanently subservient.

The dangers cited above were not, however, the most life-threatening occurrences. Fires and explosions frequently caused deaths. Peggy Hamilton, whose *Three Years or the Duration* was published in 1978, recalls that 'the slightest spark could lead to an explosion and the "canaries" wore special uniforms and walked on platforms – presumably to avoid any friction from their shoes' (Hamilton 1978: 34). In 1916, for instance, the Silvertown factory claimed twelve women's lives (Marwick 1977: 69), and Miss Olive Taylor vividly recalls in her unpublished memoir the outbreak of a fire one night at a privately owned factory near Morcambe Bay. A sprinkler system failed to contain the fire and workers were trapped inside the factory gates:

> the fire did spread rapidly and soon huge explosions shook everything. There was quite a lot of panic as the twelve foot high gates remained closed. The police on the gates were never permitted to open them until soldiers surrounded the factory & the line to the camp had been cut. The rush for the gates had the weaker people on the ground, yet still others climbed over them to try & climb the gates while the police tried to hold them back. A few girls were working to dislodge the girls on the ground & carry them into the canteen. I had no hopes of escaping that holocaust, but somehow I was not scared. We were shut in with those explosions for several hours. The

buildings had strong walls & weak roofs so that the roofs would go up rather than the walls. Truck loads of benzine & dangerous chemicals were exploding too, and several people threw themselves into a river which ran at the back of the works. We never knew how many died.[21]

The dramas of danger and heroism, however, did not entirely overrule in the shell-makers a consciousness of the ironic dislocation between their patriotic intention and its destructive effect. Peggy Hamilton analyses the connection between her motives and her actions with an unsettling awareness of their practical consequences. She expresses the 'very real guilt', not of the protected, but of the unintentionally aggressive:

> Every night I prayed for the safety of those dear to me who were at the front, and yet here I was working twelve hours a day towards the destruction of other people's loved ones. It was a terrible dilemma: indirectly I was responsible for death and misery.
>
> (Hamilton 1978: 29)

She and others took comfort in the powerful ideology that this was 'the war to end war' and that they were fighting for a better world. The articulation of her moral quandary suggests, however, a line of argument that can be taken in at least two directions. As we shall see in Chapter 4, feminist pacifists argued for the absurdity of war as a means of settling international disputes and for the value of *all* human life – a value which women, as non-combatants and child-bearers, might be particularly concerned to protect. Some propaganda writers, however, were also unsettled by the notion of women as arms producers, but went to improbable lengths to construe the activity in terms appropriate to women's more conventional roles.

How to woo the male monster . . .

Some of the propagandist texts, particularly those of Caine and Yates, are deeply troubled by the incongruity that the mothers and nurturers of the race should also be the primary arms producers. 'There is a natural antagonism between woman and war, and it is difficult to think of her as a maker of weapons of death', says Caine (1916: 66). Furthermore, 'Every instinct of our nature revolts against the thought that woman, with the infinitely delicate organization which provides for her maternal functions, should under any circumstances whatever take part in the operations such scenes require' (1916: 19). In the opening stages of his argument, then, he emphasises women's 'otherness' to war and expresses some anxiety lest the very nature of munitions making might upset their biological make-up. In order to justify their importation on a massive scale into the industry and their patriotic heroism in performing the task, then, it becomes rhetorically necessary to assign a feminine function to the filling of shells and the making of shot. The work, after all, 'looks simple enough, and seems perfectly natural to their sex', says Caine (1916: 22), and he proceeds to 'naturalise' the activity further by describing the uniform as being 'in the eyes of the male creature, [. . .] extremely becoming' (1916: 24). Moreover, it seems to involve only a minor adjustment for these attractively attired women to employ their traditional wiles in making love to powerful machinery, instead of to powerful men:

> if you show a proper respect for their impetuous organ-isms, they are not generally cruel. So the women get along very well with them, learning all their ways, their whims, their needs and their limitations. It is surprising how speedily the women have wooed and won this new kind of male monster.
>
> (1916: 23)

The entire operation is thus shielded from an interpretation concerning women's changing roles in industry by the language of the love story. Indeed, the metaphor invites visions of gothic heroes – Heathcliffs, Mr Rochesters – men who are headstrong and demand delicate and tactful handling if they are not suddenly to unleash their heinous potential. The 'monster' image is somewhat startling in this context as it invokes the threat of violence – suggesting the possibility of industrial injuries – but also of the irrational and the subversive: the machines might possibly go out of control. Caine descends further into the sexual metaphor, however, and in a move characteristic more of a dreamer than an industrial observer tells us that 'somewhere' in the 'danger zone' of the factory 'the *womb* of the shell has to be loaded with its deadly charge' (Caine

1916: 25; my emphasis). Making a bomb, it seems, is not that dissimilar to making a baby. And, as if to complete the picture by including another fetishistic vision of women, this mysterious setting is likened to a convent, where 'the shadowy figures of women workers in their khaki gowns and caps, move noiselessly about *like nuns*' (1916: 26; my emphasis). The shell, a female victim/volunteer, is thus implanted with its deadly charge by the brides of Christ, while older, coarser, witch-like women stir up great vats of boiling lead (1916: 37). This imagery – gothic, sexual, religious – releases an unsettling range of associations which, to the modern reader, might seem to question rather than confirm women's role in munitions making. Caine, however, knits together his allusions to wombs, nuns and old hags by saying that:

> For every war that has yet been waged women have supplied the first and the greatest of all munitions – men. [. . .] Therefore, consciously or unconsciously, the daughters of Britain may be answering some mysterious call of their sex in working all day and all night in the munitions factories.
>
> (1916: 34–5)

The making of shells, then, can be explained not by social, economic or political reasons, but by the unconscious lure of women's weird and murky biological function, and by the strange, devotional practices (becoming nuns or witches) to which only women succumb. This probably says more about the male than the female unconscious. In struggling to comprehend these women's 'unnatural' acts Caine appeals to a range of images that asserts women's innate mysteriousness, but which also betrays a certain anxiety on his part concerning their biological – and cultural – potency. In any case, once again, the flesh-and-blood woman worker disappears from view.[22]

The tone of Caine's piece is one of bemused awe rather than scientific cultural analysis, but he nevertheless resolves his metaphorical flights by pointing to motherhood, and the health and well-being of the race. If the countryside and the practice of thrift will ensure strong and powerful future generations, then it seems logically probable that twelve-hour shifts seven days a week in a poorly ventilated and noxious atmosphere would guarantee the opposite. There were many arguments to this effect. Working-class married women were dissuaded by journalists, eugenicists and labour spokespeople alike from entering permanent, full-time employment on the grounds that they would neglect their children, they would probably spend the money they earned on drink and they would almost certainly lead immoral lives (Braybon 1981: 116–22). The concern of such propagandists was for the future of the race. L.K. Yates, on the other hand, quotes Lloyd George as saying 'The workers of today are the mothers of tomorrow' (1918: 37). She adds the observation that 'many of the girls passing through this strange war-time adventure have assuredly gained by their pilgrimage precisely in those qualities most needed by wives and mothers of the rising generation' (1918: 63). We have an uneasy conflict here, and brought together under the banner of a single metaphor, the traditional concern for the race, the masculine concern to keep women out of the (permanent) labour force and the industrial and political necessity of employing large numbers of women in munitions factories in order to speed up production at minimum cost. Patriarchy is thus upheld, but is also undermined by its need to stick to a single image of womanhood in order to protect its own interests. The female biological functions ought to be irrelevant here. They are invoked, in all their mystery, in order to confirm women's literal and metaphorical confinement. It is simply the case that munitions work *does not* make sense in terms of maternity.

Gender: Industrial emancipation?

The prejudices surrounding women workers were complicated. The engineering unions objected to their working at all in skilled and semi-skilled areas, particularly as previously set tasks would be 'diluted' by more than one worker taking on responsibility for different elements of that task, thus devaluing and restructuring workshop practices. True, it was the Amalgamated Society of Engineers that insisted on equal pay for women performing 'diluted' labour, with the result that women fitters and tool setters could earn between £5 and £10.[23] That union's permission for dilution, however, was only given on the basis that the arrangement be seen as temporary, and should cease with the end of the war when pre-war conditions should be reinstated. Women's industrial emancipation, then, had a time limit on it.[24]

Women had hitherto been expected to be unambitious and apathetic with regard to their paid employment. The common pre-war prejudice was that they did not deserve to learn skilled jobs as they would inevitably marry and therefore leave work. Their 'real work', of course, was home-making and mother-hood. But there was also a more generalised prejudice which was based on women's supposedly innate characteristics. Boyd Cable, for example, sees women as an ideal source of cheap, docile labour because:

> they are punctual and regular in attendance; they are tractable and obedient and don't 'raise trouble'; they are amazingly keen on their work, take an interest in it, stick closely to it, and honestly do their best all the time. For munition work which is in their handling capacity they are apparently ideal workers.
>
> (1916: 77)

Like placid children, they do as they are told to the best of their ability. But when it comes to work requiring intellectual acumen, their gender weaknesses manifest themselves:

> most of the engineers I spoke with agreed that the women are not as good as the men, because the women have not the initiative or inventiveness, would not think of or suggest any alteration or improvement in machinery or details of their work. . . .
>
> (1916: 77)

Women, then, were seen to be malleable, uncomplaining, good at unchallenging tasks, ideal for low-paid, unskilled labour, but fundamentally lacking in initiative. Yates suggests that all stereo-typing has been dropped: 'War necessity has, however, killed old-time prejudice and has proved how readily women adapt themselves to any task within their physical powers' (1918: 12). Their physical powers, of course, are seen by her as extremely limited, and she goes on to contribute to the debilitating patronage of her own sex by reinforcing the stereotype of women's innate inaccuracy of mind. In training, she says, the greatest problem was 'the implanting of a feeling for exactitude in persons accustomed to measure ribbons or lace within a margin of a quarter of a yard or so, or to prepare food by a guess-work of ingredients' (1918: 22). She then attributes their ability to surmount this problem to their 'proverbial patience'. Peggy Hamilton's narrative reminds us that prejudices were by no means overcome: 'The trade unions had accepted women in the unskilled jobs but there was considerable resistance to the idea of women working in the toolroom' (1978: 44). When she makes the move from unskilled to skilled labour she has to run the gauntlet of a series of initiation ceremonies orchestrated by her male fellow workers:

> I remember showers of steel shavings pouring down on me from the gallery above as I worked at my lathe. Another time, as I was bending over my machine, a great wad of cotton waste, stuck with shavings and dripping with oil, caught me right in the face.
>
> (1978: 51)

The obsession with maternalism, then, tied to assumptions concerning women's proper place and their potential to act as blacklegs, obscures the areas of women's political relation to industrial practices that women like B.L. Hutchins, Esther Roper and Clementina Black were trying to bring into the public domain *via* the pages of the feminist journals *The Common Cause*, *The Englishwoman* and *Women's Industrial News*. Questions concerning equal pay, bargaining power and health and safety provisions were having to do battle with a monstrous metaphorical construction of women's relation to industrial practice, backed up by the politics of race and a largely conservative male workforce. When this is combined with ruling-class attitudes concerning women's proper behaviour, again the real conditions of working women's lives disappear beneath a set of values geared towards assuring women of the permanency of the underlying structure of social and industrial relations. Their apparent freedom and high wages is just a blip.

Class: Myths of mixing

The question of class here is crucial. When Yates speaks of the worker's pilgrimage through the munitions factory towards motherhood, she is, of course, speaking in terms applicable only to those who would want to cease working with the end of the war. Those were not in the majority. Her account, like Thekla Bowser's of early VAD units, suggests that equal numbers

THE SPHERE

AN ILLUSTRATED NEWSPAPER FOR THE HOME — With which is incorporated *BLACK & WHITE*

Volume LXXIII. No. 954. | REGISTERED AT THE GENERAL POST OFFICE AS A NEWSPAPER | London, May 4, 1918. | Price One Shilling and Sixpence.

IN A MUNITION FACTORY—A WOMAN MAKING 4·5 CARTRIDGE CASES

We reproduce above an interesting picture of munition-making. The girl-worker is engaged on the manufacture of 4·5 cartridge cases, and is "feeding" a Taylor and Challen drawing press. This is only one of the many operations connected with the making of munitions which are being successfully carried out by women. The metal is forced into the desired shape by great pressure. Just below the big control lever to the right of the worker are some of the dies and also the portions of cartridge casing with which she is dealing

Plate 3 Front page of *The Sphere*, 4 May 1918, showing a woman munitions worker. (By courtesy of the Trustees of the Imperial War Museum.)

of women of all classes worked side by side, united by a common cause, with no friction or difficulty:

> Even in the early days of the advent of women in the munitions shops, I have seen working together, side by side, the daughter of an earl, a shop keeper's widow, a graduate from Girton, a domestic servant, and a young woman from a lonely farm in Rhodesia, whose husband had joined the colours. Social status, so stiff a barrier in this country in pre-war days, was forgotten in the factory, as in the trenches, and they were all working together as happily as the members of a united family.
>
> (Yates 1918: 9)[25]

Social status, of course, was forgotten neither in the trenches nor in the factories. Just as the officer class in the army was privileged over the cheery British Tommy, class informed the hierarchy of labour in munitions factories. Educated women tended to be trained as forewomen and Lady Superintendents, like Lilian Barker at Woolwich who was responsible for the 25,000 women workers there in 1917. Her work was essentially welfare work and, like that of the early VADs, can be construed as the logical continuation of charity and social work performed by gentlewomen in the nineteenth century. Her principal skills are 'understanding, patience and tact', and for this she was paid much more than the working-class unskilled workers (McLaren 1917: 10–11). The propaganda, in order to justify the privileges of middle- and upper-class women, insists on reproducing the stereotyped view of their social inferiors. According to Alec-Tweedie, 'tawdry finery is the hall-mark of the usual working-class girl' (1918: 55), and Caine presents 'Tommy's Sister' as a child with 'kiss-curls twiddling over her temples' and a bag of sweets (1916: 71). Hysterical behaviour during air raids is also, according to him, exclusively the province of 'Alice and Annie and Rose' and has to be 'put down with an iron hand' – the property of the educated lady supervisor (1916: 72). Not all educated women, however, conformed to the aristocratic image that Alec-Tweedie proposes. The *Women's Industrial News*, for instance, cites a case where university women were engaged for the supervisory posts of a particular task, not, as it turned out, because it required any great intellectual skill, but because the management hoped that they would give their time for 'patriotism'. On the contrary, they held out for an increase in pay for both supervisors and workers (*Women's Industrial News* April 1916: 16). There is, then, an ideological silence here. The propaganda speaks of the breakdown of class divisions while justifying the training of educated women as leaders. The contradiction is concealed (from those at whom the propaganda was aimed) by the ideology of a natural social hierarchy, whose operations guarantee to elicit the best from each individual worker.

The fiction of the period that relates to munitions work is limited, probably because of the usual problems relating to the articulation of working-class experience (cf. for example, O'Rourke 1988) and the fact that there was only a small number of middle-class women employed. Two popular novels by Bessie Marchant and Brenda Girvin called, respectively, *A Girl Munition Worker* (1916) and *Munition Mary* (1918) do nothing to challenge stereotypical class assumptions. Like Berta Ruck's *The Land Girl's Love Story*, they reproduce popular ideologies in the setting of a developing, if troubled, romance that leads to marriage. Marchant's heroine, Deborah Lynch, is a well-to-do young thing living with two rich aunts while both father and brother are serving in the army. Her 'fiery zeal and red-hot patriotism' (1916: 1) lead her to a munitions factory, where she sets the pace, easily outstripping the production of the ordinary girls, but leading them on to better performances. She receives due reverence, particularly from Elsie Marsh, a beautiful orphan with a shifty step-father, who turns out to be a German spy and blackmails his vulnerable charge into directing zeppelins towards the munitions plant. Being a true Brit, Elsie shines the light in the wrong direction. Deborah, however, senses danger, and manages one night to shoot at the spy (who has incapacitated the guards), thus saving the plant and its night-shift from certain destruction. She later inadvertently kills the spy by knocking him down in a taxi. The munitions setting is really little more than an excuse to celebrate the patriotism and heroism of upper-class women doing their bit, and to perpetuate the myth that only those who are properly bred can properly govern and properly protect.

The heroine of *Munition Mary* is less aristocratic, but well-bred enough for all the lower-class girls to lose their hearts to her – all, that is, except one coarse-looking, brown-skinned girl, who inevitably turns out to be a German spy. The book is ostensibly about combatting the masculine prejudice of the factory owner, Sir William Harrison, whose unwillingness to admit the proficiency of the 'girl' workers coincides neatly with the spies' plan to destroy the factory. They conspire to persuade the girls that Sir William is sabotaging their work and making them ill, when the real culprits are the hostel owner and canteen manager, both members of the ring. Mary, however, realises that her employer, if somewhat gruff, is really a stout-hearted patriot. She uncovers the plot (more lights and zeppelins), traps the criminals and marries the handsome nephew, while remaining delightfully 'feminine' and not offending Sir William with any untoward bumptiousness.

These two combine the adventure of children's stories with the love interest of romantic fiction (both authors were established writers of girls' adventure and school stories). Irene Rathbone's *We That Were Young* ([1932] 1988), however, presents itself as a more serious study of the war generation and, as its title might suggest, has much in common with *Testament of Youth*. Its brief depiction of munitions work, though, does little to challenge any of the orthodoxies concerning class and industrial occupations. Pamela Butler, daughter of a county family, enters the factory in order to avenge the death of her fiancé. The work, '[d]eafening, stupefying, brain-shattering', is clearly seen as unhealthy and unnatural ([1932] 1988: 262). She sits next to the working-class, outspoken Liz Fanshawe, who 'was a good-natured creature, if a bit foul-mouthed at times' ([1932] 1988: 263). Pamela, however, who has a genteel aversion to raising her voice, communicates with her only through facial expressions. The one person Pamela does befriend is the daughter of a country vicar, Miss Fenton, and the two are left 'tacitly alone' by the others. Liz screams and sings and gulps her tea – and loses her hair in the machinery. While 'little Nellie Crewe' goes off to be quietly sick, Pamela maintains her stoical bearing: 'One did not faint' ([1932] 1988: 267). One also does not 'actually' sit on the lavatory seat. Pamela's aunt, Lady Butler, advises her niece to leave 'that dreadful munition factory' for something 'less unsuitable'. She sees 'no point in competing with the lower orders in physical endurance; they were obviously far better able to bear things than we were'

([1932] 1988: 276). The comment is undoubtedly a tongue-in-cheek rendition of the feelings of the older generation, but nevertheless, Pamela's health cannot withstand the strain. Again, however, and despite the physical arduousness of this employment, it is the soldiers on the 'desolate Front' who set the imaginary example – not her fellow workers who do not have the choice of taking up something 'less unsuitable'. It seems to be a crucial element of women's war consciousness that they compare themselves unfavourably, not with their sisters who lie across class barriers, but with their brothers, who, as members of the capital-owning class, exploit the labour and health of the working classes. The novel comes to no conclusion other than that industrial work is intrinsically bad for one's health and that Pamela is jolly brave – if slightly unhinged – to have tackled it.

Viscountess Wolsely's project of a new peasant class never came to fruition. There were more women, however, in paid employment in the metropolitan centres after the war than there had been previous to it (Braybon 1981: 173). This seems to suggest that Holtby was right: if women of that period sought liberation from limited role models, they needed to head towards the cities. The images of female alterity offered by the promoters of racial supremacy had no political value and farming communities themselves were economically too run-down to accommodate women's demands for equality. The problem here is the intersection of two different agendas: if women wanted to help to win the war they were welcome to do so, but within the boundaries of conservative definitions of femininity and on the condition that any apparently radical change was merely temporary. If they were seeking independence or emancipation, the political picture became more fraught. As we have seen, assumptions concerning women's true role were adjusted to accommodate their temporary involvement in industry, rather than being called into question by their work, and the vision of the working woman as blackleg, imposter and usurper of the breadwinner's wage was difficult to shift.

In these two instances of women's employment the changes to their gendered identities that women were experiencing – economic, social, physical – were contained by the ideology of racial supremacy and the British woman's natural role in this.

The effect of the war on women who saw their role throughout the conflict as being associated with the home, and who did not attempt even to take temporary advantage of the opportunities for war work, will be explored in the next chapter.

3

WOMEN AT HOME
Romance or realism?

This, the central chapter of this study, deals with the wartime identity of women who did no war work but structured their lives around their homes and their men. This issue acts as a pivot between the first two chapters and the last two. The image of the 'angel in the house', as we have seen, is the conservative touchstone that limits women's attempts to free themselves from cloistered domesticity by working in semi-military or industrial regimes. On the other hand, in spite of its conservatism, that image of women as mothers who were politically uncorrupted, generated an ideological stance that was deeply radical and critical of the social and political strategies that led to and governed the war. The image of the silenced, domesticated nurturer is, then, at the ideological junction of those conservative representations of women who fought for the war and radical women who fought against it.

While the war was apparently offering liberty and adventure to those who could escape the role of dutiful daughter, for those who remained the strategies of 'business as usual' prevailed. Business, in war as in peace, meant finding a husband and maintaining a home, an activity animated and invested with meaning by the seemingly universal ideology of romantic love. Many of the popular songs, posters and postcards of the war reveal that romance was necessary as a life-enhancing counterpoint to the brutalities and degradations of war: if women were to keep the home fires burning, that fire was to be as alive in their hearts as it was in their hearths. Romantic love seemed to offer both soldiers and civilians some continuity and order to their lives. This chapter will investigate the social and narrative function of romance as revealed in popular magazines and novels of the period. The magazines and some of the novels promote the myriad practical details that certify the housewife's success at her job. This can be seen as at once a form of escapism and a smoke-screen to shield women from the developments in suffragism, women's employment and the moral and political problems that the war produced for women. Women's silence on these issues is made to appear natural by the ethics of the angel in the house. The war is presented as a test which assures the permanence of womanly values, rather than as an agent for their disruption. On the other hand, as Rebecca West's *The Return of the Soldier* suggests, the ideality of romantic love, while frequently conservative, can offer a pathway to a vision of an alternative value system preferable to that dominated by the war. Furthermore, some post-war novels indicate that the loss of the romantic ideal can expose some of the patriarchal pompousities of the masculine, imperialist mentality.

HEART TO HEART CHATS

Women's magazines, not surprisingly, were reluctant to foreground the radical changes in women's lives that the war could effect. Indeed, they present the war in very low profile. The 'editresses' rather sought to absorb elements of war-specific home economy into the already-existing ideological structures that underpinned their magazines, in order to reassure their readers of the necessity not only of their occupations as wives, mothers and angels in the house, but also of the war itself. Images of the war and images of femininity are thus organised in such a way as to reflect upon each other as part of a natural order. The magazines emphasised the moral equity of women's subservience: loyalty to the country was thus equated with loyalty to the patriarchal order.

The penny-weeklies (*Woman's Own, Woman's World, Everywoman's*, for example), while they encourage women's silent acceptance of men's part in the war, toe a harsh moral line with regard to the challenges presented to women. Women are encouraged not to fall victim to glamorous images of wartime romance[1] and the sub-text of this advice centres on chastity. 'Don't be a traitor to the lad out there who loves you! Be as faithful to him as you expect him to be to his flag' is the headline for 'My Straight Talks to Sweethearts Wives and Mothers of the British Empire' in *Woman's World* (20 November 1915: 19). A reader seeking advice as to whether she should marry her soldier before or after he goes off to fight, is counselled:

> Dear girl, this is not the sort of question anyone can answer but your own heart, and, I may add, your own common sense. I am not going to give you a definite answer, but I am going to suggest just one or two things to think over. In the first place remember the glamour that surrounds all things military and war-like. I need say no more on that point, I think. Secondly, why do you hesitate and trouble to ask me at all? Does real love know such hesitancy? Thirdly, have you really considered the possibility that he may be killed? And following on that have you realised that you would then be a girl-widow – not a 'war widow', but a real, sorrowing woman whose loved one had gone beyond recall and left her to face the rest of a long life alone? I have not said all this to discourage you, dear, but in order that whatever you may do you will do it with your eyes open. For I know full well that if true love binds you together no advice, were it reiterated for ages, would keep you apart.
>
> (*Woman's Own* 11 September 1915: 8)

The tone is maternal, the advice is against the temptations of false and insincere glamour and the details are practical. A '*real* sorrowing woman', it is true, does not have the same headline-quality as a 'war widow', but this is precisely the point: the editor is discouraging women from being seduced by the specious romantic images pedalled by a sensationalist press. There is a guiding fiction, however, which ameliorates the harshness of common-sensical reality. 'True love', when attained, is not to be ignored nor overcome. It naturalises all difficulties and contradictions, and is entirely spontaneous. This is a representation of romance – the instant and inexorable resolution to all problems – which provides the 'magic agent' for many of the novels of the period and frequently forestalls the female characters' acknowledgment of the challenges to their lives – emotional, moral, practical and political – that the war provokes.

Woman's Own, Everywoman's Weekly, Woman's World and *Mother and Home* target the lower-middle classes and concentrate on advice for effective home economy in the face of war restrictions on the assumption that the ideological stronghold of 'true love' in the form of marriage is unchallengeable. They are primarily concerned to convince women of their proper duties and (which amounts to the same thing) to offer them strategies to manage the war's crises, strategies which barely redirect the readers' attention from their pre-war tasks: knitting, sewing, cooking and cleaning. The first mention of the war in *Woman's Own*, for example, comes in September 1914 (four weeks after the declaration of hostilities), when the cover shows a young woman saying 'I am making garments to help the soldiers! Are you?' (*Woman's Own* 5 September 1914). The inevitable sewing patterns are found inside. *Woman's World* provides similar designs under the heading 'Woman's Work in Wartime', thus combining the increasingly popular war work ethic with woman's traditional sphere, while reinforcing the acceptable limits of women's employment (*Woman's World* 12 September 1914: 233). All the weeklies carry home hints and recipes fired by the extra challenge of providing nourishing meals in the face of rising prices and food scarcity. The ideological forces that construct these magazines' philosophies are unmistakeable. They are based upon conventional Christian teaching and a drive to counteract the lures of sex and suffragism, but with the compensation of providing the security of a morally superior, traditional identity.

The domestic detail is sustained by the ethics of the angel in the house, delivered in editorials or 'weekly chats'. Jeannie Maitland, a major contributor to *Woman's Own*, is the embodiment of this position. The soft-spoken Christianity evident in her 'Recollections of a Minister's Wife' frequently lies behind her short story and her weekly words of wisdom on anything from war-shattered dreams to bringing up babies. Her ideals are Victorian – Dickensian, even. She believes that the wife and mother should be the heart of the home, the haven in an increasingly hostile world: 'one who believes that the sun is still shining, and that behind the black cloud the sky is still blue' (*Woman's Own* 5 June 1915: 22). In an article called 'Back to the Home' published in 1915, before the initiatives for women's war work had been fully established, she wonders 'how far we women are to blame for the loss of the old, sweet, true ideals of happiness'. Significantly, is her answer, and the neglect of the home in favour of votes, work, independence and other manifestations of Georgian pleasure-seeking must cease in the face of war's responsibilities. She concludes with the following:

> Now, again, has come the sober light of stern and awful duties upon our life. This war must pass one day, but life will never be quite the same again. Shall not those of us who are mothers determine to do what lies within us to make home – home days and home evenings – the dearest and best of all pleasures? The great responsibilities of creating that quiet, wholesome happiness lies on the wife and mother. She must be kind, tactful, wise and self-sacrificing if she is going to satisfy the heart-hunger of the young for something outside themselves.
>
> (*Woman's Own* 17 July 1915: 1)

The war, then, rather than taking women out of the home, is seen as an awesome signal to them to return to their natural duty – in what *Everywoman's Weekly* called 'The "Great Push" Towards Womanliness' – thus setting back the cause of women's emancipation by several decades. The mother is the repository of moral values: if these disappear it is her responsibility. This moral blackmail (which is still evident in our culture) is what lies behind the maternalism discussed in the previous chapter. It feeds on the fearful anticipation of their children's delinquency to persuade women to sacrifice their own personal needs to those of their family, and to blame themselves should things not go to plan. The moral blackmail works by pretending to offer women a unique *power* position. Weakness is thus constructed as power, and radical alternatives are seen as a perverse molestation of natural order.

If the tone of the above examples seems to resemble the quiet teachings of the local parson, the evangelical priest is Horatio Bottomley, the editor of *John Bull*, who offered a rumbustious, weekly dose of patriotism in *Everywoman's*. One of his 'Straight from the Shoulder Talk[s]' reads:

> If I were a woman! What a vista of glorious possibilities the very thought conjures up – for to be a woman, and a British woman during this epoch-making war is, in my estimation, one of the most glorious privileges the gods

have granted humankind since ever the spheres were set in motion, and dawn from darkness sprang. Wife, mother, daughter, sister, sweetheart – old and young, rich and poor, gentle and simple – all come within the sweep of this dawn of grace which is going to make every minute a milestone on the long-drawn-out march of womanhood towards the cloud-kissed heights where perfection of the species will be found. The march of the species from the valleys to the hill-tops is more or less instinctive; we can no more help climbing upward in soul than a lark can help soaring as it sings; it is the destiny of humanity to rise until the great and wonderful plan of the Creator is crystallised into perfect harmony, and woman, on account of her finer fibre, her higher moral endowment, her sweeter and purer sentiments, and her more clarified moral vision, is ordained by Him 'who hung the stars in translucent splendour in night's dark canopy' to carry the banner of progress towards its ultimate goal, whilst her brothers, husbands, sons and lovers attend to grosser things, and wrestle with the world, the flesh, and the devil.

(*Everywoman's* 19 February 1916: 687)

The evangelical imagery carries the piece forward by rhythm and bluster rather than by substance. The pulpit rhetoric of lyrical repetition and the quasi-poetical imagery, masquerading as philosophical and anthropological discourse, exalt women to a position far beyond the drudgery of daily life. Housework, if Bottomley is to be believed, is really nothing less than a manifestation of 'higher moral endowment' and 'more clarified moral vision', and women gloriously occupy the super-egotistical space in their culture, while men fight it out on the site of the ego, with the mundanities and corruptions of base human experience. There is no possibility that woman's exalted sphere might in any way *change* men's 'grosser' preoccupations: women are left to the larks and the stars, quite out of reach of the world and the flesh. The explanation of this is based, of course, on racial supremacy. Women have been given the task of carrying 'the banner of progress towards its ultimate goal', the 'perfection of the species': the prerogative specifically of the *British* woman, according to 'the great and wonderful plan of the Creator' – to which, one assumes, Bottomley has privileged access. The war, then, according to this ideology, has had the *beneficial* effect of affirming the God-given polarisation of the sexes. Rather than offering women the chance actively to alter the world, Bottomley, Maitland and the others spirit them further off, to higher regions, where, apparently, they were naturally bound in any case. At least it gets them out of the way.

Few other editorials are so willing to 'flatter' women. Womanly advice tends to prefer the discourse of gratitude and humility, steering away from romantic heights and dwelling instead on self-sacrifice and the need to keep going and think of others worse off than oneself. In one of *Woman's World*'s 'Heart to Heart Chats' the editress replies rather impatiently to a reader who has already lost three children and whose husband has now gone to France:

> Dear sister, I am so sorry to hear of your unhappiness. But, dearie, you must really try to be more cheerful, and face the separation from your husband a little more bravely . . .
> (*Woman's World* 15 May 1915: 540)

The appellation 'dearie' creates an atmosphere of (false) intimacy, within which it can be clearly intimated that revealing one's unhappiness is unpatriotic. Similarly, in an article entitled 'The Women England Wants – A Soldier's Wife',[2] the paragon is invited to repress her own grief and anxiety and tend to that of others:

> Brave wife, who are toiling all day and often at night, keeping the little home together while your soldier–husband answers to the call of duty, have a thought for that neighbour of yours whose husband has also been called to the front. Try to find time to see her, to comfort her, or cheer her. Do little deeds like this, and you will be as nobly doing your duty as those who are in the fighting line.
> (*Woman's World* 26 September 1914: 285)

Again this is based on the popularisation of Christian asceticism. Selflessness and community spirit, with the additional reward of being thought 'noble', like the soldiers, clinches the patriotic message. What it fails to confront, of course, is the trauma that is unleashed when the symbol of these patriarchal microcosms (the 'little home[s]') is actually killed. If the 'real

sorrowing woman' is incapable of living up to the extra-
ordinarily high ideals set for her, she is offered a sense of guilt
and worthlessness as recompense, as some of the novels of the
period reveal.

Motherhood is crucial to the identity of the 'brave wife'. We
have seen that running against the recruitment drive to get
more women producing munitions was the drive to protect and
promote the motherhood that is their natural condition. Indeed, *Woman's Own's* Jeannie Maitland adopts the position that
'no mother of children under a certain age, at least should be
allowed to go out to work' (17 April 1915: 12). And in any case,
according to the writer of the 'Patriotic Mothers' column in
Mother and Home, 'This is a "war work", a work for "King and
country"': the mother's job is to 'train that child to be of value
to the State, to help in the future to enlarge its borders and
repel its enemies' (1 January 1916: 499). A woman's social
function, it seems, is to develop her (implicitly male) children
into little Kitcheners.[3]

If the magazines aim to convince the reader of the use and
necessity of her work as mother, it falls to them also to provide
the reasoning behind the sacrifice of so many sons. In *Woman's
World* there is a weekly feature: 'Ten Minute Talks to Ladies. By
the Bachelor of Experience.' Once again it is an authoritative
male who explains to the 'ladies' the rationale behind the war.
This eminently sensible figure (who, in the caption, at first
appears as an Edwardian gentleman and then, in mid-1915,
mysteriously dons the uniform of an officer) accounts for the
necessity of the war as follows:

> The story of the war is simple enough. A cowardly bully has
> kicked a baby amongst the nations. Great Britain, your big
> boy, grown-up and strong, has gone for the bully.
> He is going to get hurt in the struggle, for the bully is
> strong and unscrupulous. And his hurts and his losses
> must come home to you – his womenfolk.
>
> (*Woman's World* 17 October 1914: 388)

We can see here the deliberate, and excruciatingly patronising,
manipulation of the stereotypical notions of female sensibilities.
Women, it is implied, can only understand such complex issues
when they are explained in nursery language. Belgium is the
baby, Germany the bully. Great Britain, our brave boy, has to

retaliate; the mother's role is to repair what are euphemistically referred to as 'hurts and losses'.

The ideologies of the magazines, then, attempt to reduce complexity and abnormality to a matter of woman's 'natural' duty. The war is seen not as a disruption but as an opportunity to rediscover the 'feminine' experience. The magazines adopt the voice of a 'pal': they appeal to their readers as young, inexperienced, in need of aid and advice, which is a subtle way of patronising a largely lower-middle-class readership. The consolation that these women are offered for relinquishing a voice in the political world, is a kind of moral superiority. Men, when not held up as figure-heads, are frequently matronised in that way which allows their power position to remain unchallenged. The women, however, have to make do with a bogus citizenship; one that has no place unless it is subordinate and supportive to imperialist ideology.

The conduct book

There is little to choose, in terms of content, between some wartime fiction and the women's magazines. Indeed, 'conduct book' seems a more appropriate term than 'novel' for many of these publications, such is their concern for the proper balance of duty and decorum. Their fictional status, though, is guaranteed by a narrative trajectory, which conventionally follows a pattern of love and marriage. The presence of the war serves to enhance this by adding tension to the primary relationship, and patriotic investment to the details of housekeeping.

Annie S. Swan was a best-selling romantic novelist, and editor of *The Woman at Home*. Her stories appeared frequently in *Woman's Own* and *The Woman at Home* as well as in book form. *Letters to a War Bride* (1915) is an epistolary text in which the letters are from an old family friend to a young and inexperienced soldier's wife. The advice is mostly practical and concerns housekeeping and servant management. It is focalised through an older, experienced woman who, like Jeannie Maitland and the others, adopts a tone of gentle and condescending authority. The similarity of the tone and material to the letters pages of the magazines is striking, yet not surprising given the editorial background of the author, and her 'Foreword' in fact states that the letters were originally written to a 'real war bride'. With its fictional status thus blurred by documentary reference, the text arrogates a certain authority to itself as realism rather than romance and, like the magazines, disguises its propagandist ideology beneath the cloak of the observation of 'natural' experience.

The narrative opens with a war wedding, not the rushed and glamorous kind – which would be as out of place here as it would be in the pages of *Woman's Own* – but one nevertheless precipitated by national events:

> If it is not exactly a case of 'We twa hae run aboot the braes, and pu'd the gowans fine', at least, you have known one another quite a respectable number of years, and it is just the war that has brought things to a crisis, as it has brought many another love-affair.
>
> (Swan 1915: 10)

The match manages to combine an appropriate measure of romance and respectability; the author is emphatically not endorsing a whirlwind romance, although this, of course, does nothing to reduce the bride's tumultuous excitement:

> If I needed any assurance that you have chosen wisely, I obtained it from your mother's letter, not from yours, which was very properly a little incoherent.
>
> (Swan 1915: 11)

Incoherence is something very far from the measured, protective tones of the letter writer. Her correspondent is notably barred from the printed word: her muddled utterances are merely alluded to.

The bride, however, must soon turn her attention to housekeeping, ever spurred on by the encouragement of her invaluable friend, who cannot quite resist allowing the jagged edge of condescension to invade her praise:

> You have made the little hired house into a home, and when a woman can do that she justifies her existence. It could not of course be called a pretty house, but you have done wonders with it.
>
> (1915: 18)

Thus rewarded, Ruth can move on to the cooking. Food shortages and the strictures of economy provide the narrative guidelines here. Recipes fill the pages. The stock pot, kept going for several days, meat pies, cheap fish and milk puddings are *de rigeur*, nourishing, inexpensive and, most important, pleasing to the masculine taste. Men, of course, are seen as little boys when it comes to puddings: 'The man of my house has never outlived his childish love of rice, and we make it as follows . . .' (1915: 37). The tone of solicitous matronage (found also in VAD and Land Army directives) authorises the plan of attack which will encourage a further generation of angels in the house to combat their more rebellious sisters.

Approximately half way through the book the plot thickens and a new dimension of married experience arises. Brian is posted to France leaving Ruth with two demanding duties: to face his departure bravely and to rise to the housekeeping challenge of finding a new house and furnishing and equipping it for her husband's return:

> I can see from your letter the shadow of the parting creeping over your dear heart. Don't let Brian see it. I know his type. It will hurt him far more than you know. Keep on smiling, my dear, and send him out with that smile, and God will do the rest.
>
> (1915: 51)

Although the narrator is completely unaquainted with Brian, she happily reduces him to an adoring but unintelligent 'type', who, for reasons both patriotic and matronising, should not be let into the secrets of the woman's heart. Ruth must be like all the other Women of England, smile, say 'go' and seek consolation in the tasks that lie ahead of her, knowing that she is fulfilling her duty and is gaining in 'womanliness' from experience:

> You, too, dearest, are in the melting-pot, and life is becoming daily more serious to you. It is very enriching however, don't let us forget that [. . .]. It [the war] is the greatest thing the world has ever seen, and you, a soldier's wife, are doing your bit, when you smile, even when the days seem dark.
>
> (1915: 50, 52)

What is important, then, is to create a conspiracy of silence, sealed with a smile, that assumes women's tacit support for the patriarchal goals of warfare, and simultaneously suppresses their reservations. The reward is access to a separate value system, specifically female, which has no interface with the real world of the war, except through deferential complicity with the apparent wisdom of the benevolent matriarchs. The material manifestation of this mysterious order, it seems, is a blind preoccupation with 'O-Cedar' mops, 'Bissell' carpet-sweepers, the duties and wages of servants and the housekeeping budget. Again, anything potentially disruptive of female gender roles is subsumed by a flight into domestic detail and abnormality is merged into normality. Ruth's real boss is not her husband, but her 'friend'.

Margaret Sherwood's *The Worn Doorstep* (1917) also follows the strategies of the conduct book, but from a different orientation. It is another epistolary novel, but this time the letters are from a 'war bride' to her husband – who has been killed. The narrative follows her attempts to come to terms with her loss through the details of her domestic life and oscillates between rational self-analysis and fairy-tale resolution.

Initially the narrator articulates the kind of loss explored in the novels to be dealt with later on in this chapter:

> The vastness of my loss I cannot even grasp; my world is swept away from under my feet, and I am alone, with nothing to stand on, nothing to reach in space. Dying myself could hardly mean such utter letting go; I am aware only of a great blankness. I have not even tried to measure my disaster, to understand.
>
> (Sherwood 1917: 27)

This temporary despair, however, soon gives way to a determination to carry on the 'quest we began together' (1917: 1): looking for a place in which to set up house. She writes to her dead husband of her own heroism: 'through the crashes of tragic rumours that have rolled through England, I have gone on and on, not running away or trying to escape, but full of the need to find the right corner' (1917: 1). In effect, she is following *Woman's World*'s instructions for 'The Women England Wants' by writing to her soldier telling him all about her housekeeping duties (*Woman's World* 26 September 1914: 285). Her task is to continue to live, with or without 'understanding', and she does this by proceeding with the domestic project as if her husband were still there and by explaining to him her apparent eagerness to let him go to the war in the first place:

> You thought I never wavered; when you were doubting, I was sure; when you were sure, – you never knew that I wrote you a note that last night and took back my decision, saying that thinkers had their own separate task, and that you should stay. I burned it . . . .
>
> (Sherwood 1917: 34–5)

Like Ruth, she conceals her misgivings behind a conventional show of patriotism, and persuades her intellectual husband that he should join up (Brooke-like) in the early days of the war. She manages to do the same to her male servant. Madge and Peter Snell are her housekeepers; she and Madge between them manage to persuade Peter to go and fight, even though, as a Socialist, it is against his principles. He returns suitably wounded (minus an arm); she keeps him on as a gardener. This sequence of events is related in terms that applaud her generosity and right thinking, and which help to confirm women as the upholders of safe, conservative values. On the subject of Peter's Socialism she says:

> From these advanced radical theories Madge and I turn back, as women will, to the old and homely needs of human life. She fingers her apron.
>
> (1917: 40)

Women, then, are portrayed as being naturally averse to 'radical' political opinion. Domesticity represents an underlying and permanent value system which is a refuge from the challenge of alternatives. In using the term 'turn back' the author is, albeit unconsciously, underlining the regressive quality of the action; in appending 'as women will' she is implying a kind of essential femininity that Horatio Bottomley applauded, but which side-steps responsibility for her own part in the war. Madge's fingering her apron suggests an awkwardness that comes from divided loyalties. She turns from the values of her own class (notably represented by her husband) towards a conservative essentialism that is symbolically reinforced, in terms of her subordinate position and its imprisoning domesticity, by the apron she is wearing. The narrator actively encourages her husband and servant to go and fight as though this were as 'natural' as her own 'homely' duties. She takes refuge in these, seeing it as unnecessary to defend or even to articulate her own ideological position.

In this text, as in *Letters to a War Bride*, the ideological silence over the major political issues is compensated for by attention to domestic detail. Instead of dwelling on the housekeeping budget, however, the narrator focuses on her role as social benefactress – and this is where the fairy-tale element comes into play. A dog, a kitten, a recalcitrant pony are absorbed into the domestic company, and the narrator chances on the needy in ways that resemble a folk-tale more than a documentary account. Once again we are reminded of the *Woman's Own* dictum that one should pay greater attention to one's neighbour's griefs than to one's own. The narrator gives shelter to a woman travelling on foot down from 'the North' with her baby to see the child's father before he goes to the Front; she discovers, in an improbable fashion, a female Belgian refugee lying asleep by the roadside and resolves to help her. 'I've got to find her lover for her, and how shall I begin? I'll go and ask the pony!' (Sherwood 1917: 87). Even more improbably, she is successful: the lover, in spite of his unfamiliarity with the language, manages to see the advertisement she has placed in a newspaper, arrives to claim his bride and the happy couple are married in her house.

The story is resolved a year after its opening with the adoption of an abandoned French baby. Although she cannot fulfil her role as wife and mother in its original romantic formulation, the conventional elements of the romantic plot – marriage and childbearing – are resolved by displacement: satisfaction is ensured by substitution. Her own loss and grief, then, are elided into a narrative of the romantic love of another couple, thus leaving that ideology and the ideology of women's separate order of experience, unchallenged.

Motherhood thus has more of a symbolic than a practical role in these texts.[4] It allows for the fabrication of a mysterious and inaccessible women's order of experience which requires of those who believe in it something resembling a leap of faith. The ideological function of this separate identity was that it ensured the preservation of a set of apparently permanent and undoubtedly conservative values, and forbade women's access to discussion of the war in practical or political terms. In offering one basic 'plot' for women's lives: romance–marriage–childbearing – these texts, and the magazine ideologies that underpinned them, refused to acknowledge the cost of romantic illusion to the relationship between men and women, and to the women for whom romance failed.

WHAT IS 'REALITY'?

I shall now turn to novels published during or immediately after the war, which are more frankly concerned to explore the moral and emotional confusion instigated in middle-class, non-working women by the clash between romance and the war. Far from resembling conduct books, these texts set out to question the kinds of roles and values established by magazines like *Woman's Own* and to confront the disruptions to the romantic myth initiated by the death or absence of husbands or lovers. The war in these texts is not seen as a stabilising force in which women can attain their true angelic potential and lead the race to greater heights of perfection. It is instead represented as a personal crisis that disrupts the conventional view of middle-class 'reality' and forces women to question their part in maintaining the conservative stronghold that ensures their dependence on a masculine partner. Simultaneously, however, they acknowledge the grip of the romantic ideology that has hitherto underpinned their gendered identity and frequently find this hard to relinquish. May Sinclair's *The Tree of Heaven* (1917), Romer Wilson's *If All These Young Men* (1919) and Rebecca West's *The Return of the Soldier* (1918) all question the nature of 'reality': is it romantic love? Is it the war itself? Or, more disconcertingly, is it the turmoil that results from resisting the false claims of war?

May Sinclair is best known for her feminism and modernism, and in *The Tree of Heaven* (1917) she does indeed fictionalise some of her experiences with the suffrage movement.[5] The text, however, is illuminated by the same patriotic spirit that characterises both *A Journal of Impressions* and *The Romantic*. That is, a profound reverence for the 'reality' of the war and for women's active but deferential part in it. This novel, while it does not entirely give in to the claims of romantic love, nevertheless diminishes women's role in suffragism and the impact and implications of the Imagist movement in art. The teleology of the novel takes us to the discovery of 'reality', where 'reality' is war, which is seen to displace the political and linguistic experimentation that preceded it.

The book opens in the late nineteenth century, and follows the Harrison family through to the middle years of the war. The first section, entitled 'Peace', introduces us to the pre-war English pastoral idyll: tea, tennis, the Englishman's home (symbolically a castle) and its 'buttresse[d]' territory. Frances Harrison is the kind of late-Victorian mother of whom Horatio Bottomley approved: she takes little practical interest in politics, believing that strikes and the British Empire will simply go on for ever and are best administered by men. Her priorities centre on 'those enduring things': her children, her home, her garden and the provision of human happiness (1917: 13). The myth of permanence, however, is at least partially undermined: children grow up and, this being a war novel, are killed. In keeping with the effects of a system of patrilineal succession, Frances has a stronger bonding with her male children: 'she loved her three sons, Michael, and Nicholas and John, with passion, and her one daughter, Dorothea, with critical affection' (1917: 25). When her second and favourite son has earache, she holds him and comforts him: 'For now she was lost to herself and utterly absorbed in Nicky. And her agony became a sort of ecstacy, as if, actually, she bore his pain' (1917: 35). This imagery of rapturous self-sacrifice is to recur in the consciousnesses of Nicky and Michael in the context of battle. The Pietà image is an anticipation of holy sacrifices yet to be made.

The second section, 'The Vortex', is set in the years 1910–14. Dorothea graduates from Newnham with a first-class degree in Economics and becomes a suffrage worker. Her 'war' is fought before the European one and concerns suffrage strategies. She is, nevertheless, unhappy with the kind of collective identity that the more militant suffrage movement represents and publically stands up to a rousing speech by the improbably named 'recruiting sargeant', Maud Blackadder:

> She says that fighters are wanted, and not talkers and writers and thinkers. Are we not then to fight with our tongues and with our brains? Is she leaving us anything but our bare fists? She has told us that she rides straight and that she doesn't funk her fences; but she has not told us

what sort of country she is going to ride over, nor where
the fences are, nor what Hell-for-leather and Neck-or-
nothing means.
We want meaning, we want clearness and precision. We
have not been given it yet.

(Sinclair 1917: 106)

Dorothea, however, does not demand precise terminology
when the 'real' war is being discussed. In the latter case
similarly bellicose terms are given credence where in this
context they are criticised for lack of definition; the distinction
she makes, it seems, is ideological, not intellectual. Dorothea is
prepared to fight – up to a point. She is involved with a
suffragette demonstration which results in a stint in prison. Her
solitary experience in a whitewashed cell inspires in her a kind
of revelation:

> The things that came to me were so much bigger than the
> thing I went in for. I could see all along we weren't going
> to get it that way. And I knew we *were* going to get it in
> some other way. I don't know how, but it'll be some big,
> tremendous way that'll make all this fighting and fussing
> seem the rottenest game.

(1917: 192)

The revelation is anti-suffragist. The anticipation of the war,
the 'big, tremendous' event that will change everything, makes
the movement seem petty – a lot of 'fighting and fussing',
reduced to the status, in the idiom of the day, of a child's game.
Her stay in prison is the pivotal point that allows her gradually
to shift allegiance from a feminist fight to the European one,
which has a vague but idealised identity in her imagination.

The war section, revealingly, is entitled 'Victory'. The war is
seen as being 'real'; a necessary focus of order and common
intention after the fragmentations caused by feminism and
artistic experimentation. The transition is symbolised by a
moment when, during the drunken celebrations in central
London on the night of the declaration of war, we are shown
the deeply serious implications of this historical moment:

> It was quiet on the south side by the Barracks. Small, sober
> groups of twos and threes strolled there, or stood with
> their faces pressed close against the railings, peering into

105

the barrack yard. Motionless, earnest and attentive they
stared at the men in khaki moving about on the other side
of the railings. They were silent, fascinated by the men in
khaki. Standing safe behind the railing they stared at them
with an awful sombre curiosity. And the men in khaki
stared back, proud, self-conscious, as men who know that
the hour is great and that it is their hour.

(1917: 249)

The 'drunken, orgiastic, somnambulistic' scenes (1917: 247) of
colourful, restless crowds waving Union Jacks give way to this
quiet vignette of discipline and monochromatic, monolithic
order, which is to be separated from the civilian world by
railings for only a short time. The war is thus seen to rescue the
world from chaos.

Dorothea's brother Michael, however, disapproves of the war,
is disgusted by patriotism and finds the bellicose mentality
opposed to his own project, which is to try, through poetic
language, to get to 'clear, hard reality'. 'Artists', he fears, with
some justification, 'will not be allowed to exist except as agents
for the recruiting sargeant' (1917: 253). Inevitably, though, he
changes his mind and, on hearing of his brother's death in
battle, decides to enlist. His speech of revelation might have
come from a propagandist pamphlet insisting that conscientious
objection is nothing but cowardice:

> What shocked Michael was his discovery, not that he
> funked it now, which was natural, almost permissible, but
> that he had funked it all the time . . . . Funk, pure funk,
> had been at the bottom of all he had said and thought and
> done since August, nineteen-fourteen; his attitude to the
> War, his opinion of the Allies, and of the Government and
> its conduct of the War, all his wretched criticisms and
> disparagements – what had they been but the very subter-
> fuges of funk?
>
> (1917: 336–7)

This is perhaps illuminated by the knowledge that May Sinclair
was one of the few women to sign Masterman's 'Author's
Manifesto' declaring support for the war. Michael comes to the
conclusion that England is fighting 'the Great war of redemption' (1917: 330). He experiences the same kind of

'ecstacy' in battle that his mother felt while tending her ill son, and finds that his search for aesthetic perfection is to be fulfilled on the battle field. 'It's odd', he writes, 'to have gone all your life trying to get reality, trying to get new beauty [. . .] and then to come out, and to find what you wanted' (1917: 349). A wave of patriotic emotion subsumes Michael's pacifist objections just as the same phenomenon demolishes Dorothea's suffragism. 'The little Vortex of the Women's Movement was swept without a sound into the immense vortex of the War. The women rose up all over England and went into uniform' (1917: 261). That final image is another cliché of wartime propaganda.

Dorothea helps Belgian refugees and drives an ambulance in London. She and her fiancé (who disapproved of her suffragist activities) overcome their differences and decide to marry. He is called up and subsequently killed, however, before the ceremony can take place, causing Dorothea to regret having spent years on suffrage work that she might have spent with him. Although she thinks that 'it is a war that makes it detestable to be a woman' (1917: 265) and laments her inability to fight, she accepts her relatively passive war role as a necessary and natural consequence of her gender. Later she comes to reflect on her thinking:

> I knew something tremendous was going to happen. I saw it, or felt it, or something. I won't swear I knew it was the War. I don't suppose I did. But I knew Frank was all mixed up with it. *And it was the most awfully real thing.* You couldn't go back on it, or get behind it. It was as if I'd seen that he and Lawrence and Nicky and Michael and all of them would die in it to save the whole world. Like Christ, only that they really *did* die and the whole world *was* saved. There was nothing futile about it.
>
> (1917: 355)

The same exalted, spiritualised vagueness that characterises Michael's change of mind (and the language of the Liberal press) informs her analysis. She is no longer asking for critical analysis of terms, but from the comfortable ideological position of being in the majority, she accepts the war as 'most awfully real' without examining it further. It is 'real' in the Romantic sense: 'proved upon the pulses'. The application to an epistemology which is external to, and greater than, that of the ordinary, chaotic, human subject – the Christian religion – confirms the unquestionable value of the war: 'the whole world *was* saved'. Paradoxically, the attention in the novel shifts, with the transition from peace to war, from the terror of being part of a massed and powerful collective body (Dorothea fears the uniform solidarity of the suffragette movement as much as Michael initially fears the manifestations of patriotism) to the rapture of individual martyrdom. Dorothea, her aunt (who is married to Lawrence) and her mother are seen as Marian figures, sacrificing their menfolk for the sake of the future of civilisation. That their losses are personal and their grief private seems to imply an acceptance of women's interiorization of the war and a rejection of the role of public commitment and open debate that an organised women's movement offers.

The 'victorious', then, emerge from the 'vortex' fully integrated into the Symbolic Order. A religious certainty replaces the confusions and fragmentations of the pre-war period, and although Dorothea escapes the cloying and conspiratorial influence of the private house by taking on independent employment, this is seen as an aspect of her individualism and her engagement with a reality 'higher' than that of the 'fighting and fussing' of feminism.

Romer Wilson's *If All These Young Men* (1919)[6] is troubled by a radical uncertainty as to the nature of 'reality' in a society in which the protagonist seems to have no proper role. In contradistinction to Sinclair's assumption that the world will be saved by a righteous war, this is one of the few novels to register the fear that England might actually lose the war. It opens in Easter 1918, when the allied troops were retreating from a powerful German offensive and Haig issued his famous order: 'With our backs to the wall and believing in the justice of our cause each one of us must fight to the end' (cf. Taylor [1963] 1966: 223). Josephine Miller, the central consciousness of the novel, is possessed by the mental agony of feeling involved in the battle but being unable to fight in it. Her identity is invaded by the imaginative enaction of battle, without its physical release:

there was no blood, no cries, no horror of war, for the

108

whole scene was a reflected conflict upon the battle ground of the mind; instead there was anguish, fear and dread from which there was no refuge.

(Wilson 1919: 11)

In a phrase that could stand as a metaphor for women's situation, she feels herself 'caught up by the intention of resistance and thrown into conflict with the intention of advance' (1919: 10). On one level this refers to the perilous defence of the allied trenches on the Western Front; on another, though, it can be seen to represent the subjective battle between the forces of permanence – of romance, of what is considered 'natural' – and those of change, whether to a personal or a political structure of belief. Josephine navigates relationships, ideas, the 'ragged ends of her convictions' (1919: 101), oscillating between the imminence of chaos and the desire for integration.

In the context of the possibility of England's invasion, though, patriotism overrides her analyses of constitutional injustices: 'she was a Socialist of Socialists and a democrat to excess, but on this today she was nothing but a part of her loved England' (1919: 70). But her agony lies in her inability to seek a conventional form of release for this passion:

'If I could only fight,' she cried to herself. 'If I could only fight,' and her spirit flew up. She heard the bayonet go in; phantasmagorically she went through the pantomime of conversion to human sanity. Finally, she emerged cleansed, and reinstated herself in the dull monotony of endurance.

(1919: 100–1)

Her vision of death as a 'conversion to human sanity' can only be seen as an index of her own sense of dislocation, having no proper role to play in her culture and forced imaginatively to undergo what others were experiencing in real life:

'Neither to love, neither to fight,' she suddenly cried to herself, 'but to live in constricted anguish, not to cry aloud, not to go mad.'

(1919: 101)

This, then, represents a typical female predicament which initiates a crisis of identity in a culture which gives priority to killing for men and loving for women. These two identities are (at least temporarily) unavailable to this apparently 'modern' young woman, leaving her in the ambiguous, war-rent position of desiring and being unable to fulfil. With 'no lover and no God' (1919: 102), lacking even the opportunity for action to obliterate her agony, she inhabits a chaotic mental landscape.

The battle, however, is averted. The allies uphold their 'intention of resistance' – and so does Josephine. Her identity as an Englishwoman is bolstered by her identification with the countryside and then given additional protection by a romantic relationship. The imagery through which this is articulated, however, suggests ultimate retreat: 'she was a dead soul gone back into the earth out of life's intricate movements, and out of the madness of war' (1919: 242). The war is 'a battle of the ants and midges' and she is:

> neither man nor woman, nor boy nor girl, but only a creature contemplating to no purpose the sky and grass, and wondering at them as if they were new sights created for her amazement and joy.
>
> (1919: 243)

In spiritual terms this may represent a numinous experience. In political terms it is an image of surrender and regression. Josephine seems to have found a position that is free from the constraints of gender and leaves her as a kind of originary innocent, communing with nature, no longer troubled by the philosophical and intellectual chaos that represents the 'real world' of the war.

Rebecca West's *The Return of the Soldier* (1918) explores and holds in balance two contrasting epistemologies. West was a socialist and a feminist, who wrote for *The Freewoman*, *The Daily News* and *The Daily Herald* amongst other journals and newspapers (her early journalism is published in Marcus 1982). She despised the intellectual laziness of some feminist pacifists (cf. her review of Ellen Key's *War, Peace and the Future* in Marcus 1982: 338–40) and presents the war as 'real' in as much as it is actual, was inevitable and could not have been prevented merely by the public acknowledgement of women's disapproval. On the other hand her novel does articulate a kind of alterity that questions the sanity of the war's demands.

The Return of the Soldier, West's first novel, is about the ambiguous value of the Symbolic Order that Dorothea Harrison finds so attractive and Josephine Miller finds so elusive. The novel offers a sharp parody of the 'angel in the house' mentality and, at the risk of merely displacing a nostalgic veneration of womanliness, presents the lower-middle-class Margaret Allington as the repository of genuine values. The kind of happiness her position represents, however, is the happiness of innocence – or of the psychotic. It cannot be integrated into the cultural and social structures that construct meaning for the majority. Whether or not this is ultimately beneficial to humankind is left open; but the process of distinguishing reality from romance, depth from decoration, is seen as being crucial to mental health even if it involves a brutal dismissal of an alternative value system and an equally brutal return to the barbarities of war.

Baldry Court occupies a similar position as bastion of class and social values as does the Harrisons' house in Sinclair's *The Tree of Heaven*. This house, however, is presented not reverentially, but ironically. It has all the up-market sparkle of a *Vogue* presentation house – and all its superficiality. Huge sums have been spent on renovations and Jenny, the narrator, who is the cousin and childhood playmate of the absent soldier, justifies the expense by seeing it as an act of love. The desire was to create a sanctuary for Chris – 'so far as surfaces could make it so' (West [1918] 1980: 16) – which, especially in war time, should provide at least a mental refuge of 'controlled beauty'. As the ideal country home is parodied, so is the aristocratic 'angel in the house', a character worshipped by magazines and fictional narratives. Kitty and Jenny are the apotheosis of expensive decorativeness:

> Exquisite we were according to our equipment; unflushed by appetite or passion, even noble passion; our small heads bent intently on the white flowers of luxury floating on the black waters of life.
>
> (West [1918] 1980: 118)

Kitty, indeed, 'looked so like a girl on a magazine cover that one expected to find a large "7d" somewhere attached to her person' ([1918] 1980: 11). She awaits Chris's return dressed in bridal white, encrusted with jewels. The imagery is of a valuable, but stiff and lifeless icon: 'she looked cold as moonlight, as virginity, but precious; the falling candlelight struck her hair to bright, pure gold' ([1918] 1980: 56–7).

The ironic description of this frigid felicity suggests its imminent disruption. This comes in the form of Margaret Allington, now Mrs Grey, who, from the minute she walks in with 'her deplorable umbrella, her unpardonable raincoat' ([1918] 1980: 33), represents opposition – but lower-middle-class opposition, and therefore, Kitty hopes, capable of being excluded. The earthy colours of red and brown and the vocabulary of staining and fouling are associated with Margaret and her home, but her eyes, unlike Kitty's, are 'full of tenderness'; her body is not lifeless, but 'long and round and shapely' ([1918] 1980: 25).

Margaret's entry into the lives of the inhabitants of Baldry Court seems improper to them and they intend to dispose of her quickly. Jenny hopes, at their first meeting, that the problem Margaret seems to have brought with her will dissolve 'and be replaced by some more pleasing compositon in which we would take our proper parts; in which, that is, she should turn from our rightness unashamed' ([1918] 1980: 31). But the natural 'rightness' of the social hierarchy is not to be upheld and Margaret is not to be so easily repulsed. She has brought to the surface a part of Chris which they thought had been decorated out of existence; she becomes 'a spreading stain on the fabric of our life' ([1918] 1980: 37).

As a result of amnesia induced by shell-shock, Chris has forgotten the war, Kitty, the renovated Baldry Court and the mature Jenny. He has mentally returned to the time when, fifteen years ago, he was in love with Margaret, then an innkeeper's daughter. This part of his life operates in a symbolic landscape entirely at odds with the cultured chill of his marital home. Kitty appropriately laments that with his loss of memory comes their loss of him: 'he isn't ours any longer' ([1918] 1980: 39). He has returned to a world uncontaminated by the war, by his business projects and by his marriage, a world which predates his own life-altering decisions and loss of innocence and in which Kitty has had no part. Margaret occupies this site. She, the lower-class woman, represents sensuality, warmth, nature, a passion of the soul which has nothing to do with appearances – values which have been 'educated out' of Chris's upper-class existence.

Kitty and Jenny find it hard to believe that after their decorative influence Chris could possibly be interested in

Margaret – 'that dowd' – but the war, it seems, has triggered a sensual impulse in him that he cannot mentally associate with his home. The Freudian implication is that it had only ever found its resting place with Margaret, and had since been repressed, only to be reactivated by the trauma of war.[7]

Margaret herself, however, is described in terms that emphasise her maternal qualities rather than her sexuality and so come close to making of her a kind of earth mother who merely fits an alternative stereotype of femininity. Chris praises her warmth and humanity: 'When she picks up facts she kind of gives them a motherly hug. She's charity and love itself' ([1918] 1980: 74). Jenny is forcibly struck by Margaret's healing powers when she sees the former lovers out in the woods one afternoon – beyond the cultivated boundaries of Baldry Court. Chris is asleep, his anxiety relieved; Margaret is watching over him. The scene has for Jenny a kind of religious significance:

> It means that the woman has gathered the soul of the man into her soul and is keeping it warm in love and peace so that his body can rest quiet for a little time. That is a great thing for a woman to do.
>
> ([1918] 1980: 144)

This image of spiritualised maternal love on one level reduces the woman to a healing womb, but on another suggests a register of communication/communion unavailable to the frigid Kitty. Margaret represents timeless values: an abstract reality that finds articulation in concrete acts of love. Under her influence, Chris's – and Jenny's – boundaries of class, gender and history temporarily melt: she symbolises a land of no differentiation; a 'magic state' ([1918] 1980: 102) like the Kristevan semiotic, where substances merge and the laws of the physical universe melt into an imaginative, sensual haze. This is a description of her at her Monkey Island home:

> In the liquefaction of colours which happens on a summer evening, when the green grass seemed like a precious fluid poured out on the earth and dripping over to the river, and the chestnut candles were no longer proud flowers, but just wet white lights in the humid mass of the tree, when the brown earth seemed just a little denser than the water, Margaret also participated.
>
> ([1918] 1980: 77)

'Solemn and beatified' ([1918] 1980: 97), despite her external dinginess, Margaret represents an alternative order of beauty, one that stands in opposition to Kitty's bright, delicate, defined perfection.

A moral question thus arises: should Chris be rescued from this timeless, innocent, blissful state so that he would be fit to return to the trenches? The dilemma is focused through the ambivalent position of Jenny. As the focaliser of the text, who attempts objectively to observe Chris's oscillations between the two worlds represented by Margaret and by Kitty, she suppresses her powerful feelings for Chris at the same time as she narrates his story. Her objectivity is blurred by the fact that she becomes at once jealous of Margaret's intimacy with Chris and profoundly grateful to her. This forces Jenny to recognise her own permanent solitariness, a result of her passionate but undisclosed love for her cousin. She is envious of the naturalness of the communion between him and Margaret, but she has a basic, animating drive in common with her: her adoration for Chris. Only in her presence can Jenny allow herself to feel 'the sense of him saturate me as it used'. At least while Margaret is there he is protected from the horrors of warfare that Jenny experiences indirectly in her dreams:

> While her spell endured they could not send him back into the hell of war. This wonderful kind woman held his body as surely as she held his soul.
>
> ([1918] 1980: 147)

The war can be seen as the apotheosis of the same kind of social and political accident that originally led Chris to leave Margaret in order to save the family business, not knowing that their communication would be severed. To bring him back to that world of commerce, warfare, loveless marriage, would mean, in reality, breaking his heart again and possibly sending him to his death in France. Paradoxically, the world he occupies in his insanity is saner than the real world, as Jenny recognises:

> It was our particular shame that he had rejected us when he had attained to something saner than sanity. His very loss of memory was a triumph over the limitations of language which prevent the mass of men from making explicit statements about their spiritual relationships.
>
> ([1918] 1980: 133)

The values that Margaret embodies, then, are seen to override even the culturally determining limits of language. This lower-middle-class woman, closer to nature, to suffering and to human passion than her superficial social superiors, is a matrix for a register of understanding that is far wiser than that of the ruling classes. This reverses the trend in contemporary ideology that assumes upper-class custody of refined sensitivity and rational thinking. Further, it destroys the fairy-tale conventions of romance: the heroine is made dingy by age and poverty, the hero has temporarily lost his sanity. Romance, in this novel, is seen as a refuge from the world's problems – not as an answer to them.

Margaret's wisdom is not merely other-worldly. If Chris is to regain the language of the conventional world, Margaret, having been the guardian of his spiritual sanctity, must now reintroduce him to the Symbolic Order. Jenny, who realises that one must 'celebrate communion with reality or else walk for ever queer and small like a dwarf' ([1918] 1980: 182), knows that, if they did nothing to restore Chris to 'sanity', with age:

> He who was as a flag flying from our tower would become
> a queer-shaped patch of eccentricity on the countryside
> [. . .]. He would not be quite a man.

> ([1918] 1980: 183)

Chris has no choice. He cannot retain his youth and 'be a man'. Jenny and Margaret agree about this, about the common sense of facing up to 'the truth', and Chris returns to the Symbolic Order, to Kitty, to Baldry Court, to the War, wearing a 'dreadful decent smile', 'Every inch a soldier', to end up in no-man's-land, where 'bullets fall like rain on the rotting faces of the dead' ([1918] 1980: 187).

The 'truth', then, does not form part of a simplistic equation in opposition to 'lies' as it does, for example, for Michael Harrison in Sinclair's novel. The kind of reality of which Margaret is the guardian is spiritually greater than, but culturally subservient to the material reality of history, social relations and mental health. 'The truth's the truth' ([1918] 1980: 184) is the kind of tautological statement that has come to epitomise the irony and absurdity of the war – like 'We're here because we're here'. Chris finishes where his story in the novel began, in a world dominated by falseness and deathly values, where he will robotically perform his duty until he dies.

115

Jenny, however, has moved on. This novel is interesting in
that it is the narrator, thought of as little more than a hand-
maid, who learns most. Kitty remains a doll and Margaret's
wisdom is a permanent fixture, but Jenny gains significantly
from her relationship with Margaret:

> We kissed, not as women, but as lovers do; I think we each
> embraced that part of Chris the other had absorbed by her
> love.

([1918] 1980: 184)

This recognition of her love for Chris and of the values that
Baldry Court glosses over, forces her to re-negotiate her own
identity. Kitty's falseness glints with a kind of predatory malice
at the end of the book, while Jenny allows herself to imagine
what they have bestowed on Chris. The narrative returns us to
Jenny's nightmare vision of no-man's-land, the Baldry Court
stage is as empty as when the book opened. If the predominant
cultural values have not been changed, they have at least been
exposed. In losing Chris, Jenny can embrace Margaret. This
gesture has implications for a female solidarity which offers
hope for the deconstruction of the male order.

LOST GENERATIONS

The last section of this chapter will deal with novels that present
a post-war perspective on the interrelation between the war and
romance. Although the historical context is different from that
of the magazines and the earlier novels, the concern with the
structure of identity through domestic commitment remains
dominant (cf. Beddoe 1989). The three novels I shall examine
deal with the heroine's uneasiness about her role in the
Symbolic Order, her bewilderment at the loss of clear role
models and her grief at what we might call the 'death of
romance'. The currency of romance, of course, remained
dominant, but it was undermined by the absence of its primary
structuring force – the right man. Lacking forceful encouragement towards independence, middle-class heroines of conservative background had to negotiate an identity from the
fragments of illusions and without the immediate emergency of
the 'reality' of war to distract them. All three novels present the
war as a central element in a tri-partite perspective which begins

116

before the war and ends some years after it. They are May Wedderburn Cannan's *The Lonely Generation* (1934), Ruth Holland's *The Lost Generation* (1932) and Sylvia Thompson's *The Hounds of Spring* (1926).

Cannan's novel is the most conservative of the three, and it also presents the most successfully 'integrated' post-war heroine. Perhaps this is because the book's cultural values are represented by a trio of patriarchal figureheads: a General, an Oxford Professor and a gentle, aged aristocrat, whose standing in the higher reaches of English life remains undisturbed by the conflict. The thread that links them is a powerful and nostalgic reverence for an England characterised by chivalric romance. Against this backdrop, and in a similar narrative pattern to the other two novels in this section, the heroine has an idyllic pre-war childhood with a perfect friend who matures into a lover and who is killed during the war. This leaves the heroine bereft of identity and ideals and faced with the challenge of reconstructing herself in an unsympathetic and alien post-war environment.

Delphine, though, is slightly different from the other heroines: she has not been indoctrinated by the angel in the house ideology into believing that her only role is to care for men and children. Brought up and educated at home by her journalist father and his artistic and intellectual friends (her godfather is Lucius Carey – an Oxford Professor, almost certainly modelled on Sir Arthur Quiller-Couch), she inhabits a 'masculine' world of ideas, personal honesty and independent thought. A further guardian figure is a military General, in whose company Delphine observes the army on manoeuvres. Delphine's response to a generally approving remark characterises her entire attitude to the war:

> Delphine looked at them and saw not a handy lot, but the armies of England. Saw Romance a sword tempered to endurance; saw the peace of Avon's woods so protected, so served.

> (Cannan 1934: 78–9)

This is a typical example of the symbolic landscape of the novel. The elaborate metaphorical construction of a group of soldiers on an exercise as the embodiment of an Arthurian strain of chivalric romance, a perfect image of protection and service, leaves little room for female endeavour and little hope for the germination of feminist ideas. Indeed, the ideological stance of the text as regards women's specific position is deeply anti-feminist although committed to the idea of *individual* women's independence. Delphine has no influential female role models and at school, for example, has no inclination to identify with the 'team spirit' of her schoolmates: her vision of independence seems to be independence from others of her sex, rather than from the opposite sex, with whom, she assumes, there will be a natural fusion. The novel presents Delphine, then, as an exception from the female 'team'; one who does not seek to bond with her own sex, but relies on the chivalric respect of an older generation of males to reinforce her value system and to help her through her moral and practical confusions.

Bobbie, her special friend, is part of the system she values with his Sandhurst education and training in India, but he is killed in the war.[8] Delphine does not think in a practical and political way about the war. She does not even want to fight in it: the adoption of an overtly masculine position would be no relief, as it apparently would have been to Josephine Miller in *If All These Young Men*. The metaphorical haze of her patriotic romanticism does not translate itself immediately into specific practical tasks with the onset of war: but the war itself becomes the focus of all that she has invested in Bobbie and in her love for England. With the death of Bobbie the war gives her an identity: 'The War in which Bobbie had died needed her, and with the first gathering of her strength, she came back to this War' (1934: 123).

She works as a VAD nurse in England and later, with the help of Lucius Carey, gets a secretarial job in the Ministry of Information and Propaganda in Paris, where she sees the war through to its end. It becomes evident, however, that, in accordance with her tendency to confuse idealisation with reality, she has transferred her identity to the war itself rather than to any particular role in it. By the end of it:

> She was two-and-twenty, and she had lost everything, everything but her work, and her work was the War. Of what should happen when that ended she could not, she dare not, think. [. . .] Afterwards she came to think that in

118

those days she had never really believed that when the War
ended it would be asked of her that she should live.

(1934: 131)

The war, then, gives her an identity. Although her patriotism
allows her a share in the victory of 'Englishness' (for which she
is grateful), the power of her gratitude immediately leads her to
dwell on the past rather than the present:

> '*Bless you they don't want us now.*' Perhaps not, but they had
> wanted one once. One had been part of it; part of this
> pageant of love and death of soldiers and kings. One
> might have been too old or too young. One might have
> missed it. One had broken one's heart, yes; but one had
> been part of it. Thank God one had been of the gener-
> ation of the War.

(1934: 152)

The tragic/triumphant nostalgia evident in this passage is
striking, perhaps even alarming in the context of the human
decimation that the war was responsible for, but, as we have
seen, not atypical of a certain kind of war experience. Delphine
does not become disillusioned with the war: it is given the status
of a life-enhancing rather than a life-destroying event. Her
problem is in dealing with the post-war world that wants to
escape the, for most people, discredited image of pageantry,
and has no interest in, or resources for, rewarding war work.
With no formal qualifications, only a small private income and
no patience to study for a degree, Delphine must try to make a
living, on her own, in London, as part of the 'surplus two
million' of women. Her aunt thinks she should nurse or teach
and disapproves of 'commercial' work, but then:

> she was of the generation of women, who, desiring desper-
> ately their financial independence, revolted from the
> means necessary to obtain it. It was 'nice' to work, but it
> was not 'nice' to work indiscriminately for women or men
> who might 'speak rudely' to you, or rebuke you 'roughly'
> or even behave in ways which she described emphatically
> as 'worse'.

(1934: 180)

It is from this point that the narrative begins to allow some

119

strategies of realism to supplant the dominating romantic nostalgia. Delphine's unconventional upbringing frees her from the constraints that sent her aunt's generation into nursing and teaching, and in any case she has not the private means to make 'nice' work a possibility. She is, however, of a class 'that asks courage of its women, no less than of its men' (1934: 206) and it is this 'spirit' that supports her as she descends into near poverty and suffers sexual harassment from her employer. This is now her war. When she loses her job with little hope of finding another, she cannot shake off her war identity:

> She was the child of her generation. The generation that had questioned and philosophied, and doubted, over its wood fires in the winter of nineteen hundred and thirteen. She had none of the restlessness or the aggression of the young of nineteen-twenty who were even then beginning to dance their way into what they imagined to be a new world, snatching at what they could get.
>
> (1934: 220)

Eventually she breaks down and has to appeal to Lucius Carey for help. He finds her somewhere suitable to stay and secures her a job with a London publisher. Delphine's old identity is maintained because she sees herself as a member of an intellectually and culturally *superior* generation – one that thinks instead of dancing – so her problem does not pivot so much on having to graft on a new identity as finding suitable soil in which to re-establish the old one. Her new employer is gentlemanly and encouraging; she publishes some of her own poetry and gradually makes a success of her job; her friend, Kitty, provides her with a social life. Kitty's brother, Hugh, forms a gentle, romantic attachment to her and, partly owing to their common reverence for Housman's *A Shropshire Lad*, Delphine decides to marry him, although she cannot forget the power of her earlier love. The tone of the novel, then, is of proud nostalgia, the implicit tragedy of which can be mitigated to some extent by the rediscovery of individuals of the heroine's own type, class and generation. Delphine's lowest point comes when she is forced to mix with socially inferior men who try to take sexual advantage of her. Once reinstated in the world of Oxford dons and the officer class, the conservative power structure to which she sees herself as belonging, she can be happy, although this is not merely a consequence of finding someone to marry: her professional and artistic identity exist independently of her married identity. This is presented as a beneficial consequence of her individualism, her idiosyncratic upbringing, and the influence of her powerful but gentlemanly patriarchal guardians rather than any new-found freedom for women in general.

Ruth Holland's *The Lost Generation* (1932) is a bleaker and more subdued novel, as the adjective in the title suggests. It has a similar panoramic perspective and describes the maturation, disintegration and attempted rehabilitation of Jinnie, who grows up in culturally and politically oppressed Wales, with her cousin Eliot. The symbolic structuring of the text is similar to *The Return of the Soldier*, where adolescent love and a familiar landscape form an apparently permanent con-stellation, signifying peace, harmony and perfect security. This set of organicist values is then made to clash with another set, grouped around images of cultural dominance. Wales is thus presented in symbolic opposition to England. Jinnie and Eliot in their late teens, before the war, learn together about their Welsh heritage and its repression by more powerful cultures:

> They were artists, musicians, and poets, who had been forced to be the servants of the more practical hard-headed races, so that they have never been able to follow the course of their true development.
>
> (1932: 85)

Fired by nationalist enthusiasm, the two lovers plan to study their country's history and folk-lore and recover 'those dim forgotten things' (1932: 85) that have been marginalised and all but obliterated by English colonisation. The war, however, provides the inevitable interruption to this subversive and absorbing project – and a new perspective on it. Both Jinnie and Eliot have to travel to London: Jinnie to be 'finished' and Eliot to attend interviews for officer training.

Their initial view of England is in keeping with its rep-resentation as oppressor: in comparison with the surging and dramatic Welsh landscape, and like the Symbolic in opposi-tion to the semiotic:

it was so wide and calm and flat, so ordered and well-kept. The fields were uniformly squared out, the hedges trimmed, the roads wide and smooth, the bridges solid.

(1932: 93)

The vocabulary of order, uniformity, smoothness and solidity ambivalently suggests something of both the security and the dull complacency of a ruling class. England is like an edifice that has withstood attack and endured for generations. It is an image of the kind of Englishness that structures Delphine's idea of reality. For Jinnie it was not 'real', 'not like her life at home': but it does, however, offer her a new identity and new roles to play which are exciting and demanding. The war years though, for all their vibrance and activity, are presented as a temporary 'eclipse' of the part of Jinnie that she has internalised in the hope of preserving it unmolested: 'That was the core of the enjoyment, none of it was real; behind the outward show, she was safe, untouched' (1932: 107).

Jinnie's experience of the war, then, is characterised by her sense of its superficiality and excitement, and simultaneously by her conscious alienation from its attractions. Unlike Delphine and Dorothea Harrison, her 'logic of identification' is not with a Holy War, but with an object of romantic love who, despite his soldierly loyalty, is also associated with an ideological position that is opposed to England's Symbolic Order. While both her London life and Eliot are available to her, Jinnie's identity can oscillate freely between them. But it is only when she is with her lover that her sense of 'lack' dissolves:

They stood laughing and talking together on the platform and immediately the focus of Jinnie's life had changed. Life was whole again. They were together, alone in their own intimate happy world.

(1932: 108)

Their relationship, like that between Delphine and Bobbie, is a blissful communion. Both understand that they have left Wales for 'a more concrete active world', yet both cling to their past life together 'because it had become as a dream' (1932: 127) and their relationship alone acts as a direct line to that world of permanent, enduring values, now sealed up by time and distance.

Eliot, of course, is killed, and with his loss, Jinnie, like Delphine, has to find a means of existence in an alienating world. Unlike Delphine, however, she has no job to give her even a temporary identity. Marriage is the only institution that seems to offer any relief and she wanders aimlessly into it, in the false belief that 'to be married and settled [. . .] would be the relaxing of an intolerable strain' (1932: 187). The stand-in figure does little to assuage the desire for her original love and when he too dies Jinnie is left sensing still greater disconnection:

> She was feeling lost, a little anxious and bewildered, looking at a world, stirred up and chaotic, in which new generations were already crowding up, pushing her back into the past; the war generation was a back number.
>
> (1932: 273)

This is comparable with a similar statement in Cannan's novel, but instead of registering a kind of cultural superiority, it signifies loss of identity. The war generation is not wanted by its more hard-headed, sybaritic successors; war-grief is unwelcome, reconstruction and forgetting are prioritised. Delphine re-integrates herself through work and friendship, Dorothea Harrison finds employment and a good use for her first-class degree. To one whose only training was at finishing school, who has no resources and no expectations other than love and marriage, the romantic myth dies hard because there is no viable alternative.

While Sylvia Thompson's *The Hounds of Spring* (1926) follows a structure and chronological arrangement similar to the other two novels in this section, its tone invites criticism of rather than collusion with the dilemmas of its heroine.[9] Delphine and Jinnie demand the reader's pity and sympathy for the war's victimisation of women. Zina Renner, the beautiful but un-educated product of the Edwardian idyll of English loveliness, is in love with romance at the expense of reality and is therefore seen to be morally at fault. But the novel's interest does not lie solely in this, for, rather like *The Return of the Soldier* (and to some extent like *The Lost Generation*), the power of romantic love, rather than buttressing conservative patriarchal struc-tures, can unexpectedly disrupt them.

123

The novel opens immediately before the war in a typical war-novel scenario of sun-soaked English pastoral beauty. The setting is Pelham Court and the family comprises Edgar Renner, an Austrian who has been made an English baronet, his English wife Cynthia, their children Zina, John and the much younger Wendy, and Zina's fiancé, Colin, newly graduated from Oxford. The women clearly are fixed in the angel in the house ideology:

> Edgar watched them as they went out into the hall, felt it as strange that he should, to such an extent, be responsible for them – for their rareness and peace and elegance, and for all their fragrant immunities.
>
> (Thompson 1926: 57)

This benignly reverential and absurdly abstracted view (what are 'fragrant immunities'?) is seen to be to some extent responsible for the intellectual weaknesses of the women. Cynthia is characterised by 'her inconsistencies, her sweet arrogance' and 'her obvious favouritism of her son' (1926: 5) – a common attribute amongst mothers in these novels, as we have seen. Zina has the 'unconscious egotism' of the secure, upper-middle-class upbringing. Her privileged lifestyle and feminine training have disabled her from confronting anything other than 'variations of the beautiful' (1926: 17). The male consorts of these protected women are seen to have the political vision lacking in their partners, who are satisfied with the peace and easiness of domestic love. Both men refer to their respective partners as children – 'Das Kind'; 'Sweet absurd child' (1926: 7, 18) – and discuss international relations against the 'fragrant' background that they support materially only to dismiss intellectually.

The war breaks out, as in *The Lost Generation*, in the second part of the novel. This part is entitled 'The "Great" War', and it is worth noting the ironical addition of quotation marks. A subtle and attenuated critique of the war punctuates this novel which oscillates between the serious, critical structures of realism and the serendipities of romance, where romance is represented as conservative and regressive, while also acting as a kind of ideological underground agent for the disruption of patriarchy.

Their initial reactions are predictable. Colin joins up, so does

Zina's brother, John. Their mother, in obedient collusion with the prevailing hegemony, feigns delight at the news: 'How thrilling!' (1926: 79) she says, maintaining the fiction of the righteous actions of manhood, only to be desolated when John is killed:

> what one can't [. . .] believe – is that something that was once such a darling baby and then such a fat, naughty little boy, and gradually grew up for us to be so proud of him – something that one loved so – and hoped and planned such a lot for, should just be broken and wasted, right at the beginning of fulfilling everything one had hoped and thought and worked for. That this baby grew up just to be killed and thrown away with millions of others – in a civilised age!
>
> (1926: 121)

Olive Schreiner and many feminist pacifists made similar observations about the role of maternity in wartime (cf. Chapter 4, below), but related their comments to the broader political structure. Cynthia, however, sees her loss as something purely personal, her grief is private and cannot even be shared with her daughter, who also suffers a tragic loss. In March 1915 Zina receives the message that Colin is missing, presumed dead. Their different objects of grief separate mother and daughter rather than forming between them a matrilineal bond: each resents the fact that the other is suffering from a different cause. All women, then, are seen to live in separate worlds, lacking the threads – the men – that once drew them together and made a social pattern.

Zina's reaction is one of numb despair, and once again the nature of reality is questioned: 'Nothing left, nothing at all, just blank darkness [. . .] was anything real any more?' (1926: 96). For Zina (as for Jinnie) the object of romantic love animates and gives structure to a life that is otherwise incomprehensible. She makes no attempt to study or understand the war: that was Colin's role. But she has also lost emotional contact with her grieving mother and, by extension, with the female community in general. This is an aspect of the romantic myth that the women's magazines struggle to compensate for. War is isolating and annihilating for women who live their lives through their men and who then lose their entire investment. Zina attempts to articulate the emotional and spiritual vacuum that was the experience of many women:

> Colin was my life . . . my real life . . . He was everything that mattered to me . . . all my youth and ideals . . . all my hopes and beliefs . . . and courage belonged to him. [. . .] But he *isn't* anymore: that's gone . . . It's no use pretending and being sentimental – one has to find a possible *modus vivendi*. There isn't religion – for our generation, as there used to be. [. . .] We only have reason left us. And if you begin to reason about the last four years it makes you a little light-headed.
>
> (1926: 145–6)

Zina abandons books and music and occupies her time working in the gardens of Pelham Court, which has been turned into a home for convalescent officers. Meanwhile she becomes aware of the attentions of her conventional, chauvinist neighbour, George Barret-Saunderson. He is sensible, reliable, reasonable-looking, liked by children and animals and Zina, again like Jinnie, thinks that married life with him 'would arrange things for one, make some sort of path for one to follow' (1926: 110). In other words, it would offer her an identity, a position from which to speak and act. She does not want him to stir her imagination: that he does not absolves her from treachery to her lover. All she feels for him are the glimmerings of sexual desire, which the text registers as an illustration of her brutalised and cynical sensibilities.

She escapes, then, into a pragmatic marriage. The ironic confrontation between the institution of marriage and the loss of romance, however, lifts an ideological veil and reveals to Zina the patriarchal interests that underpin marriage and childbirth. This is where Thompson's text becomes notably more acute than Holland's. When Zina becomes pregnant she writes to her father that: 'it is a trying situation to be treated all the time as something between an imbecile and a Madonna' (1926: 208). She is conscious that her sexuality has been colonised in order to carry on the male line (George's parents always refer to the foetus as a 'grandson'). We can read this as a recognition that her place in the social and symbolic order is that of reproducer of the phallus. While in the position of 'phallic mother' she is simultaneously in a position of strength and a position of nonidentity: a vessel for the continuation of the power structure. Her 'nature' is subordinated to a patriarchal and conservative 'culture'.

She experiences an increasing alienation from the value system that George and his family depend upon, but is unable openly to articulate this. To do so would mean to admit that she had made a mistake, and to commit herself to rectifying it. Instead she adopts the role of detached observer. In a passage that is almost Woolfian in style and political implication, she finds herself wondering of her husband:

> as his head and shoulders disappeared again behind the rustling barricade of the *Morning Post*, whether he ever deduced from words more than the actual sense that their grouping presented to him; whether he was ever aware of the shadowy play of thought and emotion beyond the defined gates of words, the half-lit garden, alleys leading to darkened distances, flickering lights on waters gleaming through trails of queer blossoms, fantastic, shuddering trees, spasmodic great stars and scudding clouds; the silence and shadows beyond the gates which seemed to hold the very essence of another Being, so that, peering between all that wrought-iron verbosity, one began in spirit to explore, and perhaps to know and understand a little.
>
> (1926: 247)

The barrier between George and Zina is both political and gendered, and is created and perpetuated by their different use of language. George is to Zina what 'words' are to the play of meaning: in Kristevan terms, the Symbolic to the semiotic. The gates of words, like George's conservative politics, hem in, institutionalise, colonise, leaving the 'other' as a potential but, in Zina's case, impotent force. She is perfectly capable of recognising – and despising – the inauthentic structures of her present life, but unable, indeed unwilling to free herself from them in order to live independently.

Had the novel ended here it would have finished with a strikingly ambivalent picture of the desolation that a conventional, conservative life can offer. The structures of romance, however, are called in to rescue Zina from this nightmare. Colin had not been killed, it turns out, but had been a prisoner of war, suffering from shell-shock in the form of amnesia. The two meet fortuitously and Zina falls back into her old passivity and wants once more to be taken over by her lover. Colin is conscious that all he has to offer her are 'sordid futile fragments' of the 'little jewelled world' (1926: 318) that once held them. That world Zina still holds within her and she can recall it to break the conventional pattern that she has allowed herself to be caught up in. The pre-war, pre-Symbolic relationship, then, is at once disruptive and regressive. She goes to Colin, as her mother says, 'hardly more than a child' (1926: 317), but that marginalised position, although insulated in powerlessness, at least gives her a perspective on the conservative, masculine hegemony.

Responsibility is left in the hands of her younger sister, Wendy. Now an Oxford undergraduate, it is up to her to think about the League of Nations and the possibility of world peace. Zina is seen as a useless – although pitiable – product of a useless ideology. Wendy, in a scene set on Remembrance Day, 1924, is seen to have a considerable task in front of her. In the context of a drunken, riotous armistice celebration she recalls Colin's words:

> 'At least you have your chance, Wendy, you and your generation, to try and straighten things out and get at life cleanly and rightly, to make for decency and beauty and peace.'
>
> (1926: 339)

This chapter has mostly been about conservatism: the strategies adopted by and experiences of those who neither threw themselves into paid employment nor openly opposed the war and women's conventional role in it. The power of romance appeared to ensure continuity and obedience to received doctrines, and often seemed an antidote to the traumas of war. In the later novels, though, the bereft war generation is seen as wrecked, helpless and regressive, capable only of hoping that the next generation will repair the ruins. There is an element in that regression, however, that has deconstructive potential. The next chapter will show that there was a generation of women who were politically active before and during the war, and who themselves sought for a version of 'decency and beauty and peace' using, as an ideological power base, images of womanhood only partially removed from those described in this chapter.

Plate 4 Women of Britain Say 'Go!', poster. (By courtesy of the Trustees of the Imperial War Museum.)

4

REACTIONARY OR REVOLUTIONARY?
The maternal pacifist

This chapter will explore what seems to be a paradox: the revolutionary potential in the apparently conservative position of motherhood. The previous chapter has examined the propagandist discourse which hails to the pride in sacrifice of England's mother-at-war: she must take a responsible part in the fighting of a just cause and encourage her grown-up soldier boy to protect the innocent Belgians from the bullying Boches. The symbol of maternity was made significantly adaptable for the purpose of prosecuting the war: 'The Greatest Mother in the World' is a nurse; the women of Britain who say 'GO!' are mother and daughter, secure in their home, watching the departing backs of their soldier heroes; Robert Graves's 'Little Mother' is a blood-curdling patriot. But the open weave of the symbol can be stretched to fit another form. From the beginnings of the Women's International League (for Peace and Freedom) (1915) to the contemporary example of the Greenham Common Peace Camp, feminist commentators have expressed the allure and plausibility of associating women, and particularly mothers, with a pacifism of such moral force that if it were mobilised politically it could change the face of international relations.

The rhetorical use in First World War peace literature of the mythical properties of motherhood forms the focus of this chapter. These properties are seen, spontaneously and universally, to align women with pacifism on the grounds that mothers have a special concern for the creation and preservation of human life. A binary opposition thus emerges: men are life-takers, women life-makers. The political potential of this deconstructible social edifice is explored in the writings of

131

Catherine Marshall, Helena Swanwick, the contributors to the feminist internationalist journal *Jus Suffragii*, and in fiction by Mary Agnes Hamilton, Rose Macaulay and Vera Brittain. They argue for the existence of a *latent* force which, if activated, could have a revolutionary impact on conflict resolution on a national and global scale, bringing the war to a decisive and humane close and substituting arbitration for war in the future.

A description of this potential is problematic, as it has only a latent mode of existence. Given this, I shall try to set out its position using Julia Kristeva's model of the Symbolic and the semiotic as broad guidelines. The political status of suffragist pacifism, then, can be compared with the linguistic marginality of the repressed semiotic. A mode of signification other to the Symbolic Order of the war prosecutors, the discourse of suffragist pacifism tried to disrupt the logical, powerful, 'obvious' position of armed civic virtue. The 'chora' of motherhood (i.e. an uncircumscribable locus of drives, both positive and negative, radical and conservative) represented the potential voice of the normally silent and normally powerless, which, to some extent, had found expression in the marginal discourses of suffragism, pacifism and socialism. Now, discourses which threaten the power of the dominant discourse tend to be carefully policed and labelled deviant or utopian – or in the context of the war, unpatriotic or pro-German. But a group of women believed that if the balance of power were to shift towards these marginal discourses, if, for example, women were to be given the vote, then (assuming the policing forces did not close ranks to absorb these new-found powers in previously existing structures) the potential for revolution would be ripe: a difference of view would have ousted dominant codes, a new way of life could begin which empowered an aspect of womanhood which carried the force of a massive political catalyst: maternity.

This chapter will focus its exploration of the discourse of feminist pacifism around the campaign for the vote for women in England. The feminist historian Jo Vellacott, in the course of her work on pacifism and suffragism, has identified three stages of suffragism that can be seen broadly to coincide with Kristeva's three generations of feminism (Kristeva [1979] 1986; Vellacott 1987b). The first is concerned primarily with gaining access to masculine systems of power, partaking in the 'logical and ontological values of a rationality dominant in the nation state' (Kristeva [1979] 1986: 194), and can be located in the Pankhursts' organisation, the WSPU. The second emphasises and accepts women's *different* role and its concerns with issues of health, welfare and childcare – 'housekeep[ing] for the nation' as Vellacott puts it (1987b: 37).[1] The third seeks eventually to deconstruct the ideological constellations patriarchal–bellicose and maternal–pacific and replace them with an internationalist feminist socialism that will undo repressive systems of hierarchy whether based on class, gender or race. All three, of course, over-lapped and co-existed prior to and during the First World War, and continue to co-exist in so far as they describe the positioning of women in relation to systems of power. The usefulness to this study of combining the insights of historical observation with theoretical generalisation is to accentuate the radical nature of the third position (something socialists and feminists are still dreaming of) and in so doing to account for the paradoxical 'conservatism' of the fundamental symbol used to convey the hope for that radicalism. The power of the image of maternity is greater than conventional explanations of its social function: the change that the pacifist suffragists envisaged was in excess of that which could be achieved by individual acts of social reform. The battleground on which idealism fights it out with the impediments of ordinary social existence is the subject of this chapter. Motherhood can stand for both idealism and its repressive opposite: the fight for the vote in collision with the fight against the nation's enemies sorted women out into warrior mothers, servants of the state and radical pacifists.

Motherhood is used, in the material that follows, as a myth: a collective and universal trope invested with the symbolic power to activate a vast potentiality of latent political activity. The discussion that follows explores the power and ambiguity of that myth.

WARRIOR MOTHERS

As we have already seen, the concept of efficient and dedicated motherhood was essential to the ideological framework of imperial England. This was brought into keen focus at the beginning of this century when Britain's population growth was judged to be lagging behind that of its rival master-races in the project of colonial expansion. Schools for Mothers and Infant Welfare Centres more than doubled during the war years as the importance of children as a national resource became more urgent.[2] Motherhood was seen to require dedication, hard work, scrupulous attention to child health and domestic management and was to be a full-time occupation; mothers' work outside the home was seen to be responsible for husbands' drinking and for street gangs of hooligans (Davin 1978: 53). The mother's job was to build and to conserve the Empire, to provide and service its citizenship. Indeed the word 'citizen' focuses many of the issues here. A 'citizen' was, strictly, a constituent element of the power of the community, i.e. in most cases (before 1918) a man rather than a woman. Women's 'power' in this situation was constructed as their responsibility to the men in power. It was women's duty to provide the (male) citizens of the future and to act as some sort of reservoir of moral value for the citizens of the present.

Against this background the famous 'Mother's Answer to "A Common Soldier", By A Little Mother', while still shocking, seems less startling as a social document. Graves's *Goodbye to All That* (1929 and 1957) quotes this letter to the editor of the *Morning Post* in full and without comment, to exemplify the 'foreign language' that civilians seemed to him to be speaking. The harnessing of what he calls 'newspaper language' with a patriotic interpretation of the duties of the mothers of the Empire results in a hot-blooded outburst which claims a unified identity for British mothers as the creators not of individual men, but of a *race*. The style is like Horatio Bottomley's: effect is gained through bluster and appeal to meaningless totalities (mothers play 'the most important part' in maintaining 'the whole civilized world') rather than to political detail. This is a Spartan Mother or a Volumnia of the kind that Jean Bethke Elshtain documents in *Women and War* (1987: 99–101, 192–3): rather than grieving over the loss of her son she would celebrate the victory of the state. A citizen by proxy, she uses her position to spur on the fighting forces, and extols the most conservative aspects of her maternal role in the context of the most bellicose flag-waving:

There is only one temperature for the women of the British race, and that is white heat. With those who disgrace their sacred trust of motherhood we have nothing in common. Our ears are not deaf to the cry that is ever ascending from the battlefield from men of flesh and blood whose indomitable courage is borne to us, so to speak, on every blast of the wind. We women pass on the human ammunition of 'only sons' to fill up the gaps, so that when the 'common soldier' looks back before going 'over the top' he may see the women of the British race at his heels, reliable, dependent, uncomplaining.

(Graves [1957] 1960: 189)

No wonder Siegfried Sassoon wrote so disparagingly of the 'Glory of Women'. This is an argument for woman-as-Mary, passing on her 'only son', fired by a 'sacred trust' which is stronger than the mere cries of agony that arise from the battlefield. It is as though the potential of imperial domesticated motherhood has finally come to fruition and all the images of woman as supporter and provider of ammunition for the Empire are seen to have purpose. Woman is fully mobilised. Her importance has finally been recognised, and it is that of dehumanised munitions factory or frankly terrifying goad.

If the mothers of dead soldiers could not be applied to for pacifist support, neither necessarily could feminists, although they allegedly sought to overthrow the system of male supremacy. The leaders of the WSPU, as has been well documented, abandoned all suffrage work at the outbreak of war and concentrated their services on the pursuit of martial victory. Under the clarion call of 'national militancy' (Liddington and Norris 1978: 252) they called for conscription for men, for women to replace men in the munitions factories and for industrial peace, and they were the first – although encouraged by a man – to hand out white feathers to men not in uniform (Liddington and Norris 1978: 252; Garner 1984: 55; Holton 1986: 132).

The Suffragettes' militancy gave way to patriotic support of militarism, a shift of allegiance that is neatly symbolised by the change in title of their campaign journal from *The Suffragette* to *Britannia* in October 1915. It has been argued that it would have been inconsistent for Suffragettes to become pacifists as physical force had hitherto been part of their own polemical method

(Vellacott 1987a: 86).[3] Christabel Pankhurst, though, gives her own 'reasoned' account of the natural patriotism of militant women, maintaining that 'quite naturally and logically, in the present national crisis, our appeal is to the patriotism of women. In militant women, the love of country is necessarily strong' (*The Suffragette* 16 April 1915: 3). The autocratic insistence on the naturalness, logic and inevitability of the switch from militancy to patriotism exemplifies what Kristeva calls the 'logic of identification' with dominant values in the nation state on the part of women who wish to insert themselves into the project and history of that state on its own terms (Kristeva [1979] 1986: 194). Why, for instance, should militant women necessarily have a strong love of country when the ideological values of that very country are what they have hitherto been combating? From a revolutionary position of seeking equality with men, the Suffragettes slipped back into the discourse of the good soldier and warrior mother. 'The least that men can do', said Mrs Pankhurst, 'is that every man of fighting age should prepare himself to redeem his word to women, and to make ready to do his best, to save the mothers, the wives, and the daughters of Great Britain from outrage too horrible even to think of' (*The Suffragette* 23 April 1915: 25). An activity, once marginal, is thus absorbed into the dominant discourse, and the reward is the relief of no longer being 'deviant' while retaining the pleasure of the fight.

SERVANTS OF THE STATE?

By the outbreak of war the WSPU had purged itself of dissident members such as Charlotte Despard, Sylvia Pankhurst and Emmeline Pethick Lawrence who had left to form, respectively, the Women's Freedom League (1907), the East London Federation of Suffragettes (1913) and the United Suffragists (1914), which all opposed the war. The non-militant National Union of Women's Suffrage Societies (NUWSS), however, remained a site of potential conflict with figures as diverse in interests as Millicent Fawcett, Catherine Marshall and Helena Swanwick all trying to operate through the dictates of the same rulebook. The war functioned for the NUWSS as a crisis point, dividing and regrouping its most prominent members according to the structure of their political beliefs. Mrs Fawcett was a stalwart

Liberal and believed that although war was not to be desired, women's most positive contribution should be to the relief of its effects. Marshall and Swanwick held more radical views, believing that the structure of international politics should be changed to erase physical force as a primary negotiating tool and to produce the machinery to work towards permanent peace.

The split was to occur over the Hague Peace Congress of April 1915. This international women's peace conference was attended by over 1,000 delegates representing twelve countries – a considerable feat in war time. Its resolutions concerned women's suffrage, the transference of territory, democratic control of foreign policy, disarmament and the machinery for international arbitration. It had two concrete results: envoys were sent to governments to persuade them to agree to a neutral conference for mediation, and the Women's International League for Peace and Freedom was established, of which Marshall, Swanwick, Kathleen Courtney, Emmeline Pethick Lawrence, Maude Royden and Irene Cooper Willis were prominent British members.[4] In March 1915, following a confused and divided NUWSS Council meeting, Mrs Fawcett received the resignations of Maude Royden, editor of *The Common Cause*, Kathleen Courtney, Honorary Secretary, and Catherine Marshall, Parliamentary Secretary and coordinator of the Election Fighting Fund.

In *The Common Cause* (organ of the NUWSS) of 7 August 1914, Fawcett made a statement regarding the position of the NUWSS and the war. She is careful not entirely to discredit those who work for peace, but makes clear the direction of her own allegiances:

As long as there was any hope of peace most members of the National Union probably sought for peace and endeavoured to support those who were trying to maintain it. But we have another duty now. Now is the time for resolute effort and self-sacrifice on the part of every one of us to help our country: and probably the way in which we can best help it is by devising and carrying through some well thought out plan which can be worked at continuously over many months, to give aid and succour to women and children brought face to face with destitution in consequence of the war [. . .]. Let us show ourselves

worthy of citizenship, whether our claim to it be recognised
or not.

(*The Common Cause* 7 August 1914: 376)

She uses a discourse of devotional humility – 'duty', 'self-
sacrifice', 'aid and succour' – that is not far removed from the
VAD directives, nor from the language of women's magazines.
The NUWSS was to suspend political action in favour of
providing relief for women thrown out of work by war or
otherwise adversely affected by the economic, social and industrial dislocation.[5]

The carrying out of a 'well thought out plan' clearly had
served the NUWSS well as a pre-war strategy and should continue to do so under the changed circumstances. It was, however, not the expediency of their method but their ideology that
caused Fawcett to differ from the internationalists. They were,
in her view, full of 'vague, general resolutions' that did not offer
'any guarantee of the practical sagacity or calmness of judgment
of those who had framed it' (*The Englishwoman* June 1915: 193).
Her own 'sagacity' and 'calmness' lead her entirely to mistrust
the radical perspective and to defer, instead, to the patriarchal
view that Germany and Austria must be 'humbled by defeat'
(ibid.: 199). She was not alone in this position as the pages of
The Common Cause and *The Englishwoman* verify.[6] It was not
unusual to believe that the natural 'blood and iron' character of
the Germans needed to be 'justly humiliated – Only in this way
can we English profoundly help Germans to refind their best
selves' (*The Englishwoman* February 1917: 105).

There was, then, a significant collision within the member-
ship of the NUWSS. Millicent Fawcett worked within a Liberal
imperialist tradition, loyal to the concept of 'national duty'. For
her, the awesome tragedy of the war took priority over work for
the vote; relief work could be undertaken, but with the aim of
amelioration rather than social change. Her 'plan' required
that the enemy be humbled and that English civilisation should
triumph. Only then could the business of winning the vote be
resumed. War, in her view, could justifiably continue as the
ultimate weapon of the good cause. Catherine Marshall and
Helena Swanwick, however, represented an alternative position. For them war relief was necessary but only as part of a
project for change on a scale capable of deconstructing the

oppositional conceptual framework that saw the English as unalterably virtuous and the Germans as intrinsically wicked; that saw men as fighters and women as supporters; and that associated masculinity with the public sphere, femininity with the private sphere.

Maternalism

Suffragist pacifists such as Marshall and Swanwick were committed to radical change – increased democratisation, machinery for international arbitration, the rights of small nations – and they saw women, as well as having the right and responsibility to be part of this, as having something specific to add to the process of reconstruction. That quality had as its symbol the most powerful and fertile image of womanhood: the mother.

Many women still believe that there are reasons, deriving from the practical application of women's mothering, that give women a distinctive interest in peace questions. Sara Ruddick (1989), the contributors to Joyce Trebilcot's collection of essays on the theory of mothering (1984), and some of the Greenham Common women tip the iceberg.[7] Modern psychoanalysts offer suggestions as to why women develop 'more permeable ego-boundaries' than men and why the dichotomy masculine-belligerent/feminine-pacific goes on being reproduced in the structure of our human relationships (Dorothy Dinnerstein 1976; Nancy Chodorow 1978). They also explain the power of the symbol 'mother' as both representative of a mode of being that is pacific, plural and ideal, which we have inevitably lost but desire to recapture, and simultaneously the figure of a regressive, murky, humbling limitation which we desire to supercede and replace with mastery (Dinnerstein [1976] 1987: 118–49). These two opposed but complementary images dominate the literature of the period (as Chapter 3 has shown), not because they are the product of an ahistorical myth, but because our culture continues to be structured by a division that polarises sex and gender practically, politically and psychologically, allocating nurturing and servicing tasks to women and competitive, aggressive tasks to men.

Clearly the suffragist pacifists presented themselves with problems by using the symbol of the mother to catalyse large-scale political reorganisation. The 'Little Mother's' letter demonstrates that motherhood does not universally imply pacifism; the Pankhursts and Mrs Fawcett show that 'woman's duty' can be used as a retreat from suffragism. The tendency of the image to universalise, idealise and reduce to a non-political identity was at odds with Marshall's and Swanwick's projects for democratisation and international arbitration. They used the image, though, as a literary and political device. World politics, seen through the eyes of maternalism, is defamiliarised: its destructive and oppressive capacities are foregrounded, leaving the way clear for a less barbaric, more egalitarian system to emerge. Furthermore, as a rhetorical figure, motherhood was all-embracing and unintimidating. It appealed to common experience and to what was a normal occurrence in many women's lives. The suffragist pacifists who used this image were neither entirely naive nor ruthlessly cynical: caught up in an early twentieth-century epistemology that prioritised motherhood in women at the same time as it mythologised it, they manipulated the image in a complex, if precarious, political move.

RADICAL PACIFISTS

Neither Marshall nor Swanwick was a biological mother. Nor did they operate in a political vacuum or a separatist enclave. The former was involved with the No-Conscription Fellowship (NCF), the latter with the Union of Democratic Control (UDC). The NCF was founded in November 1914 by the *Labour Leader* journalist Fenner Brockway to oppose conscription. After its introduction in 1916 the organisation became a welfare body for all conscientious objectors: meetings were held, material sent out, advice centres established, funds raised, leaflets planned and speakers organised (Vellacott 1980: 34). Marshall was responsible for persuading Bertrand Russell to become involved; Helena Swanwick was amongst the speakers. The UDC was the leading pacifist society from 1914 to 1924 through its influence in Labour and radical circles. It was established immediately after the outbreak of war by Charles Trevelyan, E.D. Morel, Arthur Ponsonby, Ramsay MacDonald and Norman Angell, and took the position that there should be greater parliamentary control over foreign policy and that secret diplomacy should be prevented, that international understanding should be along democratic lines with emphasis on popular parties rather than on governments, and that the war should be ended by negotiation and compromise rather than military victory in order to secure lasting peace (Swartz 1971: 42–66). Feminist pacifists, then, although they maintained a separate organisation (the WILPF), by no means isolated themselves from the other pacifist movements in Britain during the war.

They did, however, adopt particular rhetorical strategies with the aim of changing the approach of women to their relation to politics in the context of war. And in so doing they effected a remarkable transformation: with the help of tactful argument and passionate belief, a conservative essential became a political ideal.

The essential difference

The argument that women know the cost of human life as they are responsible for bearing it forms the root of many of the writings on woman-centred pacifism. Olive Schreiner, author of *The Story of an African Farm* and critic of British colonial rule, articulates this emotively in an essay called 'Woman and War' (1911):

> There is, perhaps, no woman, whether she have borne children or be merely potentially a child-bearer, who could look down upon a battle field covered with slain, but the thought would rise in her, 'So many mothers' sons! So many bodies brought into the world to lie there! So many months of weariness and pain while bones and muscles were shaped within; so many hours of anguish and struggle that breath might be [. . .].' And we cry, 'Without an inexorable cause, this should not be!' No woman who is a woman says of a human body, 'It is nothing!'
>
> (Schreiner [1911] 1987: 206–7)

The 'woman who is a woman', then, is a child-bearer who has already suffered 'weariness and pain' in making her contribution to humanity. Human life is her costly production and she therefore knows its true value: but her suffering, unbearably, is not only renewed but rendered worthless when that life is discarded. While this may seem to over-essentialise women's role, it was not an uncommon position for women to hold,

141

especially in wartime, when it seemed that what bound women together across national boundaries – not motherhood alone, but the fight for the vote – was more powerful than the patriotic loyalties that divided them. Emmeline Pethick Lawrence in *Votes for Women* (organ of the United Suffragists) points to the 'solidarity of women' saying that their interests 'are so universal that no national distinctions can cut deeply into them as may possibly happen [. . .] between men' (*Votes for Women* 16 October 1914). The journal *Jus Suffragii*, organ of the International Woman Suffrage Alliance, committed to suffragism and internationalism, carries in 1915 a letter by 'An English Soldier's Mother' (printed alongside a letter from a French soldier and a French mother) which may be contrasted directly with the notorious letter by a 'Little Mother'. Instead of the 'white heat' of patriotism, it calls for the warmth of a compassion that crosses national boundaries:

> As each month has passed I have felt more and more the horror and anguish of the war – the universal anguish. For one feels deep down in one's heart that the German mothers and wives are suffering just as much as those amongst one's friends who have lost sons and husbands, or the brave French women who are equally desolated. My heart goes out to them all. We all sorrow alike and together. My dearly loved eldest son who has been killed is but one among thousands [. . .]. It is my Hugh; it is their Jacques, their Fritz, their Nicholas. What does nationality matter! All mothers feel for each other in sorrow; it binds them together in spite of all differences of nationality or rank or religion. The mother's heart is the same throughout the world.
>
> (*Jus Suffragii* 1 February 1915: 236)

The allure of the proposition that 'The mother's heart is the same throughout the world' was easily capable of outstripping its detractions in an international crisis that threatened the lives and welfare of millions of men and women. The 'Mother of humanity', the 'motherhalf of the nation', 'the life force and the future' (*Jus Suffragii* 1 March 1915 and 1 September 1914) are further phrases used in pacifist journalism which, in another context, might appear to promote the imperialist cause. The difference lay not in the image itself, but in the ideologies with which it intersected. In the context of a feminist internationalist pacifism, the presence of a vast, collective m/other was summoned which had to negotiate its way out of sentimentality into universal sorrow and thence into the political arena.

When used in more sustained political writings the image of the life-endowing mother acted, not so much as a message in itself, but as a rhetorical motif which could be used as a way in to more radical analyses of women's position in wartime. Mary Sargant Florence and C.K. Ogden's *Militarism versus Feminism* was published by Allen and Unwin in 1915, material from it having appeared in *The Cambridge Magazine, The Common Cause* and *Jus Suffragii.* Florence was a painter, a suffragist and a member of the committee for the Hague Peace Congress; Ogden was a Magdalene College scholar, founder of the Heretics and editor of *The Cambridge Magazine* (Kamester and Vellacott 1987: 22). Their thesis is that the militarisation of society historically has degraded women, but that now they alone have the responsibility and the prerogative to combat the latest form of international barbarism. This contention is so placed as to clinch the argument of the book's introduction:

> Science, labour, religion, all have failed; but that silent half of humanity, permanently non-combatant, on whom the horrors of war fall with equal severity in all nations alike, bringing to all the same sorrows and the same sufferings, may through these very sorrows and sufferings find a new and real bond of unity for the redemption and regeneration of the civilised world. Here at last it is clear that the higher ideals and aspirations of women coincide with the future welfare of the whole of humanity.
>
> (Ogden and Florence [1915] 1987: 61–2)

The encouragement and endorsement of women's 'silence' by patriotic ideology has been discussed in the previous chapter. Within that silence, however, are seen to lie the 'higher ideals and aspirations', the Christ-like power to effect 'redemption and regeneration' on the rest of humanity. The religious vocabulary and narrative of 'progress' again has something in common with that of Horatio Bottomley (see Chapter 3); the difference, however, resides in a sustained political and historical argument that exhorts women to act as agents of change. They are not expected to *remain* 'silent', and their grief, rather than being experienced privately, is to find public articulation and political mobilisation.

Catherine Marshall in 'Women and War' (1915), her talk for a Collegium Meeting, uses a less declamatory style.[8] She urges all women to 'look steadfastly at war and the consequences of war, with our women's eyes – our mother's eyes – and tell the world what we see' (Marshall [1915] 1987: 41). The technique of aligning herself with her readership suggests a commitment to equality consonant with her broader political aims of encouraging co-operation rather than conflict. Helena Swanwick, however, does play to the gallery. She begins 'The War in its Effect upon Women' (1915a) with a rhetorical flourish clearly aimed at securing readers' sympathetic attention, a device justified by the development of a provocative and challenging argument:

> When they see pictures of soldiers encamped in the ruins of what was once a home, amidst the dead bodies of gentle milch cows, most women would be thinking too insistently of the babies who must die for need of milk to entertain the exhilaration which no doubt may be felt at 'the good work of our guns.' When they read of miles upon miles of kindly earth made barren, the hearts of men may be wrung to think of wasted toil, but to women the thought suggests a simile full of an even deeper pathos; they will think of the millions of young lives destroyed, each one having cost the travail and care of a mother, and of the millions of young bodies made barren by the premature death of those who should have been their mates. The millions of widowed maidens in the coming generation will have to turn their thoughts away from one particular joy and fulfilment of life.
>
> (Swanwick [1915a] 1971: 3)

The passage is packed with archaisms and verbal embellishments that produce a sense of pathos and tragic nostalgia: '*gentle* milch cows', '*kindly* earth', 'wasted *toil*' ('labour' is the word used to denote hard work in the rest of the article), '*travail* and care of a mother' and, of course, 'widowed *maidens*' tragically deprived of their particular service in life. In the context of the rest of the piece (which analyses women's position in industry and attacks the principles of capitalism) this can be seen as a rhetorical device strategically applied. The series of deeply conventional images of women, while it risks

144

being criticised for sentimentality, nevertheless creates an atmosphere, in the opening stages of a political pamphlet, that might seem unthreatening to women not yet won over to the cause and might even persuade them to read on.[9]

Political theory

I shall now turn to the area of 'political theory' that sets out to transform the woman governed by an aching maternal heart into an informed and potentially active citizen. The argument begins from a small seed: in societies built on a militarist structure women can only be oppressed. Ogden and Florence argue in *Militarism Versus Feminism* that militarism permeates every social institution from education to religion, creating a competitive infrastructure that relies on a permanently exploited class – not a social class in their terms, but a gendered one: women. This runs the risk of developing into a conspiracy theory where all men are ranked against all women, irrespective of social background. There is, of course, a fundamental naivety in this, which is brought home by Sylvia Pankhurst's East London Federation of Suffragettes (ELFS) and its paper the *Woman's Dreadnought* (later the *Workers' Dreadnought*). The ELFS envisaged a conflict based on the intersection between class and gender and symbolised it in terms of the battle between working women and the male government for an equal distribution of food: [10]

> Dear women, are you prepared to go on tamely starving as though you and your children do not matter? The men in power have plunged us into war for their commercial interests. They pass Bills in the interests of financiers. What will they do for you?'
>
> (*The Woman's Dreadnought* 8 August 1914: 82)

The language used and the issues confronted bear little resemblance to the utopian discourse of the middle-class suffragists. Where the latter are speculative and theoretical, the East End women are more concerned with ameliorating immediate hardships: instead of the discourse of the 'other' there is a call for a 'No Vote, No Rent' strike and the demand that food prices be centrally controlled.

Having said this, though, the concerns voiced in the quotation above tally with the general proposition that militarism is sustained by oppression. The difference of view is founded on the personal experience of this reality that arises from class position and on the structure of political belief that is mobilised to combat its effects. Catherine Marshall was opposed to the kind of militancy that the ELFS gradually became involved with. In July 1917 *The Woman's Dreadnought* changed its name to *The Workers' Dreadnought*, the ELFS having already become the Workers' Suffrage Federation in February 1916. This signalled a change of direction that was reinforced by Pankhurst's involvement with George Lansbury's syndicalist Daily Herald League (Holton 1986: 127). Marshall, however, was opposed to militancy in any form. Her notion of revolution was one more concerned with alternative principles of organisation – in particular co-operation – than with the spontaneous overthrow of the reigning power system. Like Pankhurst, she was working to 'creat[e] a new social fabric', but by 'find[ing] some other way' than violence ([1915] 1987: 39). This pacifist orientation was reinforced by her work with the socialist and Christian NCF, which articulated a 'deeply held belief in the sanctity of human life' and a 'loyalty to the principles of peace and human fellowship' (Vellacott 1980: 48). In her view politics by domination entailed the subjection of women, of the working classes, of small nations (cf. Marshall [1916] 1987: 45–6) – but it was not, however, associated exclusively with those who held power positions. The combative methodology was seen to infect socialist and suffragist campaigners as much as it structured the activities of their oppressors:

> The mark of your militarist is that he would rather get what he wants by fighting than by any other way. He wants to force his enemy to yield, so that he may have him at his mercy and be able to impose what terms he chooses. I have heard trade unionists talk like this of trade union rights. I have heard socialists, who were ardent pacifists on international questions, talk like this of class warfare. I have heard suffragists talk like this of the struggle for sex equality. *They were all talking pure militarism* – they were all moved by the desire to dominate rather than to co-operate, to vanquish and humiliate the enemy rather than to convert him to a friend.
>
> (Marshall [1916] 1987: 47)

She aimed, then, at eliminating militarism from every element of the political structures she involved herself in: this was seen as the only way forward for women in politics. Marshall, like the ELFS, believed that the international solidarity of workers, had it been sufficiently developed, might have prevented the outbreak of war ([1916] 1987: 50), but wanted to seek a way other than class warfare to change the social structure. Her vision was for a radical restructuring of the methods of political activity, based on co-operation rather than confrontation.

Helena Swanwick was also involved in a pacifist political organisation which went beyond the brief of suffragism: the Union of Democratic Control. She too saw the recognition of the subjection of women as a vital starting point in the project to dismantle militarism – and applied an aggressive form of satire to the so-called progressive men who were just as guilty of patronising women as the imperialists:

> When war broke out, a Labour newspaper, in the midst of the news of men's activities, found space to say that women would feel the pinch, because their supply of attar of roses would be curtailed. It struck some women like a blow in the face. When a great naval engagement took place, the front page of a progressive daily was taken up with portraits of the officers and men who had won distinction, and the back page with portaits of simpering mannequins in extravagantly fashionable hats; not frank advertisement, mind you, but exploitation of women under the guise of news supposed to be peculiarly interesting to the feeble-minded creatures.
>
> (Swanwick [1915a] 1971: 4)

While Marshall concentrates on the political equation between women and small nations to advance the feminist pacifist argument, Swanwick looks directly at women's position in industry. Like Marshall, she sees the need for 'co-operation rather than conflict' in solving industrial problems ([1915a] 1971: 6). If women and industry are to thrive 'Men and women must take counsel together' ([1915a] 1971: 6). Her argument, however, is a basic socialist one: the capitalist system down-grades women's indispensable economic contribution as care-takers for the working forces and reduces women to domestic slaves. Their work 'returns to the nation as a whole and only in

small and very uncertain part to the women themselves'
([1915a] 1971: 9). The working housewife is universally penal-
ised: she receives no tangible reward for her work in the home,
her work outside the home is poorly paid and the effort to do
both can only result in exhaustion. Capitalism, then, results in
the slavery of women even in peace time: war pushes the
argument to its extreme form and unveils an ideological
silence:

> What the war has put in a fresh light, so that even the
> dullest can see, is that if the State may claim women's lives
> and those of their sons and husbands and lovers, if it may
> absorb all private and individual life, as at present, then
> indeed the condition of those who have no voice in the
> State is a condition of slavery, and English men don't feel
> quite happy at the thought that their women are still
> slaves, while their Government is saying they are waging a
> war of liberation. Many women had long ago become
> acutely aware of their ignominious position, but the jolt of
> the war has made many more aware of it.
>
> ([1915a] 1971: 25)

She arrives at the same conclusion, then, as Ogden and Florence, although from a different direction; her argument is
based on the current practical experience of working women in
industry, rather than cultural and religious history. The thesis,
then, has moved on significantly from the 'gentle milch cows'
and 'widowed maidens': women have become political beings
rather than abstracted absolutes and the theorisation of their
position in a hierarchy which privileges physical and economic
strength opens up discussion to include all oppressed minorities
and to demand a 'true democracy, free and informed' ([1915b]
1971: 3–4).

Essentialist practice

The essentialist and political theories both articulate a fundamental difference between men and women, a difference which
situates the women as life-givers rather than life-takers and
therefore opposed to the use of physical force as a governing
structure if the world is not forever to be subject to the
barbarism of war. 'Maternal thinkers' from the First World War

Plate 5 Helena M. Swanwick, pacifist and suffragist by Lizzie Caswall Smith. (By courtesy of The Mary Evans Picture Library/Fawcett Library.)

to the present day have argued that women as mothers see things differently and have the ability to value difference and to act in a way which accommodates it without repressing the interests of the weak. What women lacked in the second decade of this century (and what they often still lack) was (is) representation in policy-making bodies. If they could translate their skills as human nurturers into the political arena, the inbuilt oppressiveness of the system might be dismantled:

> To a woman every man is a mother's son – not as her possession, but as her gift of great price which must not be wasted, her great adventure on which she has staked her all. This involves a revaluation indeed, based not on power or on wealth but on humanity; not on getting but on giving; not on domination, but on service.
>
> (Marshall [1916] 1987: 48–9)

The rhetoric here has Christian inflections but, rather than suggesting, as the women's magazines do, that women's service should be towards maintaining the patriarchal status quo, it leans towards the alternative, revolutionary side of Christianity that during the war was opposed to fighting, and aimed to replace aggressive and materialistic values with a Christian form of socialist pacifism.[11]

In an attempt to forestall her critics, Marshall addresses the question of women's traditional conservatism, which logically could be construed as a serious obstacle to the kind of challenge to the existing order that she is suggesting:

> It is true that women are by instinct conservers – but of Life, not of the status quo; and life means inevitably growth and change, as all their experience has taught them. A mother is used to providing for the needs of a growing child. She does not say to the child: 'You must not grow, because I have made clothes for you of a certain size, and I do not want the trouble of altering them or making new ones.' The wise mother makes those clothes with tucks that can be easily let out; and when they can be let out no further she starts on a new garment so as to have it ready when needed. Always *human need* is the first consideration, not the maintenance of things as they are at least cost to herself.
>
> ([1916] 1987: 49)

She grafts this argument onto practical politics by saying that democracies and many nations are comparable to growing children and the function of statesmanship is to provide for their healthy growth. The pitfall of this rhetoric, as some modern critics have pointed out, is that it sounds patronising, insular and politically naive. 'The trouble is', Jean Bethke Elshtain remarks, 'children are not grown-ups, and mothering is not and never has been a *wholly* beneficent activity' (Elshtain 1987: 239). Sara Ruddick in her essay 'Preservative Love and Military Destruction' (1983) agrees that maternity in itself is not unproblematically virtuous and also points out that conflict is not avoidable. She does, however, believe that aspects of maternal practice can be thought to be compatible with an activity which tends towards peace rather than destruction: 'In a less hierarchical society, disciplined imagination and moral reflection could reveal the interconnectedness of children's interests with the causes of peace, ecological sanity, and distributive justice' (Ruddick 1983: 239). With the benefit of a later perspective on feminism,[12] she is willing to run the risks involved with associating maternity with pacifism.

Marshall, who has neither the hindsight nor the philosophical training of Ruddick or Elshtain, is presenting a practical, political case in a cultural crisis where men are being killed and women are not recognised as responsible citizens. What the modern reader may see as naivety may be explained as political strategy based on an earlier form of feminist epistemology.

The mothers' vision, then, tends away from that which is repressive and towards that which is enabling. The system applied to international relations, however, has its roots in capitalist practice which is, according to Helena Swanwick, impersonal, ruthless, 'rapid with a senseless haste to get nowhere in the end' ([1915a] 1971: 32). In this there can be no lasting place for 'the right mother':

> Human life is and should be sacred to her, and individual character infinitely precious and desirable. If she bear ten children, she knows that each one is distinct, separate, a person; the fruit of individual pangs, the object of individual loves. Regimentation is – and one hopes always will be – an abomination to her. She sees diversity, variety, adaptability, freedom, as the salt of life and the condition

151

of development. To her, organisation will appeal only if it is directed to maintain freedom and to nourish life and love.

([1915a] 1971: 32)

Unless something fundamental is to change, then, industry and political life cannot thrive and may indeed end in the kind of devastation embodied in the war. The key to the problem as far as Swanwick and her fellow suffragist pacifists are concerned is the integration of women into public life on all levels – the symbolic representation of this being the vote.

Political practice

The suffragist pacifist rhetoric carried the energy of a self-fulfilling principle. It was the rhetoric of hope. The Women's Movement, the Hague Congress, the Labour movement and, in the early stages of the war, the likelihood of America maintaining a neutral position,[13] all seemed to stand as a symbolic cluster, offering, from some undetermined place within its structure, a promise that human progress could and would be made.

Mary Sheepshanks,[14] editor of the International Woman Suffrage Alliance's *Jus Suffragii*, in a 1914 editorial entitled 'Patriotism or Internationalism', lamented the dissolution of the idealism to be found at former internationalist conferences, and placed responsibility in the hands of women:

> In all this orgy of blood, what is left of the internationalism which met in congresses, socialist, feminist, pacifist, and boasted of the coming era of peace and amity? The men are fighting; what are the women doing? They are, as is the lot of women, binding up the wounds that men have made. Every country tells a stirring tale of the devotion and efficiency of its women. But that is not enough. Massacre and devastation continue, and the world is relapsing into a worse, because a more scientific, barbarism than that from which it sprang. Women must not only use their hands to bind up, they must use their brains to understand the causes of the European frenzy, and their lives must be devoted to putting a stop for ever to such wickedness.
>
> (*Jus Suffragii* 1 November 1914: 184)

Women, then, must commit themselves 'earnestly [to] study the causes of the present criminal madness' (ibid.). Sheepshanks's prescription for future civilisation is as follows:

> False patriotic pride and love of conquest, the oppression of nationalities, must go. No race must be conquered or dominated, but must have full and free right to self-government. True democracy in every country must give the whole nation, men and women, the right to control their own destiny; secret diplomacy and alliances must go. Armaments must be drastically reduced and abolished, and their place taken by an international police force. Instead of two great Alliances pitted against each other, we must have a true Concert of Europe. Peace must be on generous, unvindictive lines, satisfying legitimate national needs, and leaving no cause for resentment such as to lead to another war. Only so can it be permanent.
>
> (*Jus Suffragii* 1 November 1914: 184)

The emphasis, then, is on the dismantling of the hierarchical opposition oppressor/oppressed in favour of plural and democratic access to power, to include not only working men and all women, but also small nations and all races. *Jus Suffragii* did not limit itself to the statement of women's quasi-mythical opposition to war. It frequently published practical proposals as to what should be done to bring the war to a close and to prevent wars from happening in the future. A crucial element in this is the audibility of women's voice. 'For the first time, so far as I am aware' says the poet Margaret Sackville, 'the voice of organised womanhood finds expression' (*Jus Suffragii* 1 October 1915: 3). Women, crucially, have 'discovered the vital, easily ignored truth that man's business and woman's business cannot be separated – that any separation such as war creates is stultifying and ruinous' (*Jus Suffragii* 1 October 1915: 3).

The idea of responsibility is recurrent. Marshall uses it to stand for a motivating force, in combination with the political education that the women's movement has provided. In former wars, she says, there was no organised women's movement 'to give expression to the passion of horror in the women's hearts, to be fired by it to co-operative action' ([1915] 1987: 40). 'Today' there is one:

153

organised, articulate, in almost all the belligerent and most of the neutral countries. And I believe the great call to the women's movement, if we have ears to hear and the courage and faith and love enough to respond to it, is that we should face and visualise the full horrors of war, accepting our share of responsibility as those who might have helped, had we cared enough, to save the world from this tragedy.

(Marshall [1915] 1987: 40)

The political development of the women's movement transforms women's silence by enabling their maternal skills to become a political tool. In 'The Future of Women in Politics' Marshall's call is to internationalism and to the Labour Party to demand the introduction of a Franchise Bill that will include women. Marshall accepts that the potential of women's international strength could be added to the international solidarity of workers in a fruitful and natural alliance: but she then goes on to ask 'can we act? Are we going to be given a direct voice in politics? Are we going to be given it in time?' ([1916] 1987: 51).

A similar kind of urgency inspires Swanwick's message to women:

I am one of those who believe that women have a great opportunity, if they will take it. If they would put all their fire and passion at the service of the forces among men that are making for reconstruction; if they would outmatch the enthusiasm of women in the past for the soldier by the enthusiasm of women in the future for the fighters in the liberation of humanity, they would be helping to make the world anew.

([1915a] 1971: 29–31)

The women's movement had not only encouraged the articulation of women's views, it had also encouraged women to believe that no area of politics need necessarily be beyond their sphere. Foreign policy was hitherto considered to be so. The convergence of war and suffragism, however, resulted in the emergence of study circles formed by the Women's Co-operative Guild, the Workers' Educational Association, the Association for the Study of International Relations and the Union of Democratic Control. If the key to the future lay in democratic reform, there was another development taking place which had a tremendous symbolic impact in political and fictional writing alike:

> As I write, a new women's organisation is being born called the Women's International League, which will have as its object 'to establish the principles of Right rather than Might, and co-operation rather than conflict'.
>
> (Marshall [1916] 1987: 51–2)

The language of birth emphasises the optimism with which the Women's International League was greeted. Ellen Key ends her *War, Peace and the Future* (1916) with reference to the Hague conference; Swanwick's *The War and its Effects upon Women* also uses it to act as a unifying matrix for women's responsibility, their hatred of war and their newly educated interest both in women's politics and in their potential influence on foreign policy:

> This congress may be considered as marking an epoch, for it was the first congress of women held in war-time, and including women from both belligerent sides, to consider the basis of a permanent peace.
>
> ([1915a] 1971: 31)

A conservative position is thus transformed into political challenge.

'A DREAM LACKING INTERPRETATION'

One of the extraordinary things about the women's pacifist fiction of the period is its proximity, in terms of strategy and motifs, to the political writing. In novels by Mary Hamilton, Rose Macaulay and Vera Brittain, for example, the figure of the mother has a forceful role, both symbolically and narratorially, and the texts oscillate between political and narrative drives: strategies must be found to communicate arguments, but plots must explore the ambivalence in women's minds between the pull of private life and the lure of the public cause. All three novels play out the troubled route of maternal thinking from private concern to political tool, and conclude with the recognition that an alternative value system might at least change the world in the future, if not stop the fighting immediately.

Of course, in concentrating on maternalism there are many elements of pacifist rhetoric that this chapter leaves out.

Theodora Wilson Wilson, for example, was a Quaker who financed and edited the Christian revolutionary journal the *New Crusader* (cf. Ceadel 1980: 5), and who published a novel entitled *The Last Weapon: A Vision* in 1916, proclaimed by *The Woman's Dreadnought* as 'The most powerful peace book yet published'. Its 'power' lies in its allegorical simplicity. The message, a religious one, is conveyed as follows: the Prince of Fear presently rules the earth by making available his weapons of Darkness to the warring factions. The Prince of Peace sends down his representative to dismantle the resulting deadlock, which threatens universal destruction, with his Last Weapon – Fearless Love. The outcome is seen to lie in the hands of the people, but authority, uncomplicatedly, lies in Christ alone. Christian pacifism is also represented in Rose Allatini's novel *Despised and Rejected* (1918), which was originally banned under the Defence of the Realm Act (cf. Hynes 1990: 232–4; Tylee 1990: 121). The symbol of alterity in this novel is broader than in Wilson's: pacifism is a cause adopted by homosexuals, Jews, socialists, internationalists and artists, who all congregate in London, seat of government, but also of organised resistance.[15] In a figurative representation of repression, the 'social deviants' meet in a cafe that is literally underground. Here they make their plans while observing the passing 'strange, bodiless legs' ([1918] 1975: 204) of their more conventional compatriots, agents and victims of the Symbolic Order, who lack the human apparatus of thinking and feeling.

Most of the political content of *Despised and Rejected* is relayed through set piece political speeches and debates which take place in the cafe. This is a narrative strategy that recurs in the novels that I shall shortly move on to examine in more detail, and it raises an interesting point. Are the conventions of realist fiction too restricting to express the massive complications of the political objection to war? Theodora Wilson Wilson makes use of allegory – and so does Vernon Lee, a UDC member, whose writing had no religious principle to guide the choice of its form. In the introduction to her *Satan the Waster* (1920), Lee advances what may be seen as an explanation, or an apology, for its dissociated form. It is:

> merely such an extemporized shadow-play as a throng of
> passionate thoughts may cast up into the lucid spaces of

one's mind: symbolical figures, grotesquely embodying what seems too multifold and fluctuating, also too unendurable, to be taken stock of.

(1920: vii)

This sets up an opposition which throws an interesting light on both political and fictional writing. The 'lucid spaces of the mind' are contrasted with 'fluctuating' and 'unendurable', just as the purity of an idealistic form of alterity in the political writing is set against the practical details and acute losses of motherhood. In the fictional writing, moreover, the complexity and detail of the realist mode is persistently fractured by the intrusion of clear, detailed speeches, conference reports or letters of primarily political content. Lee's comment, then, seems to suggest a general sense of collision and confusion of principles and practicalities that was a problem as much in fictional as in political narrative. It is the dialogue between 'lucid space' and prosaic humanity that the novels try to play out.

The mother figures in Mary Hamilton's *Dead Yesterday* and Rose Macaulay's *Non-Combatants and Others* (both 1916) are extraordinary figures. Austere role models rather than angels in the house, they are political mothers, working not on the home front but on the international front, trying to alter the world rather than children's clothes. They are, in fact, more like Marshall and Swanwick than Frances Harrison or Cynthia Renner. Their daughters, the moral and psychological centres of the novels, find themselves caught up in a battle between the claims of heterosexual romance, which they eventually reject, and political justice. Their decision is governed by maternal identification instead of patriarchal choice. Extraordinary mothers, perhaps, demand extraordinary devices to make clear their position. In a later novel, also about the conflict between socialism and capitalism, Hamilton has one of her characters say: 'Women in novels [. . .] never have any minds; not what I call operative minds; not minds that matter' (Hamilton 1922: 237). Aurelia Leonard in *Dead Yesterday* certainly is seen to have a mind that matters.

Aurelia Leonard, then, is like a beacon, radiating the pure, uncorruptible light of suffragist socialist pacifism, so that it may guide her more troubled compatriots. She is unambiguously anti-Liberal, and it is perhaps worth remembering that Hamilton was a friend of Irene Cooper Willis, the thesis of whose *England's Holy War* (1928) is traceable in Aurelia's disdain for the British Liberal press. Aurelia propounds some of the major arguments of the UDC (of which Hamilton was a member) – that a representative democracy should be established, that all diplomacy should be under parliamentary control and that international understanding should be along democratic lines – but the trajectory of the novel concerns the intellectual and social space between the lucidity of the uncluttered, political mind that can perceive these goals and the prosaic, baffled nature of the ordinary individual. Aurelia Leonard, writer, pacifist and Internationalist Socialist, represents the former and her daughter, Daphne Leonard, the latter. Nigel Strode, a journalist on a Liberal paper, represents a kind of impassioned shallowness. He concentrates his efforts on writing 'holy crusade' propaganda that makes heroes and martyrs out of those who kill and are killed. Daphne falls in love with him and has to struggle to displace an unworthy romantic attachment with a vigorous and committed understanding of the wrongs of war.

The political agenda is set up in the first twenty-five pages, when Strode is sent to interview Aurelia for his newspaper. Her answers to his questions take the form of short speeches, not dissimilar in content to those of Marshall and Swanwick: 'How can we get the money [for social reform] – in any country in Europe – if we have to go on pouring millions into armies and navies?' (Hamilton 1916: 20). Peace is 'long endurance, labour, sacrifice, conquest of the unwilling soil, just as self-control is conquest of the unwilling self. And there's no short road to it. You have to want peace passionately, with all the hardest feeling and thinking you've got' (1916: 22). The formality of the device makes it clear that she is an idealist with faith in the workers and contempt for the press and the government. But she has one area of profound naivety: she is unaware of the seductive power of war. Nigel, on the other hand, is a bored, not-so-young man (thirty-seven) seeking adventure. The omniscient narrator intrudes to tell us a little more about him:

> A contempt for reason was part of the fundamental creed of the younger generation, and to that generation Nigel essentially belonged. They claimed to know things more immediately. Hence they went about incessantly in search

158

of the personal experience, above all of the personal thrill, that could alone give them such knowledge.

(Hamilton 1916: 119)

A debate thus emerges in the novel centred on the opposition of organisation and control against freedom and passion, with reason as the mediator. At first (as traditionally the left/right wings are represented) Aurelia seems to stand for the former and Nigel for the latter, but in the context of war they and their positions are seen to switch roles. This is largely conveyed by the operations of the press, the government and the vast machinery of mobilisation. 'Passion' is co-opted by organisation and control. Rational thought then ceases to function:

> Incessant activity made thought unnecessary: war news supplied a daily false stimulus to dull imaginations: the passion of hatred gave an energy to sterile emotions.

(1916: 314)

Daphne, too, is propelled into this intellectual no-man's-land by falling in love with Nigel. The two become engaged in May 1914 and from that point Daphne's love renders her morally and socially blind: 'The difficulty with me is, you know, that I'm not really, deep down, half as wretched about [the war] as I ought to be. I've got you – and that means so much that I can't take it in, that all the rest of the world has gone' (1916: 258). These are sentiments echoed by Zina and Jinnie in *The Hounds of Spring* and *The Lost Generation*, and like them Daphne spends some time being simply 'stunned', while Nigel is transported by a 'religious exaltation'. Elated by the spectacle of Britain's unanimous enthusiasm for the fight, he writes patriotic leaders for his paper. The view articulated in Sinclair's novel perfectly describes Nigel's mood: 'After all these years of unreality and sham a big thing like this gives one the sense of having escaped out of a tunnel into the air' (Sinclair 1917: 233). He easily falls in with the majority view: '[The Germans have] been drilling and training while we've been making ourselves too jolly comfortable, with pensions here and insurance there' (Hamilton 1916: 211) and helps to brew what Lee satirises as the 'Vitalizing Lies, Alcoholic Syrup of Catchwords' that are seen as the answer to the torpidity of the Victorian Age (Lee 1920: 8). Symbolically, the newspapers, cluttered with war-mongering

159

news, impede Aurelia as she walks around her room, trying to come to terms with the fact that 'the people' *do* seem to want war. The power of propaganda and of the Liberals' use of holy, sacrificial language thus become an obstacle to the freedom of the dissenter.

Daphne, unlike Zina and Jinnie, is not to remain a prisoner of 'false consciousness'. Inspired by her mother's example she works in the East End in workrooms for girls,[16] where she is constantly exposed to the human toll of war on mothers, wives and children crying out for their dead fathers. It is through this experience that she negotiates her way out of the 'passionate delusion' of romantic love towards the more honourable compassion for the victims of war's horrors. The 'rending pain, final and appalling' (Hamilton 1916: 323) comes when she hears of the death in battle of a friend whose wife, Jane, has just given birth, prematurely, to their baby. Moved by the intensity and authenticity of the mother–child relationship, Daphne breaks her engagement, recognising Nigel's own insipidity and seeing it as an index of moral weakness on a national level:

> as I see it, the war has come because so many people are like Nigel . . . . He can't feel, you see, and of course he wants to feel; and so must grope after things and seize them before he knows what they are.[. . .] He got hold of me [and] I wouldn't let go, because I loved him, and love seemed a short cut to everything.
>
> (1916: 410)

In this novel, then, romantic love is seen as little more than a cheap thrill. There is no short cut to the important things – peace, or a more balanced and rational civilisation – and what Nigel thought was passion was really desire for organisation and control. Aurelia, on the other hand, has to admit that the government holds the monopoly on control in wartime and the only weapon with which to combat this is passion for freedom. Their positions are thus reversed. The novel, like the political writing, finally aims for the 'conquest of the ideal over all the narrowing conditions of human existence' (1916: 357), although it might be thought that the text's manifestation of that ideal hardly rises to its challenge.

The final scene takes place at Aurelia's country home, the appropriately named 'Wending End', where sexual love has been excluded and replaced by maternal love and friendship. The two mother–daughter pairs – Aurelia and Daphne, Jane and her baby Leonora – are linked by political sorority, mutual concern and the earnest conclusion that 'to love something small and pretend it's great' (1916: 358) is the destruction of true passion. The ending, then, is earnest and radical in its refusal of heterosexual love and its positioning of maternity as something exclusive of and more powerful than patriarchy, rather than subservient to it. But this minor women's peace party takes place within an image of seclusion and retreat. While on the one hand this reinforces its alterity and gives the impression of strength through female bonding, it also creates a symbol of profound isolation. The end of the war is not yet in sight: its presence is registered in the nearby valley, which 'resounded with its agony' (1916: 411). The means by which to fight militarism, then, are theoretically available, but they are pleasantly concealed in a rural retreat. There is a kind of ideological smugness about this that assumes that once individuals have been given their proper labels and been allotted their proper places, the battle has been won. The seeds for a radical dismantling of the militarist ethic are seen merely to lie dormant while the battles, both ideological and martial, rage around them.

The narrative trajectory of Rose Macaulay's *Non-Combatants and Others* (1916) is similar to that of *Dead Yesterday*, although the stance of its narrator is far more sceptical and, in the end, more subtle. Daphne Sandomir, the mother of Alix, Nicholas and Paul, is a figure similar to Aurelia Leonard: she represents the vigour and determined optimism of the (fictional) Society for the Promotion of Permanent Peace, and it is towards her that her daughter Alix gravitates at the end of the novel, shrugging off her individualist irresponsibility enough to join a society dedicated to fostering international peace and understanding. More specifically than *Dead Yesterday* this text articulates the mental and moral dilemmas involved in making a transition from a position of indifference to the war to one which demands a positive commitment to opposing it and all future conflicts. Alix's problem is not that she is blinded by passion, but that she is made numb by disinterest. She has always had a sceptical reserve about her mother's political activities and it is only the discovery of the pain and eventual suicide of her younger brother in the trenches that leaves her unable to maintain her imperviousness. The novel is set in 1915, and opens in April, shortly after the Hague Peace Congress. 1915 saw the Bryce Report on 'German Atrocities', the zeppelin raids on London, the Gallipoli Campaign, the deadlock at Loos and the increasing industrial organisation for war production. It also saw the rise of the Women's International League, their deputations to national leaders and their programmes for education for peace. It is against this background that Macaulay's drama of military stagnation and political mobilisation is played out.

Mary Hamilton has written of Rose Macaulay that she was not a pacifist in 1914 (Hamilton 1944: 139). Like many others, such as Vera Brittain and Storm Jameson, she was converted by Dick Sheppard's Peace Pledge Union and became an absolute pacifist in the 1930s. Hamilton insists that Macaulay, unlike herself, was always politically disinterested. Their difference as novelists is notable in this: where Hamilton's narrator is earnestly instructive, Macaulay's is ironic and detached. But disinterest is a position that the book ultimately deems to be untenable in the face of the horrors of war and, while Alix, the protagonist, may not have unreserved faith in the power of religious and political forces, she asserts their value as a means of thinking constructively about bringing an end to war.

As in *Dead Yesterday*, the argument is conducted between the opposed poles of idealism and individualism. Alix's mother, Daphne, represents idealism; her cousins, the Framptons, with whom Alix lives, are apathetic, small-minded individuals who believe every word printed in the '*Evening Thrill*' and reduce all points of general principle to the mundanities of their own experience. For some time Alix risks slipping into this mental void, but her initially regressive tendency is stopped when she hears, by accident, of the events that surrounded her brother's death in the trenches. She talks to someone who was at the Front in the same company as a young man straight from school, whose nerve collapsed when his best friend was blown up in front of him. This young man, who had shot himself in the shoulder and died, was Paul, Alix's sensitive, younger brother. The shock of this incident brings into violent and nauseating focus all that she has been trying to ignore. The advice she receives from her cousin is 'not to *think*. Not to *imagine*. Not to *remember*' (Macaulay 1916: 102). This advice, she discovers, is wholly inappropriate to her own artistic activity and to political awareness. As with Daphne Leonard, an event that sends the Jinnies and Zinas into a kind of mental oblivion rescues Alix from hers.

Abandoning disinterest, Alix also gives up her pursuit of heterosexual romance (although not without some humiliation) in favour of seeking political justice. 'Something *against* war, I want to be doing, I think. Something to fight it, and prevent it coming again' (1916: 141). Two people have solutions. One is her remaining brother's flat-mate, the Reverend West, a UDC member who reads the 'heretical' *Cambridge Magazine* and whose approach to religion is revolutionary: '[I]t was West's religion which thought it was going to break up the world in pieces and build it anew' (1916: 107). The other is Alix's mother.

Daphne offers an alternative approach, not based on religious practice but on revolutionary feminist pacifism. She dominates the final part of the novel, having been a peripheral but energetic and rather eccentric presence in the first two parts. She represents internationalist pacifism, is a member of the Society for the Promotion of Permanent Peace, has attempted to attend the Hague Peace Conference, has been on a world tour to persuade the major European leaders of the benefits of peace by negotiation, and specialises in the education of children in ways that undermine the use of physical force as a means of settling disputes.[17] In other words, she stands for the same things and has taken part in similar enterprises as the Women's International League. Furthermore her position in the trajectory of the novel is similar to the rhetorical placing of the League in the political writing: final, optimistic, the possible bearer of new ways of organising the world.

She is a figure rather larger than life. Vigorous and positive, she sweeps in from the margins of the text and effectively takes over, providing the answer to Alix's dilemma in terms that challenge her daughter's selfishness, scepticism and carefully nurtured insularity. Daphne's advice undermines that of Alix's cousin's 'Thinking's no good anyhow' (1916: 103). Like Aurelia Leonard, she speaks against laziness, selfishness and stupidity. 'It's those three we've got to fight. We've got to replace them by hard working, hard living, and hard thinking.

163

And the last must come first. We've got to *think*, and make every one think. . .' (1916: 163).

Alix is taken to a meeting of the SPPP. Here the dominantly realist mode of the novel is constantly interrupted by documentary interpolations. Alix's thoughts and comments on the proceedings occupy a significant section of the novel. She dislikes the 'sentimental rubbish', the propensity to generalise, and points out some, to her, particularly dubious propositions: 'That women are the guardians of life, and therefore mind war more than men do.' 'That women are the chief sufferers from war. A debatable point, anyhow; and what did it matter, and why divide humanity into sexes, further than nature has already done so?' (1916: 164–5). She agrees with the speaker's points against capitalism, is interested in the influence of secret *ententes*, the possibility of disarmament and a Concert for Europe – but she craves practical details. Like Mary Hamilton some years later (Hamilton 1944: 68), she finds the arrogance and exclusivity of some pacifists intolerable. They seem to imply 'We, a select few of us called Pacifists, hate war. The rest of you rather like it. We will not allow you to have it. WE will stop it' (1916: 166).

Alix is nevertheless attracted by the idea of continuous mediation without armistice, a subject spoken to by a 'young, keen-faced, humorous woman, with a charming voice'. The combination of personal appeal and practical planning unites Alix's concern for the individual with her growing political awareness. She is also struck by her mother's speech on principles of non-belligerent education. 'Daphne wasn't running away from things, or from life: she was facing them and fighting them.' The account of the meeting as a whole, then, resembles a digest of the editorials of *Jus Suffragii* – with personal, sceptical commentary. At the end of it, however, there appears an almost apologetic interjection:

> Enough, more than enough, no doubt, has been said of a meeting so ordinary as to be familiar in outline to most people. That it was not familiar to Alix, who had hitherto avoided both meetings and literature on all subjects connected with the war, is why it is here recorded in some detail. There was some more of it, but it need not be here set down.
>
> (1916: 171)

Throughout, there is a similar uncertainty in the narrative voice. It almost seems to be apologising to a pacifist audience for stating the obvious. But then the ironic tone lends a confidence that belies any need to apologise, suggesting that the narrator really knows that the readership has not thought about things before in the way that Alix has done. The combination of evasive irony and documentary explication destabilises the tone of the novel. Macaulay here does not use irony to undermine an object of attack in the way Woolf does, for example, in *Jacob's Room*; instead it is used to mock commitment to a political position. On the other hand, the documentary element provides a counterweight to this scepticism. The problem revolves around a debate between art and politics. Alix has had to give up her art; can she take up politics in its place? And similarly, can an aesthetically viable novel, which seems to rely so much on detachment and irony, undermine its own mode of existence by espousing a political cause? The dialogue is never resolved. This is a novel *about* uncertainty: that very uncertainty disrupts its apparently urbane surface.

The novel ends on a note of decision but with a hint of sceptical reserve. Alix accompanies her mother on a tour of Cambridgeshire during which Daphne addresses meetings on the principles of the SPPP and receives a mixed reception. As a result of this tour, Alix makes the decision to join not only the SPPP but the church. It is a decision made in the knowledge of the complexity of the issues involved – not with the arrogance of self-righteousness. Daphne's conclusion is less absolute than Aurelia Leonard's 'conquest of the ideal over all the narrowing conditions of human existence' (Hamilton 1916: 357). She says: 'there's no fighting with whole truths in this life, and all we can do is to seize fragments of truth where we can find them, and use them as best we can. Poor weapons, perhaps, but all we've got' (Macaulay 1916: 173). Alix watches the sun set at the end of 1915 in a mood of ambivalence:

> The face of Cambridgeshire, the face of the new year, the face of the incoherent world, was dim and inscrutable, a dream lacking interpretation. So many people can provide, according to their several lights, both the dream and the interpretation thereof, but with how little accuracy!
>
> (1916: 183)

This amounts to an assertion that, although there can be no absolute values, one cannot simply give in to the chaos. The image of the dream could be replaced, in modern discourse, with the term 'ideology' to mean 'the imaginary relationship of individuals to their real conditions of existence' (Althusser 1971: 153). The 'realities' of socialist suffragist pacifism, and the systems of oppression which produce these dissident movements, appeal to Alix's subjectivity, which has been stranded and deprived of a plausible belief system as a result of the outbreak of war. She goes some way towards identifying with a system that her mother represents, thus acting out a drama of the psychological bond that psychoanalysts assume to exist between mothers and daughters. Unlike Daphne Leonard, however, she does not relinquish herself to this 'dream': she also identifies with revolutionary Christianity, which her mother rejects. On a conscious level, then, she is aware of a jostling network of doctrines and ideologies, seeking to claim her as their representative, but over which she has some degree of choice. That she does not collapse into her eventual decision with the 'jubilant assumption' that she has found a unified and dominating truth may be seen as a product of the psychology of the barren mid-war years, but also as a function of her own uncertainty about the role of the artist in political activity. Finally, however, it is a case of having to make a practical choice either to ignore the war or to try to prevent its horrifically destructive effects from devastating civilisation again. Fully aware of the limitations of an idealistic project, Alix thinks that a choice worth making.

Twenty years later . . .

Vera Brittain's *Honourable Estate* (1936) appeared twenty years after the novels by Hamilton and Macaulay, in the aftermath of Brittain's success with *Testament of Youth*. By this time the principles of the democratic suffragists and the UDC were seen to have been, if not discredited, at least disregarded: the peace treaty set out to humiliate the enemy, the League of Nations was ineffective in cases of international violence, women had gained the vote, but this did not guarantee them equal access to Parliament, the professions or industry. Brittain's novel nevertheless articulates a case for a pacifism based on women's distinctive values and marginalised political position. The argument is similar to that of Hamilton and Macaulay, but its perspective is different. The maternal pacifist is not a 'first generation' suffragist who sees the Hague Congress as the symbol of progress, but a grown-up daughter, Ruth Alleyndene, who probably knew nothing of the Women's International League during the war, and who worked as a VAD instead. Ruth, however, occupies alone the position negotiated between mother and daughter in the two earlier novels. She becomes integrated into the structures of love and marriage and into the political life of the Labour Party. Rather than being a novel about political uncertainty, *Honourable Estate* maintains that women can and must combine political awareness with motherhood – and that implies campaigning for peace.

The novel's schematic structure (Ruth and her husband 'resolve' the problems of gender and class generated by their parents) leads into a third section which is dominated by arguments that link together pacifism and motherhood. Again, much of the political argument of this section is delivered in the form of letter or public speech, a technique which recalls that of both *Dead Yesterday* and *Non-Combatants*. In this novel, however, the mundanities and trivialities of ordinary existence are settled by a good income and a devoted nanny, leaving room primarily for the 'lucid spaces' occupied by a clear political platform. Although in her non-fiction Brittain was to refer to the political blindness of the typical married woman (Brittain 1937: 60), in her fiction everything seems possible for the young, educated, experienced 'second-generation' feminist. Ruth writes to Denis about maternal involvement in politics:

I can't see how any intelligent mother nowadays dare refuse to be interested in politics, since politics are shaping our children's lives whether we like it or not. If our own mothers had been encouraged to learn what was going on in the world, instead of being told that their place was the home, the War might never have happened [. . .]. They were not allowed the knowledge or the chance to influence international relations, but I believe that *we* could prevent another war if we really put our backs into it. What's the use of having ideal children and a perfect

167

nursery, if you do nothing to stop them from being blown
to bits within the next twenty years!

(1936: 550–1)

The assumption is that the battle may be an old one but that
there are new weapons to hand – *newly*-enfranchised women, in
this case, just as there had been *nearly*-enfranchised women in
the literature written before 1918. It may seem odd that in 1936,
when the Second World War seemed inevitable to others, a
social-realist novel should present a world sealed in an earlier
period of political optimism. It is not, however, a satisfactory
explanation of this disjunction to dismiss it as romantic escapism. Brittain, in the mid-1930s, continued to believe just as
fervently in her pacifist ideals, and this novel, as much as her
anti-fascist writings, is a potent warning against allowing the
forces of masculine aggression to run unchecked. Pacifism, far
from being an escape, was a form of attack.

To be so single-mindedly optimistic and to celebrate the
success of her individualist heroine (Ruth Alleyndene becomes
a Labour MP as a result of the 1929 election) might be seen to
be, as Woolf's Mr Ramsay puts it, '[flying] in the face of facts'
(Woolf [1927] 1964: 37). The symbolism of the mother as a
new, humane, non-violent, progressive power relied on a dyadic
relationship between fact and fantasy which fulfilled a need: to
find a radical alternative to legalised slaughter in the affirmation
of life through the potent emblem of motherhood. The oscillation in the novels between realist narrative and pacifist
oratory, between heterosexual yearning and maternal-political
bonding, between the turgidity of the present and the hope for
the future, articulates the powerful but precarious nature of
that relationship. The next chapter examines the relationship
further, but with the emphasis on the politics of art, rather than
on the art of politics.

5

WOOLF, WAR AND WRITING
New words, new methods

Virginia Woolf did not join the VADs, the Land Army or the munitions workers. She knitted no socks, mourned no good soldier and didn't even participate in the political campaign against the war. Woolf came from a literary family and associated predominantly with an elite circle of writers and intellectuals, suffragists, socialists and pacifists with whose politics she broadly agreed. She was, however, no practical politician herself.[1] Although she encouraged the kind of political change that would eradicate patrilineal militarism, she was unwilling to engage with the systems that might enforce change. Her profession was that of writer, and it is the female literary artist's rendering of the war that will be examined here.

This is not to suggest that Woolf saw herself as a luminous creature existing above and beyond her own cultural conditions. I shall argue for three of her fictional texts to be read as 'war books', but not in the conventional sense of that term. They do not deal with trenches, bayonets and barbed wire, or even hospital discipline, munitions making or conditions on the home front. Woolf, in her writing, exploits the metaphorical over the metonymical potentialities of language. Rather than trammelling her characters in an associative sequence involving their appearance, possessions, friends and politics, she develops a narrative perspective which defamiliarises this realist mode of presentation. Moreover, she sees the obsession with linearity and unity as a peculiarly masculine condition. Woolf wrote as an 'outsider'. Her vision of the world that led to, and recovered from, the catastrophe of the First World War is fragmented, multiple-visioned, detached, ironic – the stuff, indeed, of literary modernism. It is also saturated with a desolate compassion for the grief that individuals suffered as a result of those four years. Woolf herself was not one of those individuals. Her vision is fuelled not by tragic personal experience in a sequence of cause and effect, but by the desire to expose the series of false constructs and dangerous values that produced one war and that underpinned the same social system that was heading relentlessly towards another. Her feminism and pacifism, then, find articulation in formal experiment.

Although Woolf was acquainted with Beatrice Webb, Pippa and Ray Strachey, Vernon Lee, Mary Hamilton and even Helena Swanwick, and greatly admired their courage and their commitment to instigating social change, she saw her own position differently. She made no effort to conceal the 'disillusion' that succeeded her first 'satisfactory thrill' when confronted with 'bodies of human beings in concert' (Bell 1979 [9 March 1918]: 125; [17 December 1918]: 229). Furthermore she had an instinctive distrust of politicians whether or not she supported their aims:

> these social reformers and philanthropists get so out of hand, and harbour so many discreditable desires under the guise of loving their kind, that in the end there's more to find fault with in them than in us [the artists].
>
> (Bell 1979 [11 July 1919]: 293)

Her artistic method was not to consolidate and defend a unitary position, but to create a system of multiple focus – 'one wanted fifty pairs of eyes to see with' (Woolf [1927] 1964: 224). In so doing, however, Woolf invites criticism from contemporary political philosophers like Jean Bethke Elshtain for 'derealizing the citizen' and from literary theorists like Elaine Showalter for 'fleeing into androgyny' or 'uterine withdrawal'.[2] This kind of criticism, while liberating for feminists seeking to fend off the image of 'woman' as the etherealised site of cultural excess, frequently speaks to the concerns of its own age and political orientation more clearly than it engages with the dilemmas of its subject. Woolf, in the 1920s, was attempting to create a radical critique of imperialist, Victorian structures of perception and evaluation. She relied on an ideological position not far removed from that in which Marshall and Swanwick were operating, and on a literary form that was similarly concerned to disperse the precepts of the prevailing patriarchal hegemony.

Woolf was all in favour of transgressing the boundaries of sexual codes, but not by violence. If the tools of one generation were seen to be useless for the next, the tools of one sex, equally, were useless for the other, if they were to be used only to build a similarly belligerent culture. Seen in the context of the thinking of Marshall, Swanwick and other feminist pacifists, Woolf's position seems less fugitive than her critics suggest. Like her contemporary pacifist role-models, she relied on the symbolism of women's alterity to confront and dismantle a linear, hierarchical, competitive system that was predicated on the repression of women and women's values. Unlike them she did not develop a programme of constitutional reform to enable these changes to take place.

MASCULINE FICTIONS

Woolf's best-known statement about the war is to be found in a letter to Margaret Llewelyn Davies, the secretary of the Women's Co-operative Guild. The letter was written in January 1916, when the Military Service Bill, which was to introduce the first wave of conscription, was in its final stages:

> I become steadily more feminist owing to The Times, which I read at breakfast and wonder how this pre-posterous masculine fiction [the war] keeps going a day longer – without some vigorous young woman pulling us together and marching through it – Do you see any sense in it? I feel as if I were reading about some curious tribe in Central Africa.
> (Nicolson 1976 [23 January 1916]: 76)

This statement, for all its flippancy, contains the nucleus of Woolf's association of feminism with anti-militarism. The war, as represented by the most powerful national newspaper, seemed an outrageous display of masculine pomposity that bore little relation to the complexity of reality – and needed to be exposed as such. Sybil Oldfield in her recent study of women pacifists interprets Woolf's use of the word 'fiction' in terms of Woolf's apparent inability to comprehend that there were indeed men screaming and dying in no-man's-land (Oldfield 1989: 104). This seems on the one hand to be too rigid an interpretation of 'fiction' as Woolf uses it, and on the other to involve a shift of focus on Oldfield's part from Woolf's object of attention – the newspaper – to the horrific scenes so inaccurately represented there. It is true that, living in Richmond in 1916 and recovering from mental illness, Woolf had little opportunity to engage with the war's more vibrant experiences. There were no men at the Front with whom she had a significant relationship. Leonard's brothers, Cecil and Philip, who were respectively killed and wounded in December 1917, were her only contacts of that kind. It is important to note, however, that her social and intellectual milieu was one of conscientious objectors and pacifists. Her brother, Adrian, was an NCF activist; Leonard Woolf, although not an absolutist pacifist, lectured for the UDC; Bertrand Russell was connected with both of these movements; other friends and acquaintances were accommodated at Philip and Ottoline Morrell's haven for conscientious objectors, Garsington Manor. Woolf occupied a marginal position as an opponent of the war, as a woman and as a practising writer, which allowed her to see the war as represented in *The Times* as a loathsome ideological construct. It is in this sense that the war seemed, to her, a fiction.

An examination of the pages of *The Times* sheds further light on Woolf's derisive attack. The newspaper was owned by Lord Northcliffe. He also owned and created the *Daily Mail*, was the most powerful Fleet Street figure and became director of enemy propaganda in 1918.[3] *The Times* of 22 January 1916 (presumably the issue to which Woolf was referring in particular) is given over almost entirely to war news. Interspersed with stories from the Russian Front, the German trenches, the dilution of labour at home and the dangers of rumour in wartime, are adverts for uniforms and for glorifying histories of the military victories that had been achieved during the previous year. The story that might have prompted Woolf's comment, though, was that of a crucial development in the militarisation of civilian life. The Military Service Bill, which was to introduce the first stage of conscription, was at that time before the House of Commons, and the Government was resisting an amendment which would provide for the granting of absolute certificates of exemption from military service. 'Obviously', says the report, 'this would have been fatal'. Fatal, one could argue, is precisely what such an amendment would not have been for those who had a principled objection to war. The Bill even received the support of the Labour leader and president of the Board of Education, Arthur Henderson, whose letter, published on the same day, reads: 'I do not see how any man can set his opinion on a military question against the conclusion of Lord Kitchener and the General Staff' (*The Times* 22 January 1916: 9). The voice of education and labour, then, advocated submission to military might. Civilian opinions were inadmissible. Women's opinions were nowhere to be found.

Celebrations of glory and honour were inscribed in the whole structure of the paper. Early war issues published patriotic poems by Kipling, Hardy and others, voicing proud, self-righteous sentiments in jaunty, quick-stepping rhythms:

> For all we have and are,
> For all our children's fate,
> Stand up and meet the war
> The hun is at the gate!
>
> (Kipling *The Times* 2 September 1914: 9)

Hardy's 'Song of the Soldiers' invokes a similar enthusiasm and the belief in England's righteousness:

> In our heart of hearts believing
>   Victory crowns the just,
>   And that braggarts must
>   Surely bite the dust
> March we to the field ungrieving
> In our heart of hearts believing
>   Victory crowns the just.
>
> (Hardy *The Times* 9 September 1914: 9)

Even the list of the dead – 'The Roll of Honour' – is named in terms that reflect chivalric discourse, and a ubiquitous vocabulary occurs in the description of those awarded military decorations. 'Conspicuous gallantry and devotion', 'fine offensive spirit', 'courage and endurance' unite and privilege those awarded DSOs over the variety of human experience omitted from the paper (*The Times* 18 September 1917: 2). The discourse of triumph is reinforced by the general usage of the pronouns 'we' and 'our' to give a sense of unity and common purpose. 'Our tactics in France', 'cost us very little in men', 'all we need is patience' are phrases used in an interview with General Smuts in *The Times* (19 September 1917: 6). The illusion created is one of intimacy, total participation and complete control, a mystique necessary in the prosecution of a successful war, as Eric Leed has pointed out (Leed 1979: 41). This, alongside lists of 'the fallen' often taking up five columns out of six of a page in *The Times*, can be seen as a reduction of human and social life to the dictates of a single national enterprise, which was, as far as Woolf was concerned, not only meaningless in the face of female experience, but largely irrelevant to the complexity of reality. 'The Northcliffe papers do all they can to insist upon the indispensability & delight of war' she noted in her diary (Bell 1979 [12 October 1918]: 200). This, then, was the 'preposterous masculine fiction' of the war. Militarism symbolised, not glory and liberation, but, as she observed having witnessed soldiers traversing a square, 'A disagreeable impression of control and senseless determination' (Bell 1979 [14 October 1917]: 59).

Woolf took issue not only with the ideological dominance of war reporting, but also with the literary fictions that gave it prominence. Her on-going battle with Wells, Bennett and Galsworthy, enacted through the pages of what are now conceived of as modernist manifestoes, 'Modern Fiction' and 'Mr Bennett and Mrs Brown', can be seen as something greater than a clash of literary styles if we turn once more to *The Times*. Irene Cooper Willis's analysis of newspaper propaganda in *England's Holy War* (1928) and the journalistic excesses of Nigel Strode in Mary Hamilton's *Dead Yesterday* illustrate the chivalric appeal of newspaper language at the beginning of the war. This was not, however, the language only of journalists, military men and politicians. On 18 September 1914, there appeared in *The Times* a letter vigorously supporting the war. Published simultaneously in the *New York Times*, and entitled 'A Righteous War', the letter argues that Britain could 'not without dishonour' have refused to defend the neutrality of Belgium, the 'weak and unoffending country'. It is a statement of the British subject's obligation to defy 'the iron military bureaucracy of Prussia', and is couched not in militaristic terms but in the form of a moral tract on Britain's 'destiny and duty', pitting the 'brute force' of Prussia against the 'free constitutions' of Western Europe. The letter was signed by fifty-two well-known authors including Wells, Bennett, Galsworthy, Hardy, Kipling, A.C. Bradley, Sir Arthur Quiller-Couch – and May Sinclair. Brought together by C.F.G. Masterman, the head of the British War Propaganda

Bureau, these celebrated writers produced pamphlets, articles and books, specially commissioned then distributed by commercial publishers, in an effort to win the war by propaganda (cf. Buitenhuis [1987] 1989: 14–20).

Wells, Bennett and Galsworthy, as well as being signatories to the above letter, were members of Charles Masterman's War Propaganda Bureau. Wells composed numerous newspaper articles, particularly attacking the pacifist movement, and was the celebrated author of *The War That Will End War* (Buitenhuis [1987] 1989: 120–1). Galsworthy's propaganda was widely published in the United States as well as in the British press (Buitenhuis [1987] 1989: 43) and Bennett, who figured most prominently as an object of Woolf's attack, was the most diligent and productive of the three. Author of over 300 propaganda articles, he, by October 1918, was running the Ministry of Information, in sole charge of British Propaganda (Buitenhuis [1987] 1989: 138). Woolf's question 'what is reality? And who are the judges of reality? (Woolf [1924] 1966: 325) is generally thought to reveal the heart of her feminist aesthetic. In the specific context of war propaganda, however, it is even more illuminating. If 'reality' is not what we have been led to believe – the biographies of great men, the stories of battles, the material details of Mrs Brown's income and her hot-water bottle – its self-appointed judges, when they are also the perpetrators of the 'preposterous masculine fiction' of war, are barbarously misguided.

It is not difficult to see, then, a link between 'masculine fiction' and war propaganda. There is a double focus on the word 'fiction': it is at once a cultural construct and a literary convention. Woolf's literary confrontation with the war is based on a search for alternative figurations, a refusal to heroicise and to reduce to a single Symbolic Order the 'myriad impressions' that the mind receives. With her privileges of class and capital, Woolf could afford to situate herself in opposition to the dominant Symbolic Order in terms of political allegiance, occupation and publishing practice. She had not only her room and her money, but also her own press. The rest of this chapter will examine Woolf's novels of the 1920s – *Jacob's Room, Mrs Dalloway* and *To the Lighthouse* – in relation to the way the independent artist's vision of the war informs the development of her feminist pacifism. Underlying her writing is a distrust of

175

political institutions as intrinsically 'masculine', and a desire to create alternative, subversive strategies. Her texts, then, in their representation of feminist identity, their attention to the war-induced breakdown of the social construction of gender and their rendering of the question of inheritance, will be seen to enact a paradox: they perform a radical critique of existing power structures while avoiding an aggressive methodology. They are not confrontational.

JACOB'S ROOM

Jacob's Room can be read as a mock obituary. Obituaries of fallen officers (not their men) regularly accompanied *The Times*' Roll of Honour and adhered to a hierarchy of social indicators to establish the status and identity of their subject. If these were not, as in 'Mr Bennett and Mrs Brown', house, income and hot-water bottle, they were school (public), university (Oxbridge) and military rank and regiment. Woolf despises those masculine institutions, not only because they are governed by a certain class and gender, but because they are the producers of an insular, self-aggrandising, monolithic persona – the 'monstrous male' – whose identity and traditions will lead him to accept war as a natural and honourable way of resolving disputes.

The feminist pacifist argument in the novel arises from the dialogic relationship between the narrator and her subject. The narrator is of the same class as Jacob, but of the opposite sex, and therefore she lacks access to his institutions and mental habits. This rather baffled narrative stance is an early manifestation of that of the 'Outsider', developed by Woolf in *Three Guineas* (1938), another text written in the shadow of war (the Spanish Civil War was in progress and the Second World War imminent). The argument of *Three Guineas* is that there is a certain masculine line of progression, from public school to university to the professions, which encourages exclusiveness, proprietorship and prejudice, attitudes which, in their turn, generate a predisposition towards war. Women can subvert the latter tendency by practising resistance, which will reveal the manifest absurdities of masculinist ideology. The absurdity exposed by *Jacob's Room*, for instance, is that Jacob, the perfect product of this ideology, should be killed by it in the 'Great' war. The ideology thus consumes itself and war becomes a metaphor for this monstrous cycle of self-destruction. Trapped within its internal logic, its victims see war (and male dominance) as inevitable and reasonable. Woolf sought ways of standing outside it to reveal it as madness.

Reading *Jacob's Room* as a satire on the convention of obituary writing suggests the double focus of Woolf's critique. The masculine 'procession' towards death in battle parallels the effacement of individual characteristics by the institutions of social privilege. The following is a typical *Times* obituary:

> Lieutenant Thomas Gair, RFA, who was killed on September 9, aged 28 was the only surviving son of the late John Hamilton Gair and of Mrs Gair, of Brunt How, Skelworth Bridge, Westmorland. He was educated at Malvern College, where he gained an entrance scholarship, and at New College, Oxford, where he graduated with second class honours in history, and was articled to Sir Harcourt Clare at the County Council offices, Preston. When the war broke out he obtained a commission in the RFA, and had been at the front since last January.
>
> (*The Times* 19 September 1917: 9)

Such writing posits an unchallenged relationship between class and education and class and bravery, but not between class and self-destruction. In Woolf's work, however, the social structures that produce school, university, profession and regiment are seen as having a causal relation to each other, as if operating on a metonymic line of progression which embodies a self-fulfilling principle: if Rugby and Cambridge, *therefore* death in battle.

Woolf, by turning this convention inside out in *Jacob's Room*, is challenging both the phallocentric order that has produced these self-destructive categories and the reliability of these markers as indicators of 'character'. Thus we only hear of Jacob's going to Rugby, glimpse him through estranged eyes at Cambridge, and merely guess at the nature of his employment – 'while letters accumulate in a basket, Jacob signs them' ([1922] 1976: 19; 40–2; 87). It is left to the reader to interpret the historical events, to deduce that war has been declared and that Jacob has fought and been killed in it. We have seen Catherine Marshall and Helena Swanwick celebrating women's capacity to value 'diversity, variety, adaptability, freedom' over the strictures of regimentation or organisation for production

(Swanwick [1915a] 1971: 32). Woolf pursues a similar line of argument through her self-consciously literary form. Disconnected fragments of Jacob's personal, social and intellectual life are vividly presented in chronological sequence but without a naturalising teleology that alerts us to the tragedy and pathos of Jacob's death. The book pretends not to know that Jacob will die. Sentimentalism, heroism and pity do not clog up the text. An attitude of narrative indifference to conventional masculine pieties means that the war appears at the end not as a resolution nor a justification, but simply as shocking by virtue of its irrelevance to the female gaze.

The significance of this, surely, is that although the war appeared suddenly to plunge Europe into darkness, patriarchal consciousness was already in so benighted a state as to be unable to perceive the course of events as inevitable. An alternative consciousness reveals that the war is imminent in Edwardian culture just as it is present throughout *Jacob's Room* – not overtly, but embedded in the texture of its imagery. The very name 'Jacob Flanders' maps out his teleology. 'Jacob' means 'follower' or 'supplanter'; Flanders, obviously, refers to the slaughter of the battlefield. Woolf's novel builds on the concerns articulated in, for example, *Dead Yesterday* and *Non-Combatants*, but it employs different narrative strategies. Instead of having an Aurelia Leonard or a Daphne Sandomir as an authoritative, female, pacifist seer, there is a multiplicity of female characters each of whom sees different things and a female narrator who claims no great responsibility for her subject on the grounds that 'it's no good trying to sum people up' ([1922] 1976: 28; 150). The oscillations are not between the personal and the political, but between the uncolonised narrator and her elusive, colonised subject; the text closes on a note of loss rather than of resolution. The argument does not take place through the consciousness of a central character, but in the dialogic spaces between characters and narrator, and through the cultural inflections of the images. The narrator is anonymous, a space, like Jacob, to be filled with words; thus her criticisms are implicit rather than explicit, her challenges oblique rather than inflammatory.

The narrator, by her own admission, is older, female, and not entirely reliable. The focalisation is external – there is no distinction between the narrator and the focaliser – but that which is focalised shifts between external and internal view points. The narrator adopts a particular ideological stance. As she is female, her narration *has* to be partly imagined. She is forced into the modernist stance of alienation and plurality rather than dogmatic unity, and her 'realist' descriptions are thus parodic of the masculine 'materialists', whose dominance she sought to subvert. A female consciousness, she slips into the minds of some to allow them to speak, but is refused admittance to others; nips in to Jacob's room when he is not there, but is unquestionably outside when it is populated by his male friends. It is as though she has taken on the job of narrating Jacob's life without really being qualified to do it – and in that lack of qualification lies the book's ironic structure.

The narrator's relation to her subject, then, is ambivalent in terms of both her disposition towards him and her access to him. The literary privilege of free indirect discourse allows her into Mr Plumer's head on the subject of dons' luncheon parties ([1922] 1976: 31) and into Jacob's on the subject of women in chapel. She can follow the external signs of an argument 'Now . . . It follows . . . That is so' ([1922] 1976: 47). She can see part of Jacob's room:

> This black wooden box, upon which his name was still legible in white paint, stood between the long windows of the sitting-room. The street ran beneath. No doubt the bedroom was behind.
>
> (Woolf [1922] 1976: 67)

But there are certain male preserves that she cannot enter. Jacob spends some time up at Cambridge. In *A Room of One's Own* Woolf gives a lively and comic description of women's exclusion from this handsomely funded seat of learning. In *Jacob's Room* the satire is more acerbic. It is the evening. 'The young men were now back in their rooms. Heaven knows what they were doing' ([1922] 1976: 40). They are presumably reading, smoking, sprawling, talking, trying to work out the meaning of it all:

> It's damnably difficult. But, after all, not so difficult if on the next staircase, in the large room, there are two, three, five young men all convinced of this – of brutality, that is, and the clear division between right and wrong.
>
> ([1922] 1976: 41)

They are all in concert. They are all convinced, like the Northcliffe press, that there is a clear division between right and wrong and that they are aware of its nature. A common tradition binds them together. The narrator, and by implication, all women, is not part of this tradition. She stands outside and watches a scene of urbane masculine companionship, as if through a window:

> The answer came from the sofa corner; for his pipe was held in the air, then replaced. Jacob wheeled round. He had something to say to that, though the sturdy red-haired boy at the table seemed to deny it, wagging his head slowly from side to side . . . .
>
> ([1922] 1976: 41)

Eventually Jacob comes to his window and looks out over the quad, enabling his chronicler to get a better look at him:

> He looked satisfied; indeed masterly; which expression changed slightly as he stood there, the sound of the clock conveying to him (it may be) a sense of old buildings and time; and himself the inheritor; and then to-morrow; and friends; at the thought of whom, in sheer confidence and pleasure, it seemed, he yawned and stretched himself.
>
> ([1922] 1976: 42)

Jacob drinks in the way of thought, the way of life, and with it a sense of possession and authority. Interestingly, the text does not allow a distinction between the narrator's actually witnessing these scenes and her imagining them. The parenthetical '(it may be)' and 'it seemed' defamiliarise Jacob's authoritative stance by drawing attention to the narrative devices necessary to present the invasion of a character's consciousness. This parodic act teasingly threatens to unravel the portrait of Jacob that is being constructed. Tradition, confidence, unity of mind are not so clearly available to the woman narrator. In *A Room of One's Own* Woolf's narrator speaks of the irrelevance of the 'weight, the pace, the stride of a man's mind' ([1929] 1977: 73) to women, and of the opposite of this unified position, the division of consciousness, the multiplicity of subject positions and one's oscillation between them:

> if one is a woman one is often surprised by a sudden

splitting off of consciousness, say in walking down Whitehall, when from being the natural inheritor of that civilization, she becomes, on the contrary, outside of it, alien
and critical. Clearly the mind is always altering its focus,
and bringing the world into different perspectives.

([1929] 1977: 93)

So woman's perspective on tradition – or civilization – is,
according to Woolf, frequently assailed by the fragmentation of
that perspective and by the female subject's oscillations –
between power and denial, being the inheritor and being the
outsider. She sees masculine tradition as comparatively monolithic, female perception as capable of more variety as it is less
rigidly fixed into, and has less to gain from, patriarchal tradition. Jacob may be 'the inheritor' – but of what? A masculine
fiction, whose legacy is violent death.

This difference of view amounts to a critique of the linear,
masculine progression towards war where Jacob's name and his
fate collide. That progression starts at Rugby and continues at
Cambridge, where Jacob's sense of his own masterliness is
bound up with the blind and menacing characteristics of
militarism. This scene is in the chapel:

> Look, as they pass into service, how airily the gowns blow
> out, as though nothing dense and corporeal were within.
> What sculptured faces, what certainty, authority con-
> trolled by piety, although great boots march under the
> gowns. In what orderly procession they advance. Thick
> wax candles stand upright; young men rise in white
> gowns; while the subservient eagle bears up for inspection
> the great white book.
>
> ([1922] 1976: 29)

Even academic life implies militarism. Great boots march under
the gowns; beneath each student is a soldier. The sinister image
of gowns shrouding incorporeality suggests both the delusion
of spirituality and the lack of the sensual (one is reminded of
Cixous's call for women to 'write. . .their bodies' (Cixous [1975]
1981: 245)); authority, merely, and empty piety prevail. The
men merge into the ritual (wax candles, white gowns), the
eagle, symbol of war and imperial power, is fused with the
transmission of the Gospel, in its subservience to the rulebook.

And the procession, deathly already, is to be towards death. Woolf's tactic in *Three Guineas* is to undermine this kind of display with mockery, 'here you mount a carved chair; here you appear to pay homage to a piece of painted wood' ([1938] 1977: 24), while still associating such ceremony with bellicosity. Here the anger and disdain for absurd, exclusive practices is perhaps less outspoken, but nevertheless implicit.

Plumer is one of Jacob's tutors. General Sir Herbert Plumer, GBE, GVCO, commanded the Second Army of the British Expeditionary Force, 1915–17, and was responsible for the successful offensive on the Messines and Wytschaete Plateau. It is impossible to tell whether Woolf was fully conscious of this, but the names, nevertheless, again link Cambridge with the army. The nature of both is to constrict and mould individuality into conformity. Jacob has his youthful conviction: '"I am what I am, and intend to be it", for which there will be no form in the world unless Jacob makes one for himself. The Plumers will try to prevent him from making it' ([1922] 1976: 33–4). The 'Plumers', then, seem to represent the crippling effect of academic conventions. On Plumer's shelves stand books by Wells and Shaw: on his table are 'serious sixpenny weeklies written by pale men in muddy boots – the weekly creak and screech of brains rinsed in cold water and wrung dry – melancholy papers' ([1922] 1976: 32). But the pallor and the boots also suggest the sullen, disciplined soldier who has his roots in the student. Three professors, of Greek, science and philosophy, exemplify the strategic rigours of the academic brain. Professor Huxtable's mental activity is described in overtly militaristic terms:

> Now, as his eye goes down the print, what a procession tramps through the corridors of his brain, orderly, quick-stepping, and reinforced, as the march goes on, by fresh runnels, till the whole hall, dome, whatever one calls it, is populous with ideas. Such a muster takes place in no other brain.
>
> ([1922] 1976: 37)

Professor Sopwith is always 'summing things up'; Professor Cowan is 'the builder, assessor, surveyor, [. . .] ruling lines between names, hanging lists above doors'. A former student would eagerly send his son to these icons of intelligence in order to maintain their prestigious traditions. 'A woman,' interpolates the narrator, 'divining the priest, would, involuntarily, despise' ([1922] 1976: 39).

That Jacob has inherited this combative manner of thinking is evident from the descriptions of his own mind at work. The exercise of the trained masculine mind – its drill – takes the form of sustained rational argument and is steeped in potential violence:

> The eyes fix themselves upon the poker, the right hand takes the poker and lifts it; turns it slowly round, and then, very accurately, replaces it. The left hand, which lies on the knee, plays some stately but intermittent piece of march music. A deep breath is taken; but allowed to evaporate unused. The cat marches across the hearth-rug. No one observes her.
>
> ([1922] 1976: 47)

While on one level this is simply a paradigm of the dynamics of serious discussion, the brute force latent in the imagery is an indication of the restrictive discipline and competition that governs the mental composition of the academically 'successful'. The alternative vision of the female narrator again interrupts. The two men are sailing round the south-west coast of England while Jacob is attempting to master the argument. 'What was the coast of Cornwall' she asks, 'with its violet scents, and mourning emblems, and tranquil piety, but a screen happening to hang straight behind as his mind marched up?' ([1922] 1976: 47).

The derogatory images of discipline and militarism, then, and their feminine equivalents, structure the entire novel. Take, for instance, an apparently independent series of images centring on Jacob's boyhood passion for catching butterflies and moths:

> The upper wings of the moth which Jacob held were undoubtedly marked with kidney-shaped spots of a fulvous hue. But there was no crescent on the underwing. The tree had fallen the night he caught it. There had been a volley of pistol-shots suddenly in the depths of the wood.
>
> The tree had fallen, though it was a windless night, and the lantern, stood upon the ground, had lit up the still

green leaves and the dead beech leaves. It was a dry place.
A toad was there. And the red underwing had circled
round the light and flashed and gone.

([1922] 1976: 21)

Initially this may seem to have nothing to do with the war. An
enigmatic sequence of symbols, it might appear obliquely
elegiac, mysterious and threatening but little more. A note of
violence, however, is soon introduced when we hear that, the
next day, 'the painted ladies and the peacocks feasted upon
bloody entrails dropped by a hawk' – an uneasy description for,
as butterflies do not feed on flesh, the anthropomorphic con-
notations suggest that human beings are the veiled object of
description. It is this conflation that suggests the link with the
war. The sequence recalls (and anticipates) juxtapositions of
the evanescently beautiful and the savagely massacred in more
explicit war writing. Furthermore, the suggestion of gender
stereotyping is reiterated in the romantic sub-plot between the
conventional, 'inanimate' beauties, Helen Aitken and Jimmy.
The dance of courtship between these social butterflies is made
irrelevant by the war. Helen ends up 'visiting hospitals' while
Jimmy, recalling the entrails dropped by the hawk, 'feeds crows
in Flanders' ([1922] 1976: 93).

When the image of the fallen tree next occurs it is held in
direct contrast with the passage describing the choristers at
Cambridge. The lantern is compared with the chapel: 'As the
sides of a lantern protect the flame so that it burns steady even
in the wildest night – burns steady and gravely illumines the tree-
trunks – so inside the Chapel all was orderly.' This description
of ritualistic orderliness is linked by three points of suspension
to a further elaboration of the above episode:

If you stand a lantern under a tree every insect in the forest
creeps up to it – a curious assembly, since though they
scramble and swing and knock their heads against the
glass they seem to have no purpose – something senseless
inspires them. One gets tired of watching them, as they
amble round the lantern and blindly tap as if for admittance, one large toad being the most besotted of any and
shouldering his way through the rest. Ah, but what's that?
A terrifying volley of pistol-shots rings out – cracks sharply;
ripples spread – silence laps smooth over sound. A tree – a

tree has fallen, a sort of death in the forest. After that the wind in the trees sounds melancholy.

([1922] 1976: 30)

The lamp of learning (and, on a larger scale, the craving for unitary meaning) is thus like the lantern in the forest. The students entering the chapel are driven on by 'something senseless': the 'light' of the civilised man's ritualised drive towards self-destruction. The apparent urbanity of educated masculinity is parodied by the unfavourable comparison with the meaningless scramble of the insects and the toad, reminding one of Woolf's 'disagreeable impression of control and senseless determination' as she witnesses a company of marching soldiers.

This undignified image, then, is juxtaposed with a 'volley of pistol-shots'. This might be read simply as a metaphor for the sound of a tree finally splitting apart as it falls. But the political implication of the metaphor is surely inescapable: it recalls the sound of gun-fire in battle, or of the firing squad for cowardice and desertion. The image of 'a death in the forest' recalls the blasted forests on the Western Front. It also anticipates Jacob's death and perhaps suggests the inevitable death of civilisation which will result from the remorseless, combative, onward movement. In this symbolic context, the melancholy wind suggests a chorus of universal mourning. In the midst of a similarly senseless procession across Waterloo Bridge, reminiscent of the London Bridge scene in *The Waste Land*, hordes of commuters rush to catch the Surbiton train: 'One might think that reason impelled them', the narrator remarks ironically. 'No, no. It is the drums and trumpets' ([1922] 1976: 109). Drums and trumpets impel, just as the light of religion or patriotism attracts. They are, on the one hand, emblems of 'the ecstacy and hubbub of the soul' ([1922] 1976: 110), on the other a show of bravado used by armies to incite feelings of communal strength and invincibility. In the midst of this human scramble there passes a lorry 'with great forest trees chained to it', closely followed by a van laden with tombstones ([1922] 1976: 109). Processions, then, are metaphorically linked with fallen trees, with chains and with death. Commuters, soldiers, undergraduates, all, when viewed from the outsider's position, are no more than a cloud of besotted insects, struggling, stupidly, towards extinction.

The hints of the onset of war, the submerged images, the implicit critique, are all brought together in the final pages of *Jacob's Room*. Murmurs of Home Rule in Ireland, criticism of Asquith and the state of the British Empire ([1922] 1976: 95; 132; 135) come to a head in a description of mass slaughter:

> The battleships ray out over the North Sea, keeping their stations accurately apart. At a given signal all the guns are trained on a target which (the master gunner counts the seconds, watch in hand – at the sixth he looks up) flames into splinters. With equal nonchalance a dozen young men in the prime of life descend with composed faces into the depths of the sea; and there impassively (though with perfect mastery of machinery) suffocate uncomplainingly together. Like blocks of tin soldiers the army covers the cornfield, moves up the hillside, stops, reels slightly this way and that, and falls flat, save that, through field-glasses, it can be seen that one or two pieces still agitate up and down like fragments of broken matchstick.
>
> ([1922] 1976: 151)

The insect-like procession leads to discipline which leads to this kind of death. The young men, like Jacob, are all in the prime of life, maybe amongst them are the 'six young men' upon whom, the narrator ironically remarks, the future depends ([1922] 1976: 103). The adverbs and adjectives deliberately underplay the tragedy of the occasion with an irony that has come to be associated with First World War literature:[4] 'with nonchalance', 'composed', 'impassively', 'uncomplainingly'. The vocabulary suggests captive passivity rather than active heroism. Organicism is replaced with mechanisation and blind obedience. The absurdity that juxtaposes the precision of the destructive weaponry with the *equality* of response on the part of the soldiers comes close to bad taste in its black humour: this is the approved imperial manner of meeting one's death – with perfect mastery of machinery.

Woolf's satire goes further. Not only is it a preposterous state of affairs that elderly, 'bald, red-veined, hollow-looking' men should so calmly dispose of the lives of so many young men, but that these patriarchs should further consolidate their position by insisting that the 'incessant commerce of banks, laboratories, chancellories and houses of business, are the strokes that oar the world forward', creating an 'unseizable force' that 'the novelists never catch' ([1922] 1976: 152). A powerful description of the energy of imperialism appeared in Wells's *The New Machiavelli*, published in 1911:

> I traverse Victoria Street [. . .] where the Agents of the Empire jostle one another, pass the big embassies in the West End [. . .] follow the broad avenue that leads to Buckingham Palace, witness the coming and going of troops and officials and guests along it from every land on earth . . .
>
> (Wells [1911] 1946: 231)

This passage, celebrating the power, extent and riches of the Empire, comes to a climax with the 'challenging knowledge' that 'You and your kind might still, if you could but grasp it here, mould all the destiny of Man!' (Wells [1911] 1946: 231). Woolf's narrative is surely parodying the egotistical, colonialist arrogance of this Wellsian breed of men, who decree 'that the course of history should shape itself this way or that way, being manfully determined, as their faces showed, to impose some coherency upon Rajahs and Kaisers and the muttering in bazaars' (Woolf [1922] 1976: 168). The satirical drive behind Woolf's text is the desire not only to expose the colonising aggression of her political and literary adversaries, but also to ridicule their assumption that they exclusively know, and are capable of judging, 'reality'.

For Woolf's narrator 'a profound, impartial, and absolutely just opinion of our fellow-creatures is utterly unknown', but, simultaneously, she believes, we are capable of being surprised by a vision of a 'young man in a chair' as 'of all things in the world the most real the most solid the best known to us. [. . .] Such is the manner of our seeing. Such the conditions of our love' ([1922] 1976: 69). The text is built upon this paradox. Thus the elegiac, mourning sound 'Ja-cob! Ja-cob!' 'solitary, unanswered, breaking against the rocks' ([1922] 1976: 7) with which the book opens is repeated at the end by Clara Durrant and by Bonamy, the two people who love Jacob. Like the image of the melancholy wind in the trees, it registers a devastating loss. Meanwhile, however, lest the novel should slip into sentimentality, the tragedy is underplayed. Betty Flanders hears a noise in the distance. 'The guns?' she asks herself:

Again, far away, she heard the dull sound, as if nocturnal women were beating great carpets. There was Morty lost, and Seabrook dead; her sons fighting for their country. But were the chickens safe? Was that someone moving downstairs? Rebecca with the toothache? No. The nocturnal women were beating great carpets. Her hens shifted slightly on their perches.

([1922] 1976: 172)

At the last moment, then, Betty dilutes 'masculine' concerns with 'female' worries. Even the noise of the shells is perceived in whimsical, domestic terms. Her final gesture is to hold Jacob's shoes out to Bonamy in an act which symbolises a profound yet unromantic acknowledgement of his absence. Who, the text seems to ask, given this massive interruption of the masculine procession, is to fill these shoes? Jacob has been the inheritor merely of a deathly patriotism. This text, unlike Woolf's two subsequent novels, provides him with no suitable heir.

A detached anger and satire, then, dominate *Jacob's Room*. The narrator is by turns baffled and timid and frustrated and irritated by her exclusion, seeming to say '*This* is what will happen if you persist in your desire to dominate'. Sybil Oldfield believes that *Jacob's Room* fails because its ironies cancel each other out: Jacob is so vague a figure that we remain unmoved by his death (Oldfield 1989: 105). This reading, however, surely overlooks the structure of the novel's images, which suggests both the limitations of the rational capacity to know and the seemingly limitless human capacity to love. The problem with masculine institutions – and a national consciousness that identifies itself by them – is that they obscure the lovable with what they take to be the knowable: the principles of combat, control and competition that govern patriarchal capitalism. Thus the war is seen to be present in all masculine practices and institutions if only we care to look. The external focaliser – the female narrator – can defamiliarise what is taken to be 'normal', and 'normality' is patently absurd and destructive. Although Woolf's technique may be oblique, the effect is inflammatory: to initiate an investigation of the ideologies that structure our ways of seeing and to allow the shock of the war to *remain* a shock, rather than permitting its assimilation into the codes of sentimentality.

MRS DALLOWAY: THE WORLD HAS RAISED ITS WHIP

Mrs Dalloway (1925) is set on a June day in 1923, and simultaneously looks back to the war's destruction and forwards to the possibilities for reconstruction. The novel's major relationship is enacted in the dialogical space between two individuals who never meet – Septimus and Clarissa – and who have entirely different experiences of the way in which the Symbolic Order has apportioned meaning to their lives. The strategy is similar to that used in *Jacob's Room*. A confrontation between an older woman and a young man is established, but never depicted according to the conventions of literary realism; that is to say in terms of the verbal debate represented in reported speech between, for example, Aurelia Leonard and Nigel Strode in *Dead Yesterday*. The 'dialogue' in *Mrs Dalloway*, then, is more metaphorical than metonymic. Furthermore, the female element in this no longer operates in the privileged, directorial narrative role. Although we have a visible 'heroine', Clarissa Dalloway has none of the political vision and fortitude of the feminist pacifist sages in Hamilton and Macaulay's novels. Mrs Dalloway is a trivial woman who represents a dying age. Her own ideological position, in all its contradictoriness, is set in play with that of Septimus, Doris Kilman and the doctors Holmes and Bradshaw, with the war as an obscured but central point of reference.

The war is more clearly visible in this novel than in *Jacob's Room* as a massive social eruption which continues to interrupt daily life long after the Armistice. Like *Jacob's Room*, *Mrs Dalloway* articulates two separate value systems. One is an object of satire: the strokes that oar the world forward, the men in clubs and cabinets, the dominant masculine ideology of 'progression' through education to war. This system is characterised in *Mrs Dalloway* by the linear time which marks the progress of the day: the leaden circles (or strokes) of the phallic symbol of male government, Big Ben. The procession of imperial masculinity reforms this time under the gaze of Peter Walsh, a child-like man of 53, who is happy to have escaped a stolid masculine conformity. He is, however, arrested by a menacing image:

> Boys in uniform, carrying guns, marched with their eyes
> ahead of them, marched, their arms stiff, and on their

faces an expression like the letters of a legend written round the base of a statue praising duty, gratitude, fidelity, love of England.

([1925] 1976: 47)

Even the metaphor that figures the expression on their faces has a metonymic link with the statues they pass on their way up Whitehall, and which they already resemble. Furthermore, they are 'boys', 16 year olds, whose ordinary, diverse, rebellious civilian attitudes have been militarised so that they march:

as if one will worked legs and arms uniformly, and life, with its varieties, its irreticencies, had been laid under a pavement of monuments and wreaths and drugged into a stiff yet staring corpse by discipline.

([1925] 1976: 47)

The militarists with their imperial values, their linear time and their Acts of Parliament march straight through the centre of *Mrs Dalloway*, producing a cultural and ideological divide, with 'One Law – One, Purifying, Transcendent Guarantor of the ideal interest of the community' dominating over a 'polymorphic, orgasmic body, desiring and laughing' which provides a sublimated alternative (cf. Kristeva [1974] 1986: 19).

The alternative, and dependent, value system employs a more spatial than linear sense of time. Clarissa's consciousness flicks back through chronological time, recreates scenes at Bourton, re-lives her lesbian passion for Sally Seton and maintains this created space in the present. She feels herself and her friends to co-exist through time, to 'live in each other' ([1925] 1976: 10), so that their ego-boundaries are permeable, not incarcerated in a singular 'transcendent' identity. This joyful pluralism, though, is held in check by the strictures of the passage of time. Clarissa's sense of the past is coloured by passions irrecoverable in their entirety and, in their entirety, incompatible with the 'Mrs Richard Dalloway' that she has become.

As in *Jacob's Room* the structure of images subverts patriarchal linearity. But there is a shift in tone between the two novels. If *Jacob's Room* represents an internalized battle of the sexes, *Mrs Dalloway* is more forgiving, registering not only the absurdity but also the tragic damage of the war. The novel is also less willing to divide the social schema into a simple binary opposition between masculine militarism and feminine vitality. The events of 1914–18 may have created a chasm between 'war' and 'women' and alienated the latter further from the public world, but women in this novel are not exonerated from their share in the reproduction of social life simply on the grounds of their gender. The 'public-spirited, British Empire, tariff-reform, governing-class spirit' ([1925] 1976: 69) is embodied as much in women as in men: Mrs Foxcroft at the Embassy, Lady Bexborough, opening a bazaar with a telegram in her hand telling of the death of her son, the 'martial' Lady Bruton, talking about politics 'like a man' and trying to write letters to *The Times*. Clarissa, too, has imbibed some of it. On the other hand, Peter is a largely unsuccessful male in terms of the rigid expectations of his class, and Septimus is a sympathetic victim of the inherent violence of gender stereotyping. The lines of battle, then, are not so clearly drawn. 'Every woman' is not permitted to be 'nicer' than 'any man' (Woolf [1922] 1976: 9). *Mrs Dalloway* suggests oscillations between subject identifications in an effort to deconstruct the unified vision which, in the context of war, prioritises a version of masculinity that is inherently deathly.

In this novel the war seems to act as an ideological border, enforcing choice and allegiance, severing all links with a mythical, integrated past and insisting on a monolithic patriotism. Doris Kilman is as much a victim of this on grounds of race as Septimus is on grounds of gender. Kilman, originally the German 'Kiehlman', unlike the German governesses in the more popular war stories,[5] was not a spy and had no intention of blowing up the major lines of communication. She was, however, forced, as a result of the war, to relinquish her career and subsequently battles with the injustices of her oppression. On one level she is deeply – and offensively – patronised by the novel's narrator as one of the ugly and uncouth by the standards of the jewelled, elitist world that Clarissa inhabits. She perspires, she grasps, she tries to seduce Elizabeth away from her mother's superficial culture and parties. She wears a green mackintosh 'year in, year out' ([1925] 1976: 12) (rather like Margaret Grey's 'unpardonable raincoat' in *The Return of the Soldier*), and appears to the privileged Clarissa to be one of the 'dominators and tyrants', enforcing on the lady of the house a sense of comparative inferiority which should not 'naturally' be her due ([1925] 1976: 13).

We should not forget, however, that Kilman's career was thwarted by the war. The unifying dictates of propagandist England, where Germans were first terrorised and later imprisoned, could not accommodate her alternative views. She has lost her job in a school:

> Miss Dolby thought she would be happier with people who shared her views about the Germans. She had to go.[. . .] They turned her out because she would not pretend that the Germans were all villains – when she had German friends, when the only happy days of her life had been spent in Germany!
>
> ([1925] 1976: 110)

The imperialist procession runs her off into a side road where she has to hold fast to her God in order to survive the injustice of her situation. We have seen something of the intensely marginalised position in which pacifists found themselves. Defiled as 'pro-German', Kilman tries to educate Elizabeth in some of the ideas that her mother, ignorant and trivial representative of the governing classes, would have no interest in. 'After all' she says, 'there were people who did not think the English invariably right. There were books. There were meetings. There were other points of view. Would Elizabeth like to come with her to listen to So-and-so?' ([1925] 1976: 116). She lives in agony, struggling against egotism and self-pity to quell her 'hot and painful feelings', fighting Clarissa for Elizabeth's approbation: 'If she could grasp her, if she could clasp her, if she could make her hers absolutely and for ever and then die; that was all she wanted' ([1925] 1976: 117). She emerges as an oppressed and oppressive parody of Clarissa and Sally: 'If it were now to die, 'twere now to be most happy'. The text does not represent Doris Kilman sympathetically. There are no overt apologies for her social construction – indeed she is frequently read as a revelation of Woolf's elitism. However, a reading of Kilman in the light of Woolf's other writing about the war reveals her as a figure more troubled than simplistically repulsive: an object of nationalistic abuse, a victim of the phallocentric class system which produced the war. The text, by foregrounding this intersection of discourses, surely produces an image of humanity degraded by ideological conviction.[6]

If the war leaves Doris Kilman tormented and unfulfilled, it leaves Septimus insane. Shell-shock becomes a vital issue (and metaphor) in several women's war novels dealing with the social construction of masculinity. In Rebecca West's *The Return of the Soldier* (1918), Chris Baldry is for a long time incapable of integrating his pre-war self with the selfhood that the army has manufactured for him; in Rose Macaulay's *Non-Combatants and Others* (1916), Alix's soldier cousin screams out at night the hideous truths that he represses during the day. Septimus Smith's poetic inclinations become indistinguishable from his desire to uphold the chivalric code. Brooke-like,

> Septimus was one of the first to volunteer. He went to France to save an England which consisted almost entirely of Shakespeare's plays and Miss Isabel Pole in a green dress walking in a square.
>
> ([1925] 1976: 77)

He goes to save an image of his national origin that is rooted in the romance of Englishness. But just as the focus of the war poetry shifts from 'some corner of a foreign field that is forever England' to the 'naked sodden buttocks, mats of hair,/Bulged, clotted heads [. . .] in the plastering slime' (Sassoon, 'Counter-Attack') of the post-Somme trenches, so Septimus discards romance and develops a self-construction – 'manliness' – better suited to withstand the experience of butchery. Septimus's pre-war passions, unsuccessfully repressed, are displaced onto his relationship with his officer Evans. The discourse that articulates this relationship is warm, playful, domesticated:

> It was a case of two dogs playing on a hearth-rug; one worrying a paper screw, snarling, snapping, giving a pinch, now and then, at the old dog's ear; the other lying somnolent, blinking at the fire, raising a paw, turning and growling good-temperedly.
>
> ([1925] 1976: 77)

Fussell ([1975] 1977: 270–309) and Leed (1979) have emphasised the tradition of homoeroticism that war perpetuated, while prohibiting homosexuality as permanent or natural. When Evans dies, Septimus cannot allow himself the luxury of grief for fear of destroying his new identity. 'It was sublime. He had gone through the whole show, friendship, European War, death, had won promotion, was still under thirty and was bound to survive' ([1925] 1976: 78). He therefore 'congratulated himself on feeling very little and very reasonably'. His false war-identity becomes inflexible and destructive. Once the war-fiction is over the overt structure validating this calloused 'manliness' vanishes and his indifference seems criminally inappropriate. He therefore embarks on a course of self-punishment: for the crime of being incapable of human emotion, for his relationship with Evans, for the fact that he has married Rezia under false pretences (he can't love her – he can't love women).

War, then, teaches Septimus a certain code – the 'Law of the Father' – adoption of which necessitates the repression of his previous experience. His poetic self, however, breaks through this stultifying discourse and mentally disables him. Like Dennis in *Despised and Rejected*, Septimus emerges as a Christ figure, a giant mourner, with messages to preach to a world that cannot decode his language. That world, he fears (and this is a typical modernist predicament), no longer has intrinsic meaning. The war becomes to him 'a little shindy of schoolboys with gun-powder', and the cause of his failure, language itself, becomes multiple and diffused, over-written with different accents and plural significations in a kind of Kristevan riot of anarchic possibilities:

> The word 'time' split its husk; poured its riches over him; and from his lips fell like shells, like shavings from a plane, without his making them, hard, white, imperishable words, and flew to attach themselves to their places in an ode to Time.
>
> ([1925] 1976: 63)[7]

The treatment of Septimus's shell-shock has frequently been read as an attack on the inflexibility, imperialism and dog-matism of the patriarchal hegemony. The latter's response to Septimus's seeing the Great European War as 'a little shindy of schoolboys' is to provide brainwashing by the medical police in order to cure him of this dangerous delusion. For the con-temporary reader, however, the novel might have suggested more precise political targets. It can, for instance, be seen as a reply to the 'Report of the War Office Committee of Enquiry into "Shell-Shock"' (Great Britain, Army 1922), which was widely publicised and is, perhaps, alluded to during the novel's

194

party scene.[8] The Report recommended a 'cure' for shell-shock that was clearly underpinned by coercion and violence. The treatment of the effects of violence by yet further violence must have seemed to Woolf the apotheosis of the kind of madness that had led to the war in the first place.

The medical profession was in a confused state over shell-shock in 1922. The Report, indeed, was unwilling fully to adopt the term, although it was unable to think of a better one. Reluctant to describe this psychological disorder as specifically the outcome of war, it suggested that most of the symptoms had been recognised in civil medical practice (1922: 92). On the other hand, as Elaine Showalter has pointed out, the term 'shell-shock' provided a suitably manly substitute for what might otherwise be described as 'hysteria' – hitherto seen as an exclusively feminine affliction (Showalter [1985] 1987: 172). The hidden agenda of the Report seems to have been to absolve bellicosity from responsibility for human derangement, and to shift the blame instead onto the inadequate 'character' of individual sufferers. This opened the way for a full range of prejudices based on race, class and education to be seen as justifiable evidence to account for the superiority of the aristocratic, public-schoolboy over his 'weaker' inferiors (1922: 96, 148). It thereby condoned the use of violent coercion in the treatment of shell-shock patients as being in the best interests of the individual 'man' and, of course, of his country.

Woolf's fictional response to this kind of attitude is complex. Her antipathy towards massed activity has already been mentioned and it was an emphasis on group identity that underpinned the Report's recommendations for the prevention of shell-shock:

> A battalion whose morale is of a high standard will have little 'shell-shock'. Included under the term 'morale' are pride of regiment, belief in the cause, mutual confidence between officers and men, and the feeling that a man is part of a corporate whole.
>
> (1922: 93)

Septimus, of course, has all the 'right attitudes' which, in Woolf's view, merely increase his vulnerability to profound mental disturbance. 'Morale' in itself, if it means doing things in a group, was, to Woolf, the kind of madness that destroys, because it denies, individuality, difference and vibrant sensitivity. The treatment recommended by the Report justifies an increase in violence proportional to the patient's inability to respond to the rules of combat. In other words, the greater the patient's resistance to authoritative structures that seek to produce a violent and coercive mentality, the stronger should be the threats of loss of individual liberty. The Report expresses this benignly. Moral persuasion is the first tactic to be employed by the psychiatrist, who will appeal to 'the patient's social self esteem to make him co-operate and put forth a real effort of will' (1922: 128). We are reminded of Holmes's oafish 'So you're in. a funk', and Septimus's alienated response: 'Human nature, in short, was on him – the repulsive brute, with the blood-red nostrils' ([1925] 1976: 82–3).

Once moral persuasion has failed, though, according to the Report, 'recourse may be had to more forcible methods' and 'even threats were justified in certain cases' (Great Britain, Army 1922: 128). This next stage, in Woolf's text, requires another character. The amiable buffoon is displaced by the sinister possessor of an authoritative grey car, Sir William Bradshaw. He is described by Clarissa as 'obscurely evil, without sex or lust, extremely polite to women, but capable of some indescribable outrage – forcing your soul, that was it' ([1925] 1976: 163). It is he who issues the threat of personal violence. Septimus has talked of killing himself, therefore he must be incarcerated and taught a sense of proportion. 'Proportion' and 'conversion' are metaphors for a social process by which those who dissent from the cultural norm are labelled insane or dangerously deviant and are forcibly subjected to pressure to conform. This is the apotheosis of the masculine procession, protecting Imperial England and making it prosper. In another outburst of ironic fury similar to that which preceeds Jacob's death, the narrative voice emerges from its amused eloquence to castigate the power of the medical police in dealing with 'what, after all, we know nothing about' ([1925] 1976: 90) in so brutal and coersive a fashion – and, moreover, their being rewarded by the humility and gratitude of the public. Sir William makes a substantial living out of penalising despair, forbidding the unfit to propagate their views and restraining unsocial impulses 'bred, more than anything, by the lack of good blood', and he manages this by enforcing on his victims an ideological stranglehold enshrined in the country's legislation.

Septimus's only defence is to evade the chronological, mono-logical order and to think and speak in metaphors. The met-onymic discourse that connects him with the details of con-ventional domestic life and thereby links him to a world in which violent death is the norm, is (paradoxically) intolerably unreal. He can therefore only define himself as a 'relic', or (recalling *The Waste Land*) a 'drowned sailor, on the shore of the world' ([1925] 1976: 83), and Holmes as (metonymically) 'human nature', then (metaphorically) a 'repulsive brute with the blood-red nostrils'. It is Holmes who finally, just as Septimus is beginning to regain a sense of self in community, invades the home, overpowers Rezia and sends Septimus over the top, straight on to the bayonet-like railings. While Holmes proclaims Septimus 'The coward!', the landlady's apron takes on the symbolic significance of a flag, saluting Septimus (it seems to Rezia) as one of the war dead ([1925] 1976: 133). Although Septimus survives the war itself, he dies in a civilian metonym of war, the logical corollary to the brutal imposition of a fixed gender identity.

'The world has raised its whip; where will it descend?' asks the narrative voice ([1925] 1976: 15). At first sight the novel's answer appears to be that it falls on Septimus, Rezia, Kilman and all the others who are constricted, stereotyped and eventu-ally destroyed by the force of war. Septimus and Rezia seem to occupy an underworld and an underclass in Clarissa's secure and confident symbolic-ordered world. While for Septimus 'The world wavered and quivered and threatened to burst into flames' ([1925] 1976: 15), for Clarissa 'it was the middle of June. The War was over' ([1925] 1976: 6). Septimus is ruined by the war, Clarissa, owing to her age, class and gender, escapes its immediate personal effects. But the two are clearly linked. The element of 'monumental time' – that which is spatial rather than chronological (cf. Kristeva [1979] 1986: 191) – is available to them both as a result of their common oppositional posi-tioning to the conventional masculine order. Septimus, in his alienation from office work, experiences 'a freedom which the attached can never know' ([1925] 1976: 83): he is the eternal sufferer, the eternal mourner. Clarissa, who sits sewing, hears in the rhythm of her activity and of her heart a phrase which resonates through the text 'Fear no more the heat of the sun'. Her body 'sighs collectively for all sorrows' ([1925] 1976: 37). The book is haunted by 'the figure of the mother whose sons have been killed in the battles of the world' ([1925] 1976: 53). This cyclical and eternal time, this permanent sorrow, lodges in both of them. Both, in their different ways, are the sacrificial victims of its counterpart: the linear, deathly time of the Symbolic Order. Psychosis, though, is the penalty paid by Septimus, for knowing, in a fully present sense, the unspeakable of the world's spoken truth.

Clarissa has also experienced meaningless death, comparable to the death of Evans. She witnessed her sister being killed by a falling tree and, as a result, resolves to 'decorate the dungeon with flowers and air-cushions' – to 'mitigate the sufferings of our fellow-prisoners' ([1925] 1976: 70). While Septimus's world is 'plastered over with grimaces' ([1925] 1976: 80), Clarissa's is filled with roses. Her class position and marital status permit this. She is grateful to her servants for helping her to be 'gentle, generous hearted' ([1925] 1976: 36) and to her husband for offering her an identity ('this being Mrs Richard Dalloway' ([1925] 1976: 11)) but not forcing her to merge with his. Clarissa's parties represent her attempt to help along post-war reconstruction as far as her limited sphere will allow. Acts of Parliament are clearly inadequate to save Septimus Smith, for example, so a different strategy is needed. If party politics are futile, the politics of the party may have something to offer. On one level this can be seen as a gesture towards alterity as radical as the Women's Peace Party. An attempt to combine and create ([1925] 1976: 109), Clarissa's party seeks to provide a matrix in which individuals can harmonize and merge; it acknowledges the continuousness of human relationships and the plurality of vision. It is an exercise in the multiple and diffuse possibilities of selection and combination, opposed to the dictates of linearity, and can be seen as a metaphor for an aesthetic vision or a radical politics.

It is at this point that the novel's double focus emerges. Clarissa is not politically radical; she is ignorant and careless. Her gathering of worthies and dignitaries is limited by her own class prejudices. Her 'femininity', plural and merging though it is, is contained within a certain arrogance. She does, however, experience Septimus's death during her party. Indeed, the details of the 'blundering, bruising' rusty spikes running through his body, are narrated through her consciousness. His ability to stand true to his convictions and not to submit to the intolerable Bradshaw, Clarissa sees as worthwhile. Septimus has preserved the 'thing there was that mattered' ([1925] 1976: 163) – integrity, the embrace, the shilling in the serpentine – but at the expense of 'simply life'. Clarissa, on the other hand, recognises that she has compromised; she 'had schemed, she had pilfered. She was never wholly admirable. She had wanted success, Lady Bexborough and the rest of it' ([1925] 1976: 164). All she can do is to make vibrant gestures in the face of the bleak prospect Septimus has revealed her life to be. The text, in its apparent disapprobation of Clarissa, subverts such easy dismissal by emphasising her suffering alongside that of Septimus. *Mrs Dalloway* refuses to allow a simple, monological answer to the problems of gender and war. Its only consolation might be that the social organisation of gender allows women, for all their disreputable social coalitions, more space for plural visions and interpretations than it does men, in the context of war.

Jacob's Room leaves us with the problem of inheritance. The world of *Mrs Dalloway* cannot support the likes of Clarissa for much longer: the Conservative party is on the way out (cf. Zwerdling 1986: 120ff), the role of perfect hostess in that social milieu – which smacks, anyhow, of the angel in the house – is already an anachronism. As Wendy is the inheritor in *The Hounds of Spring*, so Elizabeth, not Clarissa, occupies this potential space in *Mrs Dalloway*. Independent both of her mother and of her father, she explores London, discovers poverty, considers the professions. In the terms of Rachel Blau Duplessis, the quest plot, in her case, is not foreshortened by a romance plot (DuPlessis 1988). Marriage is not the only career to be open to her. The novel leaves us with a defunct generation, the massacre of millions of young men, and with Elizabeth to do battle with the force of militarism symbolised by the youthful soldiers marching up Whitehall. The problem is one of handing on the gift of 'simply life' so that it may operate in the context of the material world. There are no clear answers or strategies; like Castalia's daughter at the end of Woolf's short story 'A Society' (1920), Elizabeth is left simply to be herself, in the hope that this may be sufficient.

THE WAR IN SQUARE BRACKETS

If *Jacob's Room* leads us up to the war and *Mrs Dalloway* looks back to and beyond it, *To the Lighthouse* (1927) focuses on all three perspectives in isolation and in their relation to each other. The structure is thereby similar to *The Tree of Heaven*, *The Lonely Generation*, *The Lost Generation* and *The Hounds of Spring*. In each of these the opening concentrates on the rendering of pre-war England, the war acts as a massive force of disruption and the remainder of the book concerns attempts at the relocation and restructuring of the central figure's war-torn identity. *To the Lighthouse* has a similar emphasis on the house and the family, but it differs significantly from these novels in its alternatives to heterosexual romance as the primary restructuring social de-vice. Moreover, and most importantly, the written texture of *To the Lighthouse* expands its frame of reference beyond the domes-tic to a plural and heterogeneous vision of the effects of war on life and art.

In *A Room of One's Own* Woolf speaks of 'a sort of humming noise, not articulate, but musical, exciting' which accompanied pre-war discourse, but has since ceased. 'Shall we lay the blame on the war?' asks the narrator:

> When the guns fired in August 1914, did the faces of men and women show so plain in each other's eyes that romance was killed? Certainly it was a shock (to women in particular with their illusions about education, and so on) to see the faces of our rulers in the light of the shell-fire. So ugly they looked – German, English, French – so stupid.
>
> ([1929] 1977: 16)

Romance, then, is dead. It died with war and with women's illusions that education should prevent war when in fact, as *Jacob's Room* has shown, masculine public-school education continued, relentlessly, to encourage it. The narrator goes on: 'But why say "blame"? Why, if it was an illusion, not praise the catastrophe, whatever it was, that destroyed illusion and put truth in its place?' ([1929] 1977: 16). The pre-war age is seen as both the repository of a joyful romantic passion and the seat of pernicious illusion about chivalry, the power of a classical education and the ideology that enforces a divisive sexual code inflexibly separating and containing 'manliness' in men and 'womanliness' in women. The first section of *To the Lighthouse* deals with that period, exploring the powers and limitations of the oceanic mother in conflict with the intrusive and dominating father. At the same time it is a picture of a Victorian marriage, coloured by nostalgia for lost childhood and lost integrity. This marriage, for all its idealism, is structured by the fixed sex-gender system of its pre-war age. It confronts us with a paradox: the marriage is idealistic *because of* its limitations. The war begins to disestablish the fixed orbit of gendered relations – it destroys romance – but the consequent chaos creates space for liberty at the price of uncertainty.

In this novel we are taken a stage further into the post-war world. Clarissa Dalloway is firmly locked into the imperial tradition and the rites of the Conservative party: just as it is a mistake to see her as an unqualified celebration of femininity, so is it similarly misguided to see Mrs Ramsay thus. In *Mrs Dalloway*, Elizabeth initiates her quest into areas of London and social knowledge unexplored by her parents: she is a figure of potential, a more practical and more visionary inheritor than Jacob could ever have been. In *To the Lighthouse*, a whole section is devoted to the post-war and post-heterosexual negotiations of Lily Briscoe, as she attempts to define an identity in the space offered by the traces of the deconstructed 'manly man', the 'womanly woman' and, most important, her art.

The effect of the war allows her to do this. In *Three Guineas* Woolf was to explain how the war allowed women and girls out of the confines of the private house into field hospitals and munitions factories, even if it did mean that their ticket depended on unconscious support for an institution that outside wartime inevitably oppressed them ([1938] 1977: 46). As the early chapters of this study have shown, genuine and sustained post-war freedom from domestic pressures was rarely achieved except where strong political commitment was involved. In Woolf's vision, however, and it is a vision dependent on her own class and social background, the war, perversely, did perform a lasting service to women in destroying the romance of chivalry. This, a tragic loss to those who had learned to live only by its codes, was a radical innovation to those who sought a new angle on the relationship between men, women and war. Woolf, more than Hamilton, Macaulay or Brittain, is able to render in her writing the simultaneous allure and deathliness of what we might now call maternal *jouissance*. Woolf's fiction is not concerned with access to, or ability to wield, political power. She is concerned rather with 'how to live differently' and how to render that difference in literary terms. For her the First World War, in spite of its slaughter, nevertheless offered some new possibilities to women: it altered civilisation's focus, it smashed some prohibitive traditions; it offered the means to destroy the angel in the house.

The pre-war world in *To the Lighthouse* is again divided by the binary oppositions male and female. Mr Ramsay, obsessed by classification, systematisation, hierarchisation and the desire to master philosophy, can be seen to belong to the tradition of academic discipline apparent in *Jacob's Room,* and to the same drive to suppress 'liars' and 'lunatics' that characterises the medical profession in *Mrs Dalloway:* 'He was incapable of untruth; never tampered with a fact; never altered a disagreeable word to suit the pleasure or convenience of any mortal being' ([1927] 1964: 6). But he is also a tragic figure, past his prime, limited in his need to spend his time, as Lily puts it, 'in this seeing of angular essences, this reducing of lovely evenings, with all their flamingo clouds and blue and silver to a white deal four-legged table' ([1927] 1964: 28). The provocative bathos highlights the comic side of Mr Ramsay's presentation and the combination of the dominating and the comic, coupled by recitations from 'The Charge of the Light Brigade', render Mr Ramsay a less censorious version of that preposterous masculine fiction that Woolf saw as characterising the dominant representations of the First World War.

Images of his imaginative sterility contrast with Mrs Ramsay's fertility and generosity. If Mr Ramsay is the Victorian patriarch, Mrs Ramsay is his complementary angel in the house. Like Cynthia Renner and Frances Harrison, she expects chivalry and valour and, in return, offers men psychological security, unquestioningly revering their authority in government, whether national or domestic. She tries to foster the same instincts in her daughters, who find themselves oscillating between reverence for the metonyms (ringed fingers and lace) of a rich and alluring age and a forward-looking search for alternatives. Nevertheless, the alternatives have to be repressed, for it is only in silence that they:

could sport with infidel ideas which they had brewed for
themselves of a life different from hers; in Paris, perhaps;
a wilder life; not always taking care of some man or other;
for there was in all their minds a mute questioning of
deference and chivalry, of the Bank of England and the
Indian Empire, of ringed fingers and lace, though to them
all there was something in this of the essence of beauty,
which called out the manliness in their girlish hearts, and
made them, as they sat at table beneath their mother's
eyes, honour her strange severity, her extreme courtesy. . . .

([1927] 1964: 9)

So entirely feminine is the mother's role that it even evokes a
'manly' response from her daughters. That her daughters do
not wish to merge with her suggests that Mrs Ramsay's beauty
and wisdom are sealed in an ideological position which may
have the outward appearance of a splendid, regal perfection,
but which is flawed in its inability to accept and nurture change.

In a move similar to Clarissa Dalloway's, Mrs Ramsay takes
upon herself the effort of 'merging and flowing and creating' in
order to make something memorable out of the disparate
elements at her dinner party. She succeeds, but only by
enforcing a rigid code of practice which excludes those seeking
communication that lies beyond – and threatens – Victorian/
Edwardian etiquette. Her formula is metaphorically named
'speaking French': a polite discourse is imposed in order to
facilitate a particular kind of formal exchange. Lily Briscoe does
not want to 'rescue' Charles Tansley who has marooned himself
in the conversation. She nevertheless 'speaks French', performs
what Kristeva might call 'exchange purified of pleasure' ([1974]
1986: 31) in order to mollify her hostess. 'Perhaps it is bad
French', says the narrator; 'French may not contain the words
that express the speaker's thoughts; nevertheless speaking
French imposes some order, some uniformity' ([1927] 1964:
104). Mrs Ramsay thus creates a forum in which the men can
speak and, this established, she can relinquish responsibility for
making her own contribution. Kristeva, in discussing an extreme
form of 'feminine' withdrawal, describes a tendency to 'flee
everything considered "phallic" to find refuge in the valor-
ization of a silent underwater body, thus abdicating any entry
into history' (Kristeva [1974] 1981: 166). Her metaphor of an

'underwater body' was possibly prompted by Woolf (whom she mentions in the essay), whose Mrs Ramsay imagines herself as an underwater light that steals beneath the outward articulations of the dinner party guests, suspended, inarticulate, observing – metaphorically – the effects of their conversation rather than engaging with the content. This can be seen as a further instance of her earlier descent into a 'wedge-shaped core of darkness', where she merges with the objects of her attention – the lighthouse stroke, 'trees, streams, flowers' – and her mind becomes a heterogeneous site resolved into romantic unity, 'a bride to meet her lover' ([1927] 1964: 74). This is where she most nearly approaches Kristeva's notion of *jouissance*: a site of auto-eroticism, she engulfs the lighthouse stroke and feels:

> as if it were stroking with its silver fingers some sealed vessel in her brain whose bursting would flood her with delight [. . .] and it rolled in waves of pure lemon which curved and swelled and broke upon the beach and the ecstacy burst in her eyes and waves of pure delight raced over the floor of her mind.

> ([1927] 1964: 75)

Her silent, 'underwater' climax over, she goes to her husband to reassure him of the importance of his continued presence for her.

The problem with this as a female role model is that it is ultimately disabling. Lily Briscoe is incapacitated as a conversationalist by Mrs Ramsay's rules, and also unable to communicate with her mentally absent mentor. Mrs Ramsay may be luminous and oceanic, but she is also stifling and repressive. It takes a major shift in perspective, however, to recognise this. The ambivalence is pointed up by the sea imagery with which Mrs Ramsay is associated: on the one hand the sea is consoling and protective, 'a measured and soothing tattoo to her thoughts', or conversely it is annihilating, it 'made one think of the destruction of the island and its engulfment in the sea' ([1927] 1964: 19). These two forces hold each other precariously in tension until the war forces them apart.

The Victorian wife and the *jouissante* woman, however, co-exist with the practical mother. The idealised acts of motherhood described by Swanwick and Marshall find a parallel in Mrs

Ramsay's treatment of the boar's skull in the nursery. Cam wants it removed: James clearly does not. Mrs Ramsay performs the perfect act of conciliation: she covers it with her own shawl and persuades Cam that it's a mountain with valleys and flowers and goats and antelopes, and persuades James that nothing has been done to it. There it is, safe, under the shawl. Rose or ram's skull; bird's nest or boar's skull; beauty, beastliness; laughter, anguish. *To the Lighthouse* represents the First World War as a battle between such binary oppositions, in which the former in each pair is (at least temporarily) obliterated, or repressed and relegated to the past.

The central section of *To the Lighthouse* seems to offer a dual invitation: first to see the war in the imagery and the poetic movement of the whole, and second, to note the arbitrariness of the events we select as significant. In 1934 Woolf wrote to Stephen Spender:

> I should like to write four lines at a time, describing the same feeling, as a musician does; because it always seems to me that things are going on at so many different levels simultaneously.
>
> (Nicolson 1979 [10 July 1934]: 315)

Although written some time after the novel, this suggests a helpful way of reading 'Time Passes', particularly as its invocation of the musical stave invites comparison with the interplay between the metaphorical and metonymical axes in literary study. In other words we can read the highly figurative language of this section both conceptually and contextually. We can see simultaneously (1) the war and the breakdown of civilisation, (2) the reaction of philosophical man, (3) the reconstruction by unphilosophical woman and (4) the 'facts': the births, marriages, deaths and publications. The war serves to fragment the hegemonic unity which forms protective patterns and holds chaos at bay. It kills the feminine, the conciliating angel, and for a while brutish masculinity triumphs. But masculinity's accompanying ordering, hierarchising, philosophical frame of mind does not triumph: it engages in doomed conflict with the indifference and formlessness of nature. The problem of 'subject object and the nature of reality', as posed by Mr Ramsay, is wrenched apart and opened to reinterpretation, owing to the impasse in the so-called 'development' of human civilisation caused by the meaningless carnage of the war. The myth of the unified subject is, quite simply, smashed up. The force that wins through is an eternal and cyclical life-force in the form of Mrs McNab, who is female but not 'feminine' in the sense that Mrs Ramsay is.

Houses become important symbols in women's war writing. The family house in *The Hounds of Spring* loses its identity as a country mansion, becoming transformed into a hospital and then sold off; Ruth Alleyndene's parental home in *Honourable Estate* undergoes a similar fate but is also destroyed; Delphine in *The Lonely Generation* loses her home when she loses her father and is forced to live in squalid bedsits. The decline of the house symbolised the decline of family and unity. In *To the Lighthouse* the isolated house on the isle of Skye stands as a symbol of forgotten civilisation, pitted against the intrusive and destructive forces of nature, just as western civilisation, the family, religion, art, idealism were bombarded by massive losses on the Western Front and by the disestablishment of cultural and individual identity. The opening prophetic comments by Mr Bankes and Andrew pave the way for change: 'we must wait for the future to show'; 'It's almost too dark to see' and, anticipating the deluge, 'Nothing, it seemed, could survive the flood' ([1927] 1964: 143).

An epic significance can, of course, be seen in the imagery of 'Time Passes'. It suggests apocalyptic patterns of relentless destruction, ephemerality, absurdity. A reading of it in the context of women's anti-war writing, however, reveals a more specific, feminist pacifist construction of the war as a male assault on maternal work. While this reading need not obscure the larger, metaphorical meanings that intersect in the text, it does help to bring into focus a persistent ambivalence in feminist pacifist material: in what terms is maternalism to be valued? Through what agency does its passive constructedness translate into inspiration?

Of the 'four lines' in this section I shall take first the imagery of war, clearly visible through the rendering of nature's intrusions. The early, inquisitive, path-finding airs who are to form the body of the destructive force find themselves asking of letters, flowers, books 'Were they allies? Were they enemies? How long would they endure?' ([1927] 1964: 144), thus echoing and undermining Mrs Ramsay's triumphant 'This will remain', while setting up the discourse of the battlefield. An 'aimless gust of lamentation' announces the onset of darkness, the ideological and emotional realisation that night will follow night until they are all 'full of wind and destruction' ([1927] 1964: 146), and the 'stray airs', now self-proclaimed 'advance guards of great armies', 'blustered in' discomposing the 'human shape' of the house's paraphernalia until 'once in the middle of the night with a roar, with a rupture, as after centuries of quiescence, a rock rends itself from the mountain and hurtles crashing into the valley, one fold of the shawl loosened and swung to and fro' ([1927] 1964: 148). Maternal work begins to come undone: the snout of the boar begins to reveal itself from the folds, patterns and weavings of Mrs Ramsay's protective shawl. A final spring and summer pass, with one more fold of the shawl becoming dislodged, before clear sounds of war are heard:

> But slumber and sleep though it might there came later in the summer ominous sounds like the measured blows of hammers dulled on felt, which, with their repeated shocks still further loosened the shawl and cracked the tea-cups. Now and again some glass tinkled in the cupboard as if a giant voice had shrieked so loud in its agony that tumblers stood inside a cupboard vibrated too. Then again silence fell; and then, night after night, and sometimes in plain midday when the roses were bright and light turned on the wall its shape clearly there seemed to drop into this silence this indifference, this integrity, the thud of something falling.
>
> ([1927] 1964: 152)

This is followed by the news of Andrew's death in France. Like the nocturnal women beating great carpets at the end of *Jacob's Room*, the image of the guns is distanced, domesticated. The war is registered obliquely, in terms of female non-combatant experience. The shawl is loosened, the tea-cups cracked, the glasses tinkle and vibrate. The thud of something falling brings to mind the tree falling in the forest in *Jacob's Room*, the incongruity of its happening in broad daylight marking the true beginnings of chaos. It is on the same page that we see:

> the silent apparition of an ashen-coloured ship for instance, come, gone; there was a purplish stain upon the

207

blank surface of the sea as if something had boiled and
bled, invisibly, beneath.

([1927] 1964: 152)

The suddenness, bloodiness and above all the silence recall the
drowning of the impassive young men in *Jacob's Room*: the
adjective 'ashen' linking facial pallor with the shock of meaningless death. Here, however, the ship is in the context of a sublime
landscape. It is an intrusion that upsets not only political
decorum, but also the entire and complex romantic relationship between man and nature, whereby nature acts as compensation for, and alternative value system to, the vulgarities,
banalities and inhumanities of industrial capitalism.

From this point, the natural universe transforms itself into
'gigantic chaos streaked with lightening', as:

> the winds and waves disported themselves like the amorph-
> ous bulks of leviathans whose brows are pierced by no light
> of reason, and mounted one on top of another, and
> lunged and plunged in the darkness or the daylight (for
> night and day, month and year ran shapelessly together)
> in idiot games, until it seemed as if the universe were
> battling and tumbling in brute confusion and wanton lust
> aimlessly by itself.

([1927] 1964: 154)

The metaphor 'leviathans' might stand for sea monsters, men,
ships, states – or the two opposing armies sent 'over the top' to
shoot and bayonet each other, stupidly, day and night for years.
The specifically martial language – 'battling', 'brute confusion'
– aligns the war with its universal implications of riotous,
perverse indirection.

The house, meanwhile, seems to reach a point of no return as
a haven for civilised values:

> Toads had nosed their way in. Idly, aimlessly, the swaying
> shawl swung to and fro. A thistle thrust itself between the
> tiles in the larder. The swallows nested in the drawing-
> room; the floor was strewn with straw; the plaster fell in
> shovelfuls; rafters were laid bare; rats carried off this and
> that to gnaw behind the wainscots. Tortoise-shell butter-
> flies burst from the chrysalis and pattered their life out on
> the window-pane. Poppies sowed themselves among the

dahlias; the lawn waved with long grass; giant artichokes towered among roses; a fringed carnation flowered among the cabbages; while the gentle tapping of a weed at the window had become, on winters' nights, a drumming from sturdy trees and thorned briars which made the whole room green in summer.

([1927] 1964: 157)

This passage is striking in the context of the rest of the section for its semantic simplicity. As nature releases itself from its function to reflect the gaze of humankind – that of Mrs Ramsay in this instance – the emphasis shifts from what is represented to the means of representation. The materiality of language, its phonological and rhythmical qualities, impose abstract patterns of repetition, inversion and parallelism when, at this cataclysmic stage in the war, the universe seems devoid of meaning. Assonance and alliteration suggest a harmonic structure of pure sound, while the referents of these signs indicate the increasing disorder of civilisation. The four consecutive dactyls 'Tortoise-shell butterflies burst from their chrysalis' introduce a rhythmical pattern which contrasts with the disordered chaos of nature's abundance. The 'meaning' of the words is chaos. Paradoxically, the moment when description is most detailed and semantically unadorned is the moment when it is least likely to fit into a secure, humanised, world view.

'Nature' becomes indistinguishable from 'culture' as the house and the garden become conflated, and swallows nest in the drawing room, which takes on the greenness of what previously had lain beyond its accultured boundaries. In this chaos, attention shifts to the texture, patterns and phonic quality of language itself – to 'significant form' – as the hitherto benign and accessible 'real world' increasingly resembles the meaningless haze or jumbled and conflicting drives of psychosis and chaos. The relationship between humanity, nature and language is fragmented. The illusion which the text confronts is that the relationship was ever fixed and understood. The opposed and incompatible modalities of Mr and Mrs Ramsay demonstrate that the myth of the organic world was the product of ideology, and that ideology is historically relative. The war's chaos had its roots in the earlier Victorian period.

The external manifestations of Mrs Ramsay's work are ruined

by the effects of war. It is as though the balance between refuge and threat that she perceived in nature has tilted, and the sea has indeed engulfed the land. The philosopher's passion, that desperate masculine concern with 'subject, object and the nature of reality', is also fragmented. In a second harmonic 'line', 'Time Passes' refers repeatedly to a seeker of truth, but 'no image with semblance of serving and divine promptitude comes readily to hand bringing the night to order and making the world reflect the compass of the soul' ([1927] 1964: 146). This image of organic unity is dismantled by an ironic 'divine goodness', who, offering the occasional glimpse of 'his treasures', then shatters them with hail and 'so confuses them that it seems impossible that their calm should ever return or that we should ever compose from their fragments a perfect whole or read in the littered pieces the clear words of truth' ([1927] 1964: 146). No sooner has the curtain closed on 'The Window' than it seems impossible that it were ever there.

For 'the hopeful', though, in the age that immediately precedes the war and which May Sinclair names 'The Vortex' in *The Tree of Heaven*, there come:

> imaginations of the strangest kind – of flesh turned to atoms which drove before the wind, of stars flashing in their hearts, of cliff, sea, cloud, and sky brought purposely together to assemble outwardly the scattered parts of the vision within. In those mirrors, the minds of men, in those pools of uneasy water, in which clouds for ever turn and shadows form, dreams persisted, and it was impossible to resist [. . .] the extraordinary stimulus to range hither and thither in search of some absolute good, some crystal of intensity, remote from the known pleasures and familiar virtues, something alien to the processes of domestic life.
> ([1927] 1964: 151)

Scientific discovery, the theory of relativity, social change, artistic innovation, all the things that concerned Woolf when she wrote that human character had changed 'in or around 1910' are embedded in these images of atoms and stars. Dream, desire, rejection of domestic life, these radical departures still are driven by a persistent search for an external image of 'the scattered parts of the vision within'. Nature, in the patriarchal order of things about to be destroyed, is to culture as woman is to man. In *A Room of One's Own* Woolf suggests that woman reflects man's image as twice its natural size (Woolf [1929] 1977: 36). In her fiction, egotistical, philosophical man insists that nature should reflect culture's identity. The pacer of the beach, though, finds his harmonious vision interrupted by the ashen war ship; the vision outside no longer reflects the vision within. The latter-day Casaubon has his dream of finding a key to all mythologies destroyed: 'the mirror itself was but the surface glassiness which forms in quiescence when the nobler powers sleep beneath.' And in any case 'the mirror was broken' ([1927] 1964: 153). The war, then, has shattered the possibility of finding a unified subject identity and its common forms of social communication. The 'nobler powers' will be called on to awaken and create new forms.

If chivalry and romance are dead, if nature has failed to reflect man's desired image of himself, what remains to save the house/world? An outsider. A woman with 'a sidelong glance that deprecated the scorn and anger of the world' ([1927] 1964: 148). Someone who, while the mystic asks 'What am I? What is this?', continues to drink and gossip as before ([1927] 1964: 150). Mrs McNab, who embodies the third modality of war, is in the mould of the wild, singing woman who appears in *Jacob's Room* and the singer of the lost ages in *Mrs Dalloway*. Eternal and cyclical, as in Kristeva's 'Women's Time', there is 'twined about her dirge some incorrigible hope. Visions of joy there must have been at the wash-tub, say with her children' ([1927] 1964: 149). Her song, which had been gay twenty years ago, is now 'the voice of witlessness, humour, persistency itself, trodden down but springing up again' ([1927] 1964: 149). Working-class, old, weary, a comic figure in the melancholy atmosphere of the section, it is she who revives the memory of Mrs Ramsay and sends it flickering across the walls, like a lighthouse beam, as she dusts and straightens ([1927] 1964: 156), and she who orchestrates the rescue of the house from the 'sands of oblivion'. She is a life force. Of a different class from Mrs Ramsay, she is 'not inspired to go about [her] work with dignified ritual or solemn chanting' ([1927] 1964: 158). The world/house is regenerated and reconstructed by those who have always done the reconstructing: the mothers. Devoid of aura or mystique, Mrs McNab and Mrs Bast allow the house a 'rusty laborious birth'. They achieve a 'magnificent conquest over the taps', a 'more partial triumph over long rows of books' ([1927] 1964: 159): their war is within the household, their project of reconstruction concerned literally with the fabric of domestic life. Patiently, ploddingly, unseen (Mr Ramsay never used to see Mrs McNab), unspoken of, they rescue a form of civilisation from the threat of complete disintegration.

In amongst these three modalities of war are the 'facts'. Glimpses of death, marriage, birth, publications are placed within square brackets. Mrs Ramsay dies before the war begins, Prue dies in childbirth during the summer immediately preceding the war, Andrew is killed, along with 'twenty or thirty' other young men, by a shell in France, Mr Carmichael publishes a volume of poetry inspired by the war. Woolf's method of writing as if on four lines simultaneously is an attempt to destabilise the normal hierarchy of representation. Prue's death and Andrew's are textually juxtaposed and effectively contemporaneous, suggesting that death is equally tragic whether it be caused by war or by childbirth; the one should not be glorified while the other is ignored. Military actions and domestic processes co-exist and both are, essentially, hangovers from the sex-gender system which the war, in Woolf's rendering, gradually erodes. Prue was always to be the inheritor of Mrs Ramsay's ideals; Andrew was the one who was able to explain his father's philosophy to Lily. With their deaths, the apparently natural inheritors make way for someone less conventional and less securely hailed by the ideologies of the Victorian family.

The third section, 'The Lighthouse' returns to the rescued, repopulated, post-war house and to this novel's 'inheritor', the middle-aged and 'skimpy' Lily Briscoe. It shows us Lily's struggle to negotiate renewed subject identity and refreshed artistic design from the shattered images bequeathed by the war. The paradox that emerges from the war is that it takes the fixed configuration masculine/feminine to an extreme, where it explodes and scatters seeds for reinterpretation of social norms, reconstruction of social (and other) relationships. Attention shifts not only to seeking a way to live differently in the absence of heterosexual romance, but also, in artistic terms, from the world represented to the form of representation. 'Reality' is no longer the observable 'common phenomenal world' but the intersection and arrangement of a plethora of ideologies, drives, emotions, experiences. The 'natural' world is no longer ordered, but chaotic.

Mrs Ramsay and the pre-war world, though, remain a powerful force. At the end of 'Time Passes', once the cleaning of the house and scything of the grass has been completed:

> there rose that half-heard melody, that intermittent music which the ear half catches but lets fall; a bark, a bleat; irregular, intermittent, yet somehow related; the hum of an insect, the tremor of cut grass, dissevered yet somehow belonging; the jar of a dor beetle, the squeak of a wheel, loud, low, but mysteriously related; which the ear strains to bring together and is always on the verge of harmonizing but they are never quite heard, never fully harmonized.
>
> ([1927] 1964: 161)

Like the 'musical, humming noise' that the narrator recalls in *A Room of One's Own*, this evokes the traces of a lost completeness, a lost romance. The figures 'dissevered yet somehow belonging', 'low, but mysteriously related', 'never quite heard, never fully harmonized', anticipate Lily's struggle to achieve an independent vision through and in spite of the values that have dominated the construction of her subjectivity. This section of the novel concerns the operation of desire which sets in train a yearning for an imaginary wholeness. This yearning works its way through Lily's oscillations between the desirability and perfection of the state of motherhood as figured by Mrs Ramsay and the need to escape its fundamentally limiting implications. The medium through which this takes place is art.

Significantly, the third section opens with a barrage of questions in Lily's mind: 'What does it mean then, what can it all mean?' '[W]hat did she feel?' 'What does one send [to the lighthouse]? What does one do? Why is one sitting here after all?' And, most appropriately, 'Such were some of the parts, but how bring them together?' ([1927] 1964: 167). Lily feels that 'the link that usually bound things together had been cut and they floated up here, down there, off, anyhow'. Mrs Ramsay's death means that there is no longer a reliable and recognisable force making sense of the world. 'Was there no safety? No learning by heart the ways of the world? No guide, no shelter, but all was miracle, and leaping from the pinnacle of a tower into the air?' ([1927] 1964: 204).

But Mrs Ramsay's influence is clearly not wholly beneficial to Lily. As Elizabeth Dalloway has to break away from Clarissa's limited sphere, so Lily feels Mrs Ramsay's Imperial Womanhood to be tyrannous. The war, the death of romance, the death of Mrs Ramsay all relieve Lily of the compulsion to marry, a compulsion foisted upon her by Mrs Ramsay's urging the qualities of William Bankes. Mrs Ramsay was as certain that Lily would marry him as she was sure that Paul and Minta's marriage would be a success. But the war had destabilised any sense of fixed gendered identity. For Lily it 'had drawn the sting of her femininity' ([1927] 1964: 181). The agony of the war soothes her anger at masculinist assumptions – assumptions frequently articulated by Charles Tansley. Pity for humanity replaces gender-based fury – 'poor devils of both sexes, getting into such messes' ([1927] 1964: 181) – and she even has a vision of herself and Tansley, unified, playing ducks and drakes under the gaze of Mrs Ramsay.

The metonymic link between 'woman' and 'marry', then, no longer holds. Lily feels that she 'had only escaped by the skin of her teeth' but 'she would move the tree to the middle [of her painting] and need never marry anybody' ([1927] 1964: 200). A brush is 'the one dependable thing in a world of strife, ruin, chaos' ([1927] 1964: 170), and Lily transforms her yearning for Mrs Ramsay – 'to want and want and not to have!' ([1927] 1964: 203) – into artistic energy. Mrs Ramsay never cared for Lily's painting. Her creative force, however, the 'half-heard melody', finds its way, by displacement, onto Lily's canvas: 'and so pausing and so flickering, she attained a dancing rhythmical movement, as if the pauses were one part of the rhythm and the strokes another, and all were related' ([1927] 1964: 179). So she encloses a space, and within that space finds territory for her vision.

Her difficulty is to resolve the pain and yearning into artistic form without reducing it, Mr Ramsay-style, to fixed and de-limited meanings. Femaleness offers a strategic advantage here in that it is already constructed as a kind of otherness, as we have seen in the writings of VAD propaganda, Horatio Bottomley and some feminist pacifists. If the artist can represent the 'jar on the nerves: the thing itself before it has been made anything', the moment (in Woolf's terminology) *before* drives, emotions, ideologies are pinned down by a functionalist order or a false symbolic unity, then she might be articulating that 'otherness' without defining it. Lily's theory of design is that it should be 'clamped together with bolts of iron' and '[b]eautiful and bright on the surface, feathery and evanescent, one colour melting into another' ([1927] 1964: 194). If she can achieve this it will resolve her masculine and feminine, symbolic and semiotic modalities in communicable form. At the dinner party Mrs Ramsay allows herself to be upheld by the 'iron girders' of masculine intelligence while she closes and flickers her eyes, suspended by the fabrication, floating over the top of it ([1927] 1964: 122). Lily, equally, has to resolve Mrs Ramsay into the design and thus goes through the stages of anger with her, desire for her and impatience with her, dwelling on Tansley's infuriating derogation of women's talents and, conversely, on Mrs Ramsay's 'making of the moment something permanent'. Running through this there is the tension, the search for harmony in the design, the oscillation between feminine bonding and masculine interruption: 'For whatever reason she could not achieve that razor edge of balance between two opposite forces' ([1927] 1964: 219). Her project is to achieve a sense of process before it has been unified into a monological message.

The war, then, can be seen as offering the possibility of a plural vision. 'One wanted fifty pairs of eyes to see with' ([1927] 1964: 224). Lack and desire drive the effort for restructuring, 'to want and not to have' is the elegiac realisation that the artist must remain solitary and hold fast to her personal vision, find new words and new methods. Lily achieves her vision, her rhythmic dance of blues and greens, held together – resolved – by a line down the centre (the tree), to create a form that simultaneously unites and separates masculine and feminine modalities. Mrs Ramsay, the madonna and child, becomes a purple shadow on a new canvas. The war has drawn the sting of femininity and reduced it (in aesthetic terms) to a shadow needed to balance light.

To the Lighthouse seems to express both the allure and the pitfalls of the semiotic, imaginary, radical, conservative position that associates femininity with a particularity that goes beyond its social construction, while simultaneously reacting against a too-rigid doctrinal classification of gendered behaviour which is constantly defeated by its own limits. *Jacob's Room* places femininity outside the Symbolic Order: the external position offers the power of transformation. It has the force of an uncontaminated essence. *Mrs Dalloway* begins to explore some of the implications of incorporating that 'essence' into social currency: Clarissa can be seen as simultaneously trivial, ignorant and possessed of a world vision which transcends the limitations of the system of patriarchal 'government'. Lily Briscoe, Woolf's first post-war new woman, acts out that ambiguity. But like the book in which she is a character, she contains it in aesthetic form in order that it should have some communicable meaning, as well as being an endlessly fruitful matrix of possibilities. The problem we face at the end of the book is how best to draw Lily's line between politically naive solipsism and the positive energies, and political capital, to be derived from a productive pluralism.

CONCLUSION

Woolf, Brittain, some feminist pacifists and the more successful of the VADs had faith in the argument that the war,
even if it was a manifestation of a particularly brutal kind of
masculine madness, created space for women to work, think
and practise as artists. It helped to reveal the futility of a social
and political pact that made men and women play infantile
games with each other, and to over-invest in definitions of
'femininity' and 'masculinity' which rendered the bond un-
breakable. Farm workers, however, along with munitions
workers, the less ambitious VADs and women who could find
no 'reality' beyond that of romantic love, tended to discover
that the war reinforced their identity as merely temporary
active citizens.

If one dominant theme has emerged from this study it must
be that women were defined by the ideology of the day as war's
'other'. This they could manipulate, as the VADs did; resist, as
some land and munitions workers did; passively accept, as did
the women who minded the home front; or transform into an
anti-patriarchal power-base, as did the feminist pacifists –
including Virginia Woolf. The politics of race lay behind much
of the rhetoric concerned to remind women of their 'natural
destiny and duty': the hand that rocked the cradle should not
be stained with the impurities of paid employment if the world
were to be properly ruled. But the kind of national identity that
was based on competition and the shameless pursuit of supremacy was undermined by socialist, feminist pacifists who saw
capitalism as part of the structure that encouraged war and
relied on the permanent subjection of the physically, politically
and financially powerless. A similar dilution of an accepted

217

trope occurs when we consider the notion of 'individualism'. It is a term relished by Katharine Furse, May Wedderburn Cannan and Vera Brittain as a means of distinguishing personal strength, independence and single-mindedness from the bland ignominy of ordinariness. But again it is challenged by an alternativist vision that wants to make 'the life of the individual continuous with that of the community and the life of the community itself a conscious whole' (Hamilton 1922: 237). In terms of its admission of plurality and resistance to unified definitions, this has something in common with Woolf's assertion that 'nothing was simply one thing' – which became for her an aesthetic methodology as well as an epistemology.

I should probably say at this point that each chapter in this study is potentially the nucleus of a book of its own and could easily have been expanded to include a more complex range of context and debate. I have tried to give an outline of the kind of subject positions available to women, and of the conflicts, contradictions and coalitions that existed between them. If a military metaphor may be forgiven at this late stage, I could say that although I may not have produced a detailed, strategic guide to all the battles, I hope to have outlined some of the major campaigns. But I am not about to come up with a sudden and unifying conclusion: 'women's experience of the First World War was . . . .' If I could imagine any such conclusion it would be something along the lines of needing fifty pairs of eyes to see with. And I don't mean that simply as an uncritical endorsement of a playful pluralism. Feminism is now beyond the stage of illustrating women's experience and seeing it as being unproblematically represented and universally available. I don't intend to close an open door in order to stage an elaborate re-entry. Rather, I would hope that my work might contribute to a feminist project that is taking another look at both past and present, not in an attempt to seek out role models, but to examine the texture and complexities of women's lives irrespective of their 'feminist' credentials. The point of this is to examine our own contradictions and coalitions in the context of those that have taken place, more spectacularly, in the past. In so doing it is to be hoped that we may make sense of some of the inequalities of 'progress' that presently reveal themselves.

NOTES

1 NUNS AND LOVERS
Voluntary Aid Detachment nurses in the First World War

1 As Reilly points out, the poem came to be criticised for its naivety. Its sentiments are characteristic of the Brooke-like mood of the early part of the war; they could not survive the reports of horrific slaughter. Macaulay's change of attitude is confirmed by her pacifist novel, *Non-Combatants and Others* (1916), which will be discussed in Chapter 4. See Emery (1991: 141–60) for an account of Macaulay's rapid disillusion and her relationship with Brooke.

2 For example the Women's Volunteer Reserve, the Women's Defence Relief Corps and the First Aid Nursing Yeomanry (cf. Terry 1988: 32; Summers 1988: 250). The latter was known for its particularly flamboyant uniform and its famous breakaway member, Mrs St Clair Stobart. Her *The Flaming Sword in Serbia and Elsewhere* (1916) is notable for its pacifist message (cf. Tylee 1990: 33).

3 Female military nurses were, in fact, very rare until after the Boer War. Despite the power of her legend, even Florence Nightingale was unable to fill military hospitals with potential followers in the aftermath of the Crimean War. Military casualties tended to be nursed by male orderlies. For a detailed account of British Women as military nurses see Summers (1988). She charts their history until the outbreak of the First World War and includes an account of the formation of the VAD to which I have made frequent reference. My account of VAD work after the outbreak of war is largely based on the Women at War Collection at the Imperial War Museum.

4 Cf. 'Paper to VAD members from Katharine Furse', issued to all VADs with their instructions. A copy is held in the files of the British Red Cross Society, Imperial War Museum (hereafter BRCS).

5 There were also male detachments, but these were less popular owing, probably, to the appeal of the Territorial Force Army (Summers 1988: 253).

6 Isaac Rosenberg, for example, in a letter of December 1915,

records receiving 7s per week, while a separation allowance of 16s 6d went to his mother, plus 3s 6d deducted from the 7s (Parsons 1979: 227). Cf. also Simkins (1988: 107).

7 Lloyd George turned down her suggestion of an Officer Training Corps for women in 1916 (Furse 1940: 342).

8 The Women's Royal Navy Service was founded by Katharine Furse by invitation after she resigned from the VAD organisation (Furse 1940: 360). Gould (1987) gives an account of women's military services during the war, which concentrates on the Women's Army Auxiliary Corps and women's troubled integration into the military system.

9 Dorothy Nicol, unpublished TS: 'Memoirs of a VAD 1915–1917' (nd), Department of Documents, Imperial War Museum.

10 'Paper to VAD members from Katharine Furse' (BRCS).

11 Dorothy McCann, unpublished TS: 'The First World War Memoirs of Mrs D. McCann, VAD' (nd), np, Department of Documents, Imperial War Museum.

12 See McLaren (1917: 113–16) for an account of Mrs Graham Jones's disciplinarian approach. Tylee (1990) has suggested that she bears a strong resemblance to Mrs Bitch.

13 Her exploits in the German fighting lines were reported in the suffragist journal *The Common Cause* (9 October 1914: 471. Cf. also McLaren 1917: 73–7, Carr nd: 239–52).

14 The background to this was the campaign for State Registration of Nurses, begun in 1888 with a view to producing a national register of trained nurses. At this stage there was no definition of a trained nurse. A register would regulate qualifications and make them uniform and transferable, so that a nurse could seek work where she wished rather than being forced to take a chance with a single hospital. A further aim was to get the state to recognise nursing as a *profession*, and to diminish the operations of class privilege. The point at issue was similar to that concerning 'dilution' of skilled labour in the munitions industry, which will be discussed in the following chapter. The Nurses' Registration Act was passed in 1919, but did not require the standards demanded by those who had been involved in the campaign. See Summers 1988: 289–90; Vicinus 1985: 113–15.

15 Ruth Whitaker, unpublished TS: 'The First World War Memoirs of Miss R. Whitaker' (*c.* 1970), Department of Documents, Imperial War Museum: 188.

16 The picture of the 'Edwardian afternoon' is undermined somewhat by the signals of social unrest that dominated the pre-war period. The Suffragettes, the Irish and the Trades Unionists all were helping Liberal England towards its 'strange death' (cf. Dangerfield 1935; Fussell [1975] 1977: 23–5; Keating 1989: 91–151; Hynes 1990: 3–24). Peter Simkins, however, argues that the forces holding society together were greater than those suggesting its imminent dissolution (Simkins 1988: xvi). The narratives under discussion suggest that most provincial, middle-class daughters with little

formal education and scant political or intellectual commitment would have found that their lives had more in common with a Lesley Smith than, for example, a Virginia Woolf.

17 Cf. May Sinclair, *The Tree of Heaven* (1917), Rose Macaulay, *Non-Combatants and Others* (1916), Olive Dent, *A VAD in France* (1917): 'For the first time in a happy, even life one felt bitterly resentful of one's sex. Defence was the only consideration in the popular mind in those early August days. And defence was a man's job, and I, unfortunately, was a woman' (Dent 1917: 14).

18 Yvonne A. Bennett (1987) comments on the limitations of a feminism based simply on 'equality' when that 'equality', as is so in Brittain's case, is sought at the expense of other women of lower social and educational standing.

19 The accounts by Spearing (1917) and Dent (1917) both quote in detail many letters expressing the deeply felt gratitude of the soldiers for the meticulous and good-natured care they receive.

20 Sinclair was secretary and treasurer of the convoy, but only remained with it for seventeen days (cf. Boll 1973: 106–7, Stark 1990: 107–9). Nevertheless the experience fuelled *Journal of Impressions* (1915), *Tasker Jevons* (1916), *The Tree of Heaven* (1917) and *The Romantic* (1920). Other famous members of the convoy were the 'Two Women of Pervyse' – Elsie Knocker and Mairie Chisholm – and novelist Sarah Macnaughtan, who describes its members as 'oddly-dressed ladies, [. . .] at first one was inclined to call them masqueraders in their knickerbockers and puttees and caps, but I believe they have done excellent work' (Macnaughtan 1919: 25).

21 'I should never spiritually progress if [. . .] I never had to work out my own soul's redemption "with suffering and through time"' (1981: 165); 'I felt again [. . .] the longing for a fuller realisation of my spiritual being and for the perfecting of the intellectual instrument through which it expresses and reveals itself' (1981: 166); 'the brave do not ask for respite during toil' (1981: 221). These comments were made in 1915 while Brittain was deciding whether or not to nurse full time. Such remarks are largely omitted from *Testament*, where the emphasis is more on immediate and personal rather than abstract suffering, and on the rational nature of her decision to emulate Roland – as far as circumstances would permit.

22 Cf. Sillars (1987), who sets out to examine artistic forms of all kinds in 1916 in their relation to the public events of that year.

23 Cf. BRCS 10 1/3: '4 women do the work of 3 men; 8 women take the accommodation of 14 to 25 men. Women have spring bedsteads where men sleep on boards.' This refers to women replacing male orderlies or clerks. A direct comparison with the living conditions of the soldiers was plainly impossible.

24 Cf. Barbara Hardy's introduction to the 1988 Virago reprint for an account of the novel's inception. Tylee (1990: 197–200) offers a commentary on it, describing it as a 'grovelling plea for woman's

share in the pity of war' (1990: 199). Hardy is less dismissive, recognising 'currents of feminism under the great breaking wave of its pacifism' (1988: 7).

25 Cf. the account of Charlotte Dalton, RRC (later Mrs Mackay Brown), who describes the VAD command's regulations concerning contact with men – and their loopholes. Unpublished TS: 'The First World War Scrapbooks of Mrs G. Mackay Brown' (c. 1975), Department of Documents, Imperial War Museum.

26 Cf. her *Honourable Estate* (1936), where the heroine has 'safe' sex with her hero before he goes to his death.

27 Furse went on to form the World Association of Girl Guides and Girl Scouts; Crowdy worked for the League of Nations 1919–31, where she met (amongst others) Helena Swanwick, whose work *against* the war will be discussed in Chapter 4. Thurstan became an officer in the Women's Royal Naval Service and in the Allied Commission, Austria (1946–8), and was the author of twelve further publications.

2 COUNTRY AND TOWN, AGRICULTURE AND MUNITIONS
The proper lady and the woman worker

1 *Table 2.1* Report of the Women's Employment Committee, 1919 (Employment 29/2, Imperial War Museum.)

Occupation	Estimated number of women employed in July 1914	Increase or decrease since July 1914
Clerical	452,200	+302,000
Commercial	496,000	+364,000
Agricultural (permanent)	80,000	+33,000
Industrial occupations	2,196,600	+891,000
Totals	3,224,800	1,590,000

2 Cf. Virginia Woolf's rendering of female alterity (Chapter 5); Jane Marcus, who, in 'A Wilderness of One's Own', suggests that the country, or nature, is often imagined as a predominantly female space (1984: 138; cf. also Squier 1984: 120); the Greenham Common women's concern with nature and non-hierarchised systems; Julia Kristeva's 'Women's Time', which opposes a cyclical, monumental, eternal conception of time and value to a linear, progressive model, associated with masculinity.

3 Miss Edith Airey, unpublished memoir (nd), np, Department of Documents, Imperial War Museum.

4 The National Political League, primarily for University women,

formed a Land Council, mainly for information and training. The Women's Defence Relief Corps sent out bands of women to work at haymaking, harvesting, market-gardening and fruit-picking, stipulating a minimum wage of 18s per week and advertising the tasks as vacation work. The Women's National Land Service Corps ran on a voluntary basis for educated women unwilling to sign on for the duration of the war. The Women's Farm and Garden Union was an old established institution, which was in existence before the war and carried on providing information and support for women on the land after the war-based associations had been disbanded.

5 This consisted of signing on via Employment Exchanges and then being offered an interview by a District Selection Committee which decided whether a medical check was necessary. This Committee also decided whether the applicant should be trained or sent straight to a farm. The Landworker then returned home to wait for her instructions, uniform and grants. Training was free, as was the uniform, consisting of two pairs of boots, one pair of gaiters, three overalls, two pairs of breeches, one hat, a jersey and a mackintosh. The minimum wage was 22s 6d until the completion of three months' work and thereafter 25s per week (Files of Women Land Work, hereafter Land, 6 1/4).

6 Mrs M. Harrold, unpublished MS (nd), Department of Documents, Imperial War Museum.

7 Rosa Freedman, unpublished TS, 'Memories of a Land Girl in the First World War' (1978), Department of Documents, Imperial War Museum.

8 Mrs M. Bale, unpublished MS, 'Memories of the Woman's Land Army 1916–1919' (nd), Department of Documents, Imperial War Museum.

9 C. M. Prunell, unpublished diary (1917), Department of Documents, Imperial War Museum.

10 Viscountess Wolsely (1872–1936) founded Glynde College for Lady Gardeners in 1901, was organising secretary to the Board of Agriculture of East Sussex (Women's Branch) in 1917 and published books on gardens.

11 Olive Hockin was a married woman with children who was advised by her husband to take up war work when he was ordered to the Front. She lived in Devonshire and found that being in the country meant that 'there [was] nothing for me to do but to work on the land' (McLaren 1917: 17).

12 Cf. *The Times* (19 March 1918: 3): '100 girls will be assembled in the square during the day to inform recruits about the open-air life which these girls find so attractive that they would not give it up for any other work.'

13 Edith Airey notes that one of the striking changes to the countryside was not only the appearance of women working on the land, but the conversion of large country houses into convalescent homes – usually for officers (IWM np). Cf. Thompson, *The Hounds of Spring* in Chapter 3.

14 Cf. Holtby's recollection of the lack of light and heating, the poor communication system and rigid class divisions in the Yorkshire village in which she grew up before the war, quoted in Brittain ([1940] 1980: 397).

15 Cf. the unpublished account of Miss Olive Taylor: 'On this farm [in Barrow on Humber] there was an old bewhiskered farmer who never spoke, a down trodden old lady, the wife, and two grown up sons, one of whom was mentally backward, while his brother was a heavy drinker.' She later found out that the old lady committed suicide by drowning herself in a rainwater barrel, the farmer shot himself, the alcoholic son cut his throat and the mentally afflicted one went into an asylum. 'Recollections of the Great War 1914–18' (nd), Department of Documents, Imperial War Museum.

16 For recent work on British propaganda see Haste (1977), Sanders and Taylor (1982) and Buitenhuis ([1987] 1989), who concentrates on the collaboration between leading literary figures and the government.

17 Cf. Braybon (1981: 26, 45). Braybon is the best single source on working-class women's work in industry during the war. Liddington and Norris (1978) have a useful final chapter and Rowbotham (1973) provides a general overview of the war in the context of working women's fight for the vote. For a contemporary discussion of women's position in industry during the war years see B. L. Hutchins, *Women in Modern Industry* (1915), Dorothea Barton, *Equal Pay for Equal Work* (1919), Barbara Drake, *Women in Trade Unions* (1921), Margaret Bondfield, *English Women in the Labour and Co-operative Movements* (1919).

18 Mrs Alec-Tweedie served on many charitable and philanthropic committees. Her publications include travel books (e.g. *Through Finland in Carts* (1897)) and she frequently exhibited water-colour sketches made on her travels.

19 Cf. Mun 341/2 Imperial War Museum: 'The Effects of Tri-Nitro-Toluene on Women Workers' by Agnes Livingstone-Learmonth MB ChB Edin and Barbara Martin Cunningham MD Edin.

20 Letter from Mrs G. Kaye to her sister Eileen, 24 January 1940, Department of Documents, Imperial War Museum.

21 Miss Olive Taylor, unpublished MS: 'Recollections of the Great War 1914–1918' (nd), Department of Documents, Imperial War Museum.

22 Cf. Culleton (1988), who remarks on Caine's metaphors of maternalism but concludes that they are simply reductive of women's identity, rather than being also anxiety-producing (1988: 115).

23 Braybon suggests that reports of high pay were mythical, perpetrated by those who resented the notion of working-class women's independence (1981: 166). This is backed up by Liddington and Norris (1978: 254), Miss Olive Taylor (IWM, np) and Peggy Hamilton, who says that women's pay was normally half that of men's (1978: 100).

24 Cf. *Jus Suffragii* (1 May 1918: 120) and an article by Esther Roper in *The Englishwoman* (March 1917: 206–12).
25 Cf. also Alec-Tweedie (1918: 31–2), who almost directly reproduces this romantic portrait.

3 WOMEN AT HOME
Romance or realism?

1 Cf. the first issue under British imprint of *Vogue*, May 1916, in which the romance of the war-wedding is wistfully documented: 'One sees a little group descending the steps of the Madeleine – a soldier in a mud-stained uniform, his bride in a simple *tailleur*' (1 May 1916: 48).
2 Other titles in this series are 'A Cheerful Giver', 'The Spirit of Sacrifice', 'The Girl Who Waits', 'The Girl Who is Grateful'.
3 A 'war baby' in *The Silent Legion* (1918), by popular author J. E. Buckrose, was indeed called Kitchener. It is interesting to note, though, that novels concerned more with pacifism than patriotism tend to exhibit a greater interest in the mother–daughter bond, as will be discussed in the following chapter.
4 Others like them include J. E. Buckrose's *War-Time in Our Street* (1917) and *The Silent Legion* (1918) and Annie S. Swan's *The Woman's Part* (1916).
5 Sinclair was associated with *The Egoist* and two of its major contributors, H. D. and Richard Aldington. She was a member of the Woman Writers Suffrage League and defended the suffragist cause in a pamphlet, 'Feminism', in 1912. She also became a supporter of the war and did not, as many other suffragists did, believe that women should want peace on principle (cf. her article 'Women's Sacrifices for the War' in *The Woman at Home*, February 1915: 67). For the connection between suffragists and the peace movement see Chapter 4. Stark (1990) provides a useful discussion of Sinclair's intellectual and political context.
6 Pseudonym of Florence Roma Muir Wilson (1891–1930), a novelist who studied law at Girton before the war and had worked as a civil servant. Her third novel, *The Death of Society*, won the Hawthornden Prize in June 1921.
7 West had an interest in psychoanalysis and may have been aware of Freud's 'Thoughts for the Times on War and Death' (1915) in which he says that a repressed mental state 'may at any time again become the mode of expression of the forces in the mind, and indeed the only one . . .' (cf. Schwaber 1981: 136).
8 Cannan had been engaged to Bevil Quiller-Couch, son of Arthur, who died on active service in Germany immediately following the declaration of peace. As Carey helps Delphine, 'Q' did much to encourage Cannan's literary endeavours (cf. Cannan 1976).
9 Sylvia Thompson belonged to what Vera Brittain called 'The Somerville School of Novelists' (cf. *Testament of a Generation*, (1985: 323–4)), along with Rose Macaulay, Dorothy L. Sayers, Winifred

Holtby, Margaret Kennedy and Hilda S. Reid. Brittain appears not to have been impressed by Thompson, whose *The Hounds of Spring*, written at the age of 23, she compares unfavourably with Holtby's *Anderby Wold*, written at a similarly young age.

4 REACTIONARY OR REVOLUTIONARY?
The maternal pacifist

1 This is similar to Kristeva's second generation in as far as it emphasises women's roles and interests that are distinct and separate from those of men. Kristeva refers to a feminist *separatism*, a product of the women's movement in the 1960s and 1970s, that would not have been appropriate to women seeking entry into the (male-dominated) political system by means of the vote.

2 Cf. Davin (1978: 43) for an historical analysis of the importance in public debate of infant life and child health. See also Bryder (1987) for a discussion of government reports of the nation's health during the war.

3 It is interesting to note that the 'physical force' argument was used against women seeking equal franchise by Mrs Humphry Ward and other anti-suffragists. If women could not fight, the argument went, they should not be able to vote on issues that, according to the laws of international relations, tend to be resolved by armed combat. It was an argument strenuously rejected by suffragists and pacifists who saw it as a serious threat to civilised values and as inevitably oppressive to any minority. This argument is articulated in Maria Grey's pamphlet *The Physical Force Objection to Women's Suffrage* (1901).

4 The representation at and resolutions of the Hague Conference have been documented in many sources, notably Wiltsher (1985), Bussey and Tims (1965), Addams *et al.* (1915). Jo Vellacott has written about it from the suffragists' point of view (1977 and 1987a, b) and, from the position of her ELFS, Sylvia Pankhurst comments on it in *The Home Front* (1932), emphasising her impatience with its reasonableness (1932: 154).

5 A political dilemma emerged in that although women were indeed in need of more medical care and material provision as mothers, the ideological apparatus that allowed this was still submerged in imperialism and aimed at giving mothers sole responsibility for the welfare of children (cf. *Jus Suffragii* 1 November 1915: 24).

6 *The Englishwoman*, although not the official organ of the NUWSS, acted as a forum for more detailed and lengthy discussion of issues facing the organisation than the campaign paper had space for.

7 See Lynne Jones 'Perceptions of "peace women" at Greenham Common' (1987). For an account of individual twentieth-century women opposed to militarism, see Sybil Oldfield, *Women Against the Iron Fist* (1989).

8 Collegium Meetings were concerned with peace and the religious

aspects of the women's movement. Marshall's talk is published along-side 'Militarism Versus Feminism' in Kamester and Vellacott 1987.

9 This was a tactic employed by Bertrand Russell in his pacifist writings: he frequently opened with broad statements, reserving the real challenges until he had secured an audience (cf. Moran 1985: 57–8).

10 The statement 'Our Demands' printed on the front page of *The Woman's Dreadnought* (15 August 1914) suggests, for example, that the nation's food supply should be controlled so that 'all may feed or starve together, without regard to wealth or social position' and that working women should be consulted about fixing prices. Soldiers' wives were often unjustly suspected of being drunk and unchaste and of squandering the (minimal) allowance offered to them, which could be withdrawn without trial or any opportunity for the women to vindicate themselves (Pankhurst 1932: 98–9). The ELFS did something to minimise the horror of war for women by establishing cost price restaurants, babies' milk centres and the 'Mother's Arms' – a creche that had formerly been a pub. This work was mostly financed by wealthy suffragettes, and funds inevitably ran out. For further details see the pages of *The Woman's Dread-nought*, Pankhurst's *The Home Front* (1932) and Patricia Romero's biography of Pankhurst, *Portrait of a Rebel* (1990).

11 The words 'great adventure' also call to mind Dr Maude Royden's pamphlet *The Great Adventure: the Way to Peace* (1914) in which disarmament is seen as the only way to avoid establishing the 'heresy' of militarism in Britain; overcoming evil with good is seen as the only truly Christian way forward. Royden had succeeded Swanwick as editor of *The Common Cause* and was a member of the pacifist Christian group, the Fellowship of Reconciliation. The Quakers and Christadelphians were also predominantly pacifist.

12 Her essay has been extended into a book, *Maternal Thinking* (1989).

13 The neutrality of America until 1917 was the focus of pacifist aspiration. It was hoped that President Woodrow Wilson would call together a committee of neutral representatives to meet in Norway and begin a process of continuous mediation which would allow any country at any time to accept the offer of negotiation without the stigma of humiliation (cf. *Jus Suffragii* 1 October 1914: 174). For a general picture of America's appeal in terms of gender, race and class relations, see Emmeline Pethick Lawrence in *Votes for Women* (16 October 1914: 78). Her tour of America culminated in her accompanying Jane Addams across the Atlantic to the Hague Peace Congress.

14 See Oldfield (1984) for a biographical account of Sheepshanks.

15 For a detailed exposition of the experiences, backgrounds and prison conditions of conscientious objectors, see Mrs Henry Hobhouse, *'I Appeal Unto Caesar': The Case of the Conscientious Objector* (1917) and J. Bell, *We Did Not Fight* (1935).

16 Cf. those organised by the NUWSS or the Queen's Work for Women Fund.

17 Cf. Ellen Key, *War, Peace and the Future* (1916). This was part of the platform of the Women's Peace Party.

5 WOOLF, WAR AND WRITING
New words, new methods

1 For Woolf's political profile see Naomi Black 'Virginia Woolf and the Women's Movement' in Jane Marcus (ed.), *Virginia Woolf: A Feminist Slant* (1983). See the same volume for Marcus's 'Thinking Back Through Our Mothers', in which she describes Woolf as a 'guerilla fighter in a Victorian skirt' (1); Marcus carried on her political defence of Woolf by describing her as a 'genteel Marxist' in '"No More Horses": Virginia Woolf on Art and Propaganda' (in Morris Beja (ed.), *Critical Essays on Virginia Woolf* 1985: 153): she is concerned to defend Woolf from the 'precious invalid lady of Bloomsbury' school of criticism here.

2 Jean Bethke Elshtain, *Women and War* (1987: 236), Elaine Showalter, *A Literature of Their Own* (1978: 263ff). Woolf's critical reception is covered up to its impact with the feminist movement by Hermione Lee in her introduction to *The Novels of Virginia Woolf* (1977). Toril Moi in *Sexual/Textual Politics* (1985) argues against Showalter's case (see above) by suggesting that the deconstructive position articulated by Julia Kristeva offers a way out of the ethereal/political dichotomy. Woolf's feminism as insistence on *plural* vision has been taken up by, for example, Bonnie Kime Scott (1988) and Rachel Blau DuPlessis (1988). The development of the place of French feminist psychoanalytical thinking in academic feminism has produced numerous studies that align Woolf's political strength with her proximity to the semiotic, or the Imaginary, e. g. Jean Wyatt, 'Avoiding Self-Definition: In Defense of Women's Right to Merge (Julia Kristeva and *Mrs Dalloway*)' (1986) and Makiko Minow-Pinkney, *Virginia Woolf and the Problem of the Subject* (1987). Patricia Klindienst Joplin's PhD thesis, 'The Art of Resistance: Authority and Violence in the work of Virginia Woolf' (1984), also uses concepts of dominance and marginality, but in the terms of anthropology rather than psychoanalysis. Woolf has also received a great deal of critical attention in the context of peace studies. This work tends to concentrate on *Three Guineas* rather than the fiction. See, for example, Sara Ruddick, *Maternal Thinking* (1989), Sharon MacDonald *et al.*, *Images of Women in Peace and War* (1987), Glynnis Carr, 'Waging Peace: Virginia Woolf's *Three Guineas*' (1986) and Sybil Oldfield, *Women Against the Iron Fist: Alternatives to Militarism* (1989).

3 For Northcliffe's involvement in war propaganda see Cate Haste, *Keep the Home Fires Burning* (1977), M. L. Sanders and Philip M. Taylor, *British Propaganda During the First World War* (1982) and Peter Buitenhuis, *The Great War of Words* (1989).

4 Cf. Fussell ([1975] 1977: 3–35). His study is, of course, well known

for positing irony as the dominant mode of understanding and remembering the First World War.

5 Cf., for example, Annie S. Swan, *The Woman's Part* (Hodder and Stoughton, 1916).

6 Cora Kaplan, in an essay on representations of working-class women, argues that imperilled and defensive bourgeois feminists often reinforce their own position at the expense of lower-class women, irrespective of an overtly articulated sympathy with women across the social spectrum. This she attributes to their displacing interiorised concepts of what is inadequate in their sex onto women of lower social standing (Kaplan 1988: 59–60).

7 Cf. Henke (1981) and Scott (1988), who offer, respectively, 'paraphrenic' and modernist analyses of Septimus's language use.

8 Sue Thomas (1987) had made a case for reading *MD* specifically as a retort to the Report's findings. While I am in agreement with most of her points, my reading of the subject emphasises Woolf's tendency to charge documentary details with metaphorical significance.

BIBLIOGRAPHY

UNPUBLISHED SOURCES

From the Women's Work Collection, Imperial War Museum

Files of the British Red Cross Society (BRCS), Department of Printed Books, Imperial War Museum.

Files of Women's Land Work (Land), Department of Printed Books, Imperial War Museum.

Files of Women's Munitions Work, Department of Printed Books, Imperial War Museum.

Memoirs held by the Department of Documents, Imperial War Museum

Airey, Miss Edith (nd) Unpublished memoir, MS.

Bale, Mrs M. (nd) 'Memories of the Women's Land Army 1916–1919', MS.

Cannan, May Wedderburn (1971) 'Recollections of a British Red Cross Voluntary Aid Detachment, No. 12, Oxford University, March 26th 1911–April 24 1919', TS.

Dalton, Charlotte (Mrs G. Mackay Brown) (c. 1975) 'The First World War Scrapbooks of Mrs G. Mackay Brown by Charlotte Louise Fitzgerald Dalton, RRC', TS.

Freedman, Rosa (1978) 'Memories of a Land Girl in the First World War', TS.

Harrold, Mrs M. (nd) Unpublished memoir, MS.

Kaye, Mrs G. (24 January 1940) Letter to her sister Eileen, ALS.

McCann, Mrs Dorothy (nd) 'The First World War Memoirs of Mrs D. McCann, VAD', TS.

Manning, R. B. (24 April 1917–3 September 1918) 'Diary of Ruth B. Manning, VAD', MS.

Neville, Miss Amy, Miscellaneous letters.

Nicol, Dorothy (nd) 'Memoirs of a VAD 1915–1917', TS.

Prunell, C. M. (1917) A diary, MS.

Taylor, Miss Olive M. (nd) 'Recollections of the Great War 1914–1918', MS.

Watkins, Miss Amy (nd) '1914–18 First World War', MS.

Whitaker, Ruth (*c.* 1970) 'The First World War Memoirs of Miss R. Whitaker', TS.

MAGAZINES AND JOURNALS

Britannia
The Common Cause
The Englishwoman
Everwoman's
Everywoman's Weekly
Jus Suffragii
Mother and Home
The Suffragette
The Times
Vogue
The Vote
Votes for Women
The Woman at Home
The Woman's Dreadnought
Women's Industrial News
Woman's Own
Woman's World
The Workers' Dreadnought

PRIMARY SOURCES

Addams, Jane, Emily G. Balch, and Alice Hamilton (1915) *Women at the Hague,* New York: Macmillan.

Alec-Tweedie, Mrs (1918) *Women and Soldiers,* London: John Lane, The Bodley Head.

Allatini, Rose ('A. T. Fitzroy') (1918; rpt 1975) *Despised and Rejected,* New York: Arno.

Asquith, Lady Cynthia (1968) *Diaries 1915–18,* London: Hutchinson.

Bagnold, Enid (1918) *A Diary Without Dates,* London: Heinemann.

—— (1920) *The Happy Foreigner,* London: Heinemann

Barton, Dorothea (1919) *Equal Pay for Equal Work,* London.

Bell, Anne Olivier (ed.) (1977; rpt 1979) *The Diary of Virginia Woolf Volume I: 1915–1919,* Harmondsworth: Penguin.

Bell, J. (ed.) (1935) *We Did Not Fight: 1914–1918 Experiences of War Resisters,* London: Cobden-Sanderson.

Bondfield, Margaret (1919) *English Women in the Labour and Co-Operative Movements,* London.

Borden, Mary (1929) *The Forbidden Zone,* London: Heinemann.

Bowser, Thekla (1917) *The Story of British VAD Work in the Great War,* London: Melrose.

Brittain, Vera (1933; rpt 1979) *Testament of Youth*, London: Fontana Paperbacks in association with Virago.
—— (1936) *Honourable Estate*, London: Victor Gollancz.
—— (1937) 'Why I Stand for Peace', in *Let Us Honour Peace*, London: Cobden-Sanderson.
—— (1940; rpt 1980) *Testament of Friendship*, London: Virago.
—— (1957; rpt 1980) *Testament of Experience*, London: Fontana Paperbacks in association with Virago.
—— (1981) *War Diary 1913–1917: Chronicle of Youth*, ed. Alan Bishop with Terry Smart, London: Victor Gollancz.
Buckrose, J. E. (1917) *War-time in Our Street, the Story of Some Companies Behind the Firing Line*, London: Hodder and Stoughton.
—— (1918) *The Silent Legion*, London: Hodder and Stoughton.
Bussey, Gertrude and Margaret Tims (1965) *The Women's International League for Peace and Freedom 1915–1965. A Record of Fifty Years' Work*, London: Allen and Unwin.
Cable, Boyd (1916) *Doing Their Bit: War Work at Home*, London: Hodder and Stoughton.
Caine, Hall (1916) *Our Girls: Their Work for the War*, London: Hutchinson.
Campbell, Phyllis (1915) *Back of the Front*, London: George Newnes.
Cannan, May Wedderburn (1934) *The Lonely Generation*, London: Hutchinson.
—— (1976) *Grey Ghosts and Voices*, Kineton: Roundwood Press.
Carr, Kent (nd) *Women Who Dared: Heroines of the Great War*, London: S. W. Partridge.
Dane, Clemence (1917) *Regiment of Women*, London: Heinemann.
—— (1918) *First the Blade: A Comedy of Growth*, London: Heinemann.
Dent, Olive (1917) *A VAD in France*, London: Grant Richards.
Drake, Barbara (1921) *Women in Trade Unions*, London: Trade Union Series No. 6.
Drucker, Amy J. (1916) 'A Cockney's Harvesting', *The Englishwoman* 20 (8): 13–21.
Furse, Katharine (1940) *Hearts and Pomegranates: The Story of Forty-five Years*, London: Peter Davies.
Girvin, Brenda (1918) *Munition Mary*, London: Humphrey Milford.
Graves, Robert (1929; rev. 1957; rpt 1960) *Goodbye to All That*, Harmondsworth: Penguin.
Great Britain, Army (1922) 'Report of the War Office Committee of Enquiry into "Shell-shock"', *English Parliamentary Papers XII*, Cmd 1734.
Greig, G. A. (1917) *Women's Work on the Land*, London: Jarrold and Sons.
Grey, Maria G. (1901) *The Physical Force Objection to Women's Suffrage*, London: Central Society for Women's Suffrage.
Hall, Radclyffe (1928; rpt 1982) *The Well of Loneliness*, London: Virago.
—— (1934) *Miss Ogilvy Finds Herself*, London: Heinemann.
Hamilton, Mary Agnes (1916) *Dead Yesterday*, London: Duckworth.
—— (1922) *Follow My Leader*, London: Jonathan Cape.

—— (1944) *Remembering My Good Friends*, London: Jonathan Cape.

Hamilton, Lady Peggy (1978) *Three Years or the Duration: the Memoirs of a Munitions Worker*, London: Peter Owen.

Hobhouse, Mrs H. (1917) *'I Appeal Unto Caesar': The Case of the Conscientious Objector*, London: Allen and Unwin.

Hockin, Olive (1918) *Two Girls on the Land. War-Time on a Dartmoor Farm*, London: Arnold.

Holland, Ruth (1932) *The Lost Generation*, London: Victor Gollancz.

Holtby, Winifred (1924; rpt 1981) *The Crowded Street*, London: Virago.

—— (1935; rpt 1978) *Women and a Changing Civilization*, Chicago: Academy Press, Cassandra Editions.

Housman, A. E. (1896; rpt 1947) *A Shropshire Lad*, London: The Richards Press.

Hutchins, B. L. (1915; rpt 1980) *Women in Modern Industry*, New York and London: Garland Publishing.

Kamester, Margaret and Jo Vellacott (eds) (1987) *Militarism Versus Feminism: Writings on Women and War. Catherine Marshall, C. K. Ogden and Mary Sargant Florence*, London: Virago.

Key, Ellen (1916) *War, Peace and the Future*, trans. Hildegard Norberg, London: G. P. Putnam.

Lee, Vernon (1920) *Satan the Waster: A Philosophic War Trilogy with Notes and Introduction*, London: John Lane.

Let Us Honour Peace (1937) London: Cobden-Sanderson.

Macaulay, Rose (1916) *Non-Combatants and Others*, London: Hodder and Stoughton.

McLaren, Barbara (1917) *Women of the War*, London: Hodder and Stoughton.

Macnaughtan, S. (1919) *My War Experiences in Two Continents*, London: Murray.

Marchant, Bessie (1916) *A Girl Munition Worker: The Story of a Girl's Work During the Great War*, London: Blackie.

Marcus, Jane (ed.) (1982) *The Young Rebecca: Writings of Rebecca West 1911–17*, New York: Viking Press, in association with Virago.

Marshall, Catherine (1915 and 1916) in Kamester, Margaret and Jo Vellacott (eds) (1987) *Militarism Versus Feminism: Writing on Women and War. Catherine Marshall, C.K. Ogden and Mary Sargant Florence*, London: Virago.

Nicolson, Nigel (ed.) (1976) *The Question of Things Happening. The Letters of Virginia Woolf*, vol. II: 1912–1922, London: Chatto and Windus.

—— (1979) *The Sickle Side of the Moon. The Letters of Virginia Woolf*, vol. V: 1932–1935, London: Chatto and Windus.

Ogden, C. K. and Mary Sargant Florence (1915) in Kamester: Margaret and Jo Vellacott (eds) (1987) *Militarism Versus Feminism: Writing on Women and War. Catherine Marshall, C.K. Ogden and Mary Sargant Florence*, London: Virago.

Pankhurst, Sylvia (1932) *The Home Front*, London: Hutchinson.

Parsons, I. M. (ed.) (1979) *The Collected Works of Isaac Rosenberg*, London: Chatto and Windus.

Price, Evadne ('Helen Zenna Smith') (1930) 'Not So Quiet. . .' Step-daughters of War, London: A. E. Marriott.

Rathbone, Irene (1932; rpt 1988) We That Were Young, London: Virago.

Reilly, Catherine (ed.) (1981) Scars Upon My Heart: Women's Poetry and Verse of the First World War, London: Virago.

Remarque, Erich Maria (1929; rpt 1963) All Quiet on the Western Front, London: Mayflower Books.

Royden, A. Maude (1914) The Great Adventure: The Way to Peace, London: Headley Brothers.

Ruck, Berta (1919) The Land Girl's Love Story, London: Hodder and Stoughton.

Schreiner, Olive (1911; rpt 1987) 'Woman and War', in An Olive Schreiner Reader, ed. Carol Barash, London: Pandora.

Sherwood, Margaret (1917) The Worn Doorstep, London: Hodder and Stoughton.

Sinclair, May (1915) A Journal of Impressions in Belgium, London: Hutchinson.

—— (1916) Tasker Jevons, London: Hutchinson.

—— (1917) The Tree of Heaven, London: Cassell.

—— (1920) The Romantic, London: W. Collins.

Smith, L. N. (1931) Four Years Out of Life, London: Allan.

Stobart, Mrs St Clair (1916) The Flaming Sword in Serbia and Elsewhere, London: Hodder and Stoughton.

Swan, Annie S. (1915) Letters to a War Bride, London: Hodder and Stoughton.

—— (1916; rpt 1972) The Woman's Part, Bath: Lythway Press.

Swanwick, Helena M. (1915a; rpt 1971) 'Women and War', in 'Women and War' and 'War and its Effect on Women', New York: Garland.

—— (1915b; rpt 1971) 'War and its Effect on Women', in 'Women and War' and 'War and its Effect on Women', New York: Garland.

—— (1935) I Have Been Young, London: Victor Gollancz.

Thompson, Sylvia (1926) The Hounds of Spring, London: Heinemann.

Thurstan, Violetta (1915) Field Hospital and Flying Column: Being the Journal of an English Nursing Sister in Belgium and Russia, London: Putnam's.

Wells, H. G. (1911; rpt 1946) The New Machiavelli, Harmondsworth: Penguin.

West, Rebecca (1918; rpt 1980) The Return of the Soldier, London: Virago.

Wibberley, T. (1916) War-Time Farming, London: C. Arthur Pearson.

Willis, Irene Cooper (1928; rpt 1971) England's Holy War, New York: Garland Library of War and Peace.

Wilson, Romer (1919) If All These Young Men, London: Methuen.

Wilson, Theodora Wilson (1916) The Last Weapon, London: C. W. Daniel.

Wolsely, Viscountess (1916) Women and the Land, London: Chatto and Windus.

Woolf, Virginia (1920; rpt 1985) 'A Society', in The Complete Shorter

Fiction of Virginia Woolf, ed. Susan Dick, London: Hogarth.
—— (1922; rpt 1976) *Jacob's Room*, London: Granada.
—— (1924; rpt 1966) 'Mr Bennett and Mrs Brown', in *Collected Essays III*, London: Hogarth.
—— (1925; rpt 1976) *Mrs Dalloway*, London: Granada.
—— (1927; rpt 1964) *To the Lighthouse*, Harmondsworth: Penguin.
—— (1929; rpt 1977) *A Room of One's Own*, London: Granada.
—— (1938; rpt 1977) *Three Guineas*, Harmondsworth: Penguin.
Yates, L. K. (1918) *The Woman's Part: A Record of Munitions Work*, London: Hodder and Stoughton.

SECONDARY SOURCES

Abel, Elizabeth, Marianne Hirsch and Elizabeth Langland (eds) (1983) *The Voyage In: Fictions of Female Development*, Hanover N H: University Press of New England for Dartmouth College.
Althusser, Louis (1971) 'Ideology and Ideological State Apparatuses (Notes towards an Investigation)', in *Lenin and Philosophy and other Essays*, trans. Ben Brewster, London: New Left Books.
Armstrong, Alan (1988) *Farmworkers: A Social and Economic History 1770–1980*, London: Batsford.
Beauman, Nicola (1983) *A Very Great Profession*, London: Virago.
Beddoe, Deirdre (1989) *Back to Home and Duty; Women Between the Wars 1918–39*, London: Pandora Press.
Bennett, Yvonne A. (1987) 'Vera Brittain: Feminism, Pacifism and Problems of Class 1900–1953', *Atlantis* 12 (2): 18–23.
Berry, Paul and Alan Bishop (eds) (1985) *Testament of a Generation: The Journalism of Vera Brittain and Winifred Holtby*, London: Virago.
Boll, Theophilus (1973) *Miss May Sinclair: Novelist*, New Jersey: Associated University Presses.
Braybon, Gail (1981) *Women Workers in the First World War: The British Experience*, London: Croom Helm.
Bryder, Linda (1987) 'The First World War: Healthy or Hungry?', *History Workshop* 24: 141–57.
Buitenhuis, Peter (1987; rpt 1989) *The Great War of Words: Literature as Propaganda 1914–18 and After*, London: Batsford.
Byles, Joan Montgomery (1985) 'Women's Experience of World War One: Suffragists, Pacifists and Poets', *Women's Studies International Forum* 8 (5): 473–87.
Cadogan, Mary and Patricia Craig (1978) *Women and Children First: The Fiction of Two World Wars*, London: Victor Gollancz.
Carr, Glynis (1986) 'Waging Peace: Virginia Woolf's *Three Guineas*', *Proteus: A Journal of Ideas* 3 (2): 13–21.
Carter, Ronald and Walter Nash (1983) 'Language and Literariness', *Prose Studies* 6 (2): 123–41.
Ceadel, Martin (1980) *Pacifism in Britain 1914–1945: Defining a Faith*, Oxford: Clarendon Press.
Chodorow, Nancy (1978) *The Reproduction of Mothering*, Berkeley, CA: University of California Press.

Cixous, Helene (1975; rpt 1981) 'The Laugh of the Medusa', trans. Keith Cohen and Paula Cohen in *New French Feminisms: An Anthology*, ed. Elaine Marks and Isabelle de Courtivron, Brighton: Harvester.

Clements, Patricia and Isobel Grundy (eds) (1983) *Virginia Woolf: New Critical Essays*, London: Vision; Totowa, NJ: Barnes and Noble.

Culleton, Claire (1988) 'Gender-charged Munitions: the Language of World War One Munitions Reports', *Women's Studies International Forum* 11 (2): 109–16.

Dakers, Caroline (1987) *The Countryside at War*, London: Constable.

Dangerfield, George (1935; rpt 1966) *The Strange Death of Liberal England*, pref. Paul Johnson, London: MacGibbon & Kee.

Darracott, Joseph (1974) *The First World War in Posters*, New York: Dover Publications.

Davin, Anna (1978) 'Imperialism and Motherhood', *History Workshop* 5: 9–65.

Dinnerstein, Dorothy (1976; rpt 1987) *The Rocking of the Cradle and the Ruling of the World*, London: Women's Press.

Duplessis, Rachel Blau (1988) 'Feminist Narrative in Virginia Woolf', *Novel* 21 (2–3): 323–30.

Elshtain, Jean Bethke (1987) *Women and War*, Brighton: Harvester.

Emery, Jane (1991) *Rose Macaulay: A Writer's Life*, London: John Murray.

Enloe, Cynthia (1983) *Does Khaki Become You?*, London: Pluto Press.

Evans, Richard (1987) *Comrades and Sisters: Feminism, Socialism and Pacifism in Europe 1870–1945*, Brighton: Wheatsheaf.

Falls, Cyril (1930) *War Books, A Critical Guide*, London: Peter Davies.

Fussell, Paul (1975; rpt 1977) *The Great War and Modern Memory*, New York and London: Oxford University Press.

Garner, Les (1984) *Stepping Stones to Women's Liberty: Feminist Ideas in the Women's Suffrage Movement 1900–1918*, London: Heinemann Educational.

Gilbert, Sandra and Susan Gubar (1988) *The War of the Words*, vol. I of *No Man's Land: The Place of the Woman Writer in the Twentieth Century*, New Haven, CT, and London: Yale University Press.

—— (1989) *Sexchanges*, vol. II of *No Man's Land: The Place of the Woman Writer in the Twentieth Century*, New Haven, CT, and London: Yale University Press.

Ginsberg, Elaine K, Laura Moss Gottlieb and Joanne Trautman (eds) (1983) *Virginia Woolf: Centennial Essays*, Troy, NY: Whitson.

Gould, Jenny (1987) 'Women's Military Sevices in First World War Britain', in *Behind the Lines: Gender and the Two World Wars*, ed. Higonnet *et al.*, New Haven, CT: Yale University Press.

Greene, Gayle and Coppelia Kahn (eds) (1985) *Making a Difference: Feminist Literary Criticism*, London and New York: Methuen.

Hager, Philip E. and D. Taylor (1981) *The Novels of the First World War: an Annotated Bibliography*, New York: Garland.

Hardy, Barbara (1988) 'Introduction' to *'Not So Quiet. . .' Stepdaughters of War*, by Helen Zenna Smith, London: Virago.

Haste, Cate (1977) *Keep the Home Fires Burning: Propaganda in the First World War*, London: Allen Lane.

Henke, Suzette A. (1981) 'Virginia Woolf's Septimus Smith: An Analysis of "Paraphrenia" amd the Schizophrenic Use of Language', *Literature and Psychology* 31 (4): 13–23.

Higonnet, Margaret Randolph, Jane Jenson, Sonya Michel and Margaret Collins Weitz (eds) (1987) *Behind the Lines: Gender and the Two World Wars*, New Haven, CT: Yale University Press.

Holt, Toni and Valmai Holt (1977) *Till the Boys Come Home: The Picture Postcards of the First World War*, London: Macdonald and Jane's Publishers.

Holton, Sandra Stanley (1986) *Feminism and Democracy: Women's Suffrage and Reform Politics in Britain 1900–1918*, Cambridge: Cambridge University Press.

Horn, Pamela (1984) *Rural Life in England in the First World War*, Dublin: Gill & Macmillan.

Howkins, Alan (1986) 'The Discovery of Rural England', in *Englishness: Politics and Culture 1880–1920*, ed. Robert Colls and Philip Dodd, Beckenham: Croom Helm.

Hynes, Samuel (1990) *A War Imagined: The First World War and English Culture*, London: The Bodley Head.

Jones, Lynne (1987) 'Perceptions of "Peace Women" at Greenham Common 1981–5', in *Images of Women in Peace and War*, ed. Macdonald *et al.*, Basingstoke and London: Macmillan Education.

Jones, Nora and Liz Ward (eds) (1991) *The Forgotten Army: Women's Poetry of the First World War*, Beverley, CA: Highgate Publications.

Joplin, Patricia Klindienst (1984) 'The Art of Resistance: Authority and Violence in the Work of Virginia Woolf', PhD thesis, Stanford University.

Kaplan, Cora (1988) '"Like Housemaid's Fancies": The Representation of Working-Class Women in Nineteenth-Century Writing', in *Grafts: Feminist Cultural Criticism*, ed. Susan Sheridan, London: Verso.

Keating, Peter (1989) *The Haunted Study: A Social History of the English Novel 1875–1914*, London: Secker and Warburg.

Kennard, Jean (1985) 'Feminism, Pacifism and World War One', *Turn-of-the-Century Women* 2 (2): 10–21.

Kristeva, Julia (1974; rpt 1981) 'Oscillation between Power and Denial', trans. Marilyn A. August, in *New French Feminisms*, ed. Elaine Marks and Isabelle de Courtivron, Brighton: Harvester.

—— (1974; rpt 1984) *Revolution in Poetic Language*, trans. Margaret Waller, New York and Guildford, Surrey: Columbia University Press.

—— (1974; rpt 1986) *About Chinese Women*, trans. Anita Barrows, London: Marion Boyars.

—— (1977; rpt 1980) 'From One Identity to Another', trans. Thomas Gora and Alice Jardine, in *Desire in Language*, ed. Leon S. Roudiez, Oxford: Basil Blackwell.

—— (1979; rpt 1981, 1986) 'Women's Time', trans. Alice Jardine and Harry Blake, in *The Kristeva Reader*, ed. Toril Moi, Oxford: Basil Blackwell.

Lawrence, Margot (1971) *Shadow of Swords: A Biography of Elsie Inglis*, London: Michael Joseph.

Layton, Lynne (1987) 'Vera Brittain's Testament(s)', in *Behind the Lines*, ed. Higonnet *et al.*, New Haven, CT: Yale University Press.

Lee, Hermione (1977) *The Novels of Virginia Woolf*, London: Methuen.

Leed, Eric J. (1979) *No Man's Land: Combat and Identity in World War One*, New York and London: Cambridge University Press.

Levenback, Karen L. (1981) 'A Chasm in a Smooth Road: A Study of the Effect of the Great War on Virginia Woolf', PhD thesis, University of Maryland.

Liddington, Jill and Jill Norris (1978) *One Hand Tied Behind Us: The Rise of the Women's Suffrage Movement*, London: Virago.

Light, Alison (1991) *Forever England: Femininity and Conservatism Between the Wars*, London: Routledge.

Macdonald, Lynne (1980) *The Roses of No Man's Land*, London: Michael Joseph.

Macdonald, Sharon, Pat Holden and Shirley Ardener (eds) (1987) *Images of Women in Peace and War*, Basingstoke and London: Macmillan Education.

Marcus, Jane (1983) 'Thinking Back Through Our Mothers', in *Virginia Woolf: A Feminist Slant*, ed. Jane Marcus, Lincoln, NE: University of Nebraska Press.

—— (1984) 'A Wilderness of One's Own: Feminist Fantasy Novels of the Twenties: Rebecca West and Sylvia Townsend Warner', in *Women Writers and the City*, ed. Susan Merrill Squier, Knoxville, TN: University of Tennessee Press.

—— (1985) '"No More Horses": Virginia Woolf on Art and Propaganda', in *Critical Essays on Virginia Woolf*, ed. Morris Beja, Boston: G. K. Hall.

—— (1989) 'The Asylums of Antaeus. Women, War and Madness: Is There a Feminist Fetishism?', in *The Difference Within: Feminism and Critical Theory*, ed. Elizabeth Meese and Alice Parker, Amsterdam/ Philadelphia: J. Benjamins.

Marwick, Arthur (1977) *Women at War 1914–18*, London: Fontana.

Mellown, Muriel (1983) 'Reflections on Feminism and Pacifism in the Novels of Vera Brittain', *Tulsa Studies in Women's Literature* 2 (2): 214–28.

—— (1985) 'One Woman's Way to Peace: the Development of Vera Brittain's Pacifism', *Frontiers* 8 (2): 1–6.

Meyers, Judith Marie (1985) '"Comrade-Twin": Brothers and Doubles in the World War One Prose of May Sinclair, Katherine Anne Porter, Rebecca West and Virginia Woolf', PhD thesis, University of Washington.

Minow-Pinkney, Makiko (1987) *Virginia Woolf and the Problem of the Subject: Feminine Writing in the Major Novels*, Brighton: Harvester.

Mitchell, David (1966) *Women on the Warpath: the Story of the Women of the First World War*, London: Jonathan Cape.

Mitchell, W.J.T. (ed.) (1981) *On Narrative*, Chicago, IL: University of Chicago Press.

Modleski, Tania (1982) *Loving With a Vengeance: Mass-Produced Fantasies for Women*, London: Methuen.

Moi, Toril (1985) *Sexual/Textual Politics: Feminist Literary Theory*, London and New York: Metheun.

Moran, Margaret (1985) '"The World as it Can be Made": Bertrand Russell's Protest against the First World War', *Prose Studies* 8 (3): 51–68.

Newton, Esther (1984) 'The Mythic Mannish Lesbian: Radclyffe Hall and the New Woman', *Signs* 9 (4): 557–75.

Oldfield, Sybil (1984) *Spinsters of this Parish: The Life and Times of F. M. Mayor and Mary Sheepshanks*, London: Virago.

—— (1989) *Women Against the Iron Fist: Alternatives to Militarism 1900–1989*, Oxford: Basil Blackwell.

O'Rourke, Rebecca (1988) 'Were there No Women? British Working Class Writing in the Inter-War Period', *Literature and History* 14 (1): 48–63.

Radford, Jean (1986) *The Progress of Romance: The Politics of Popular Fiction*, London: Routledge.

Romero, Patricia W. (1990) *E. Sylvia Pankhurst: Portrait of a Rebel*, New Haven, CT, and London: Yale University Press.

Rowbotham, Sheila (1973) *Hidden From History*, London: Pluto Press.

Ruddick, Sara (1983) 'Preservative Love and Military Destruction', in *Mothering: Essays in Feminist Theory*, ed. Joyce Trebilcot, Totowa, NJ: Rowman and Allanhead.

—— (1989; rpt 1990) *Maternal Thinking: Towards a Politics of Peace*, London: Women's Press.

Sanders, M.L. and Philip M. Taylor (1982) *British Propaganda During the First World War, 1914–1918*, London and Basingstoke: Macmillan.

Schwaber, Paul (1981) 'Freud and the Twenties', *Massachusetts Review* 22 (1): 133–51.

Scott, Bonnie Kime (1988) '"The Word Split its Husk": Woolf's Double Vision of Modernist Language', *Modern Fiction Studies* 34 (3): 371–85.

Sebba, Anne (1986) *Enid Bagnold – A Biography*, London: Weidenfeld and Nicolson.

Showalter, Elaine (1977; rpt 1978) *A Literature of Their Own, British Women Novelists from Bronte to Lessing*, London: Virago.

—— (1985; rpt 1987) *The Female Malady: Women, Madness and English Culture, 1830–1980*, London: Virago.

—— (1990; rpt 1992) *Sexual Anarchy: Gender and Culture at the Fin de Siecle*, London: Virago.

Sillars, Stuart (1987) *Art and Survival in First World War Britain*, New York: St Martin's.

Simkins, Peter (1988) *Kitchener's Army: The Raising of the New Army 1914–1916*, Manchester and New York: Manchester University Press.

Spearing, E.M. (1917) *From Cambridge to Camiers Under the Red Cross*, Cambridge: Heffer and Sons.

Squier, Susan Merrill (1984) 'Tradition and Revision: the Classic City Novel and Virginia Woolf's *Night and Day*', in *Women Writers and the City*, ed. Susan Merrill Squier, Knoxville, TN: University of Tennessee Press.

Stark, Susanne (1990) '"Exits" from Victorianism', Dissertation, University of Leicester.

Summers, Anne (1976) 'Militarism in Britain Before the Great War', *History Workshop* 2 (Autumn): 104–23.

—— (1979) 'A Home from Home – Women's Philanthropic Work in the Nineteenth Century', in *Fit Work for Women*, ed. Sandra Burman, London: Croom Helm.

—— (1988) *Angels and Citizens: British Women as Military Nurses 1854–1915*, London: Routledge.

Sutherland, Kathryn (1991) 'Hannah More's Counter-Revolutionary Feminism', in *Revolution in Writing: British Literary Responses to the French Revolution*, ed. Kelvin Everest, Buckingham: Open University Press.

Swartz, Martin (1971) *The Union of Democratic Control in British Politics During the First World War*, Oxford: Clarendon Press.

Taylor, A.J.P. (1963; rpt 1966) *The First World War: An Illustrated History*, Harmondsworth: Penguin.

—— (1965; rpt 1975) *English History 1914–1945*, Harmondsworth: Pelican.

Terry, Roy (1988) *Women in Khaki: The Story of the British Woman Soldier*, London: Columbus Books.

Thomas, Sue (1987) 'Virginia Woolf's Septimus Smith and Contemporary Perceptions of Shell Shock', *English Language Notes* 25 (2): 49–57.

Trebilcot, Joyce (ed.) (1984) *Mothering: Essays in Feminist Theory*, Totowa, NJ: Rowman and Allenhead.

Tylee, Claire M. (1990) *The Great War and Women's Consciousness: Images of Militarism and Womanhood*, Basingstoke and London: Macmillan.

Vellacott, Jo (1977) 'Anti-War Suffragists', *History* 62 (206): 411–25.

—— (1980) *Bertrand Russell and the Pacifists in the First World War*, Brighton: Harvester.

—— (1987a) 'Feminist Consciousness and the First World War', *History Workshop* 23 (Spring): 81–101.

—— (1987b) 'Historical Reflections on Votes, Brooms and Guns: Admission to Political Structures – On Whose Terms?', *Atlantis* 12 (2): 36–9.

Vicinus, Martha (1985) *Independent Women: Work and Community for Single Women 1850–1920*, London: Virago.

Walkowitz, Judith (1980) *Prostitution and Victorian Society*, Cambridge: Cambridge University Press.

White, Hayden (1978) *Tropics of Discourse*, Baltimore, MD: Johns Hopkins University Press.

Williams, Raymond (1973) *The Country and the City*, London: Chatto and Windus.

Wiltsher, Anne (1985) *Most Dangerous Women*, London: Pandora.

Wyatt, Jean (1986) 'Avoiding Self-Definition: In Defense of Women's Right to Merge (Julia Kristeva and *Mrs Dalloway*)', *Women's Studies* 13 (1–2): 115–26.

Zwerdling, Alex (1986) *Virginia Woolf and the Real World*, Berkeley, CA: University of California Press.

INDEX

241